A Queer and Pleasant DANGER

Other books by Kate Bornstein

Gender Outlaw: On Men, Women, and the Rest of Us

Nearly Roadkill: An Infobahn Erotic Adventure
(with Caitlin Sullivan)

*My Gender Workbook: How to Become a Real Man,
a Real Woman, the Real You, or Something Else Entirely*

*Hello, Cruel World: 101 Alternatives to Suicide
for Teens, Freaks, and Other Outlaws*

Gender Outlaws: The Next Generation
(ed. with S. Bear Bergman)

A Queer
and
Pleasant
DANGER

KATE BORNSTEIN

Beacon Press
Boston

Beacon Press
25 Beacon Street
Boston, Massachusetts 02108-2892
www.beacon.org

Beacon Press books
are published under the auspices of
the Unitarian Universalist Association of Congregations.

15 14 13 12   8 7 6 5 4 3 2 1

This book is printed on acid-free paper that meets the uncoated paper
ANSI/NISO specifications for permanence as revised in 1992.

Text design by Yvonne Tsang at Wilsted & Taylor Publishing Services

Many names and identifying characteristics of people mentioned
in this work have been changed to protect their identities.

Library of Congress Cataloging-in-Publication Data
Bornstein, Kate.
A queer and pleasant danger : a memoir / by Kate Bornstein.
pages cm.
Includes bibliographical references.
ISBN 978-0-8070-0165-3 (alk. paper)
1. Bornstein, Kate. 2. Ex-church members—
Church of Scientology International—Biography.
3. Male-to-female transsexuals—Biography. I. Title.
BP605.S2B68 2012
305.3092—dc23 [B]   2011048448

Dedicated with all my heart
to my daughter, Jessica,
and to my grandchildren,
Christopher and Celaina.

Small as my home may be,
it's bigger on the inside and
my door is always open for you.

Contents

PROLOGUE

The Kiss of Death

The last time I looked into a mirror and I saw daddy? It was the last time I tried to phone my daughter. It was the day I got an ankh tattooed onto the back of my hand. Now, hand tattoos skate the fine edge of legality/illegality across the United States. So hand tattoos are hard to get, unless you know the right people. It was 1996. I was living in Seattle, back when the city was still gritty. I was far enough underground to know someone who knew someone, and presto: a hand tattoo was mine for twenty-five dollars. I tipped the guy another five bucks because people say it hurts to get a tat that close to the bone—but it didn't hurt me.

Thousands of years ago, North African priests, priestesses, and holy people of genders neither male nor female used the ankh to mean something along the lines of *Eternal Life, The Divine Androgyne,* or *The Power of Sex.* Take your pick. To me, it seemed like just the right mix to mark the place where Death—sweetheart that She is—kissed me on the hand.

Earlier that day, the free queer clinic had called to confirm my diagnosis of chronic lymphocytic leukemia, and I didn't yet believe the doctors when they told me that CLL is a slow-moving cancer and probably wouldn't kill me. I was forty-eight years old, Lady Death had just kissed the back of my hand, and I wanted to make peace with my daughter, with whom I hadn't spoken for nearly sixteen years.

It wasn't that I hadn't wanted to speak with her for all these years—it was that she most likely didn't want to hear me. My best educated guess is that she believes—with all her heart and soul— that I am completely and irredeemably evil. Fact is, there are many reasons that people would agree with her. Permit me to count the ways:

I'm sixty-three years old, and for the past quarter of a century I've been living in queer subcultures out on the margins of America. I write books that have been condemned by Pope Benedict—and those are just the books that are taught in universities around the world. I don't think the pope knows about all the porn I've written, but he'd probably condemn that too.

There are a great number of people in the world—I dare say most of 'em—who would say I'm a pervert and a bad person because I'm a transsexual woman. I was born male and now I've got medical and government documents that say I'm female—but I don't call myself a woman, *and* I know I'm not a man. That's the part that upsets the pope—he's worried that talk like that—*not male, not female*—will shatter the natural order of men and women. I look forward to the day it does.

I call myself *trans*, or a *tranny*—and the latter angers a small but vocal group of transsexual women who see *tranny* as the equivalent of *kike* to a Jew. Right, I'm a Jew, and everyone knows someone who's got a thing about Jews. I'm also a tattooed lady—which in most cases means I can't be buried in a Jewish cemetery. But that's OK, because after the doctors harvest whatever's useful, I wanna be lit on fire. My girlfriend knows where to scatter my ashes. Right, I'm a dyke on top of all this. Constant through my incarnations as *man* then *woman* then *neither*, it's always been women who've made me weak in the knees . . . well, knee, singular, nowadays. My right knee is titanium and space-age plastic and it never gets weak, and that makes me the bionic tranny. My daughter doesn't know any of this about me, and even if she does, none of what I've told you so far is why she thinks I'm evil.

And—full disclosure—there's more. I'm a sadomasochist. I enjoy mixing up pleasure and pain. I'm not a sadist—strictly a masochist. I'm the one who gets whipped, paddled, cut open, and pierced. I like it when people cut on me—I've been a cutter since I was a teenager. As for piercings, I've got 'em in body parts I wasn't born with.

And I live with borderline personality disorder (BPD). This gives me a whole lot to write about as a performance artist, and as an advocate for queer youth, freaks, and other outlaws—which are all more reasons some people think I'm a bad person.

In 1970 I ducked out of military service in Vietnam with a psychiatric deferment. It was an act back then, but today? On good days, I'm merely depressed, and more than one therapist has considered a diagnosis of bipolar disorder—but they've finally settled on BPD. Well, I settled on it as soon as I heard that the "borderline" they're talking about is the impossible state of mind that exists between neurosis and psychosis—not unlike the impossible state of gender that exists between man and woman. Several doctors have developed theories of borderline archetypes. I'm the waif. For some real fun, google Princess Diana AND Borderline AND Waif . . . that's us. My eating disorder is a lot like hers. I love food—can't get enough of it. And I love to starve myself long enough to see bones poke up just under my skin—and that's yet another borderline.

And still . . . in my daughter's eyes, none of this matters much, if at all. There's a whole other reason I'm bad. I'm a certified post-traumatic stress survivor—no, that's not the reason my daughter Jessica thinks I'm a bad person. Surviving my trauma, though—that's what makes me evil in her eyes.

———

A few hours after the guy drew the ankh into the back of my hand, it was throbbing. It occurred to me for the first time that because of my leukemia, I no longer have enough mature white blood cells to go after possible infections. I had to call Jessica, let her know that this disease was lurking in her own blood. I wanted to say . . . I didn't know what I wanted to say. I hadn't thought about it much before that moment—I'd always assumed we'd always be out of touch. But I wanted to say, *Hello.* I wanted to say, *I've always loved you.* I wanted to say *goodbye.* I didn't know how to reach her. I'd sent letters and cards and cash to several addresses, but they'd all come back to me with *Addressee Unknown* scrawled across the envelope. Like me, my daughter has moved around a lot in her life, and I didn't know where she was living at the time. I couldn't afford a private detective and no amount of Internet sleuthing had revealed her whereabouts. This was 1996—there were no sophisticated people-finding websites yet.

But the back of my hand was still bleeding from where Death had just kissed me, and I couldn't go another day without trying to reach her. After a few hours, I managed to squeeze a phone number out of the Internet for Jessica's mother, my ex-wife Molly. She answered the phone after three rings. I recognized her voice from the single word:

"Hello?"

"Hey, Molly. It's Kate Bornstein."

I heard the slightest intake of her breath . . . then the soft click, and a dead connection.

I wasn't surprised. I would have been surprised if she'd said something like, "Kate! Hi! It's so good to hear from you! How's life now as a performance artist after all those years you and I spent in uniform? And the woman thing . . . how's that going for ya?"

Molly hung up on me because that's the way Scientologists are supposed to deal with me. In their language, I'm a suppressive person, an SP, and simply put that means I'm bad to the bone—that's the kind of bad my daughter sees when she sees me in her mind's eye, because my daughter was born into the Church of Scientology and to this day she's a member in good standing. Me? I'm an excommunicated, decertified, and defrocked minister of the Church of Scientology. My eleven plus years as a Scientologist is my life's trauma, and leaving the Church is what makes me a suppressive person.

Scientologists believe that 80 percent of the population of all universes everywhere is made up of good and decent people, probably like you. Twenty percent of us are more or less nutty. And 2 percent of all sentient beings are suppressive persons, and we are completely and irredeemably evil. L. Ron Hubbard, the founder of Scientology, is always precise with the numbers he uses—2 percent, roughly the same number of people who live with borderline personality.

SPs like me are so evil, simply talking with one of us can be enough to make you seriously ill. Reading any further in this book just might set you on a road leading to places far more horrible than any hell the old-time religions have managed to come up with. Aren't I a fun person to know?

I come with a warning label: Scientologists believe that if you keep reading, you will likely become what they call a *potential trouble source* (PTS). You'd be trouble, and the Church has never taken kindly to troublesome people. This book, for example, is likely to be troublesome for the Church. Well, it won't be too much trouble for them—who's going to believe a freak like me? Besides, the Church has enough heavyweight troublemakers making trouble for them than to worry about *me*. Still, no Scientologist—including my daughter and her two children—will be permitted to read this book that I've written for them. That's too bad, because I just want to let them know what's become of their daddy and grandpa—and I'm sorry. I am truly sorry. Because by writing this book, I've put my daughter and grandchildren in the impossible conundrum of choosing to satisfy their curiosity about me, only to become PTS, or possibly even a full-fledged SP like their daddy and grandpa turned out to be.

———

So, Molly had hung up on me and I just stood there stupidly, holding the phone at my side. That's when I realized I couldn't contact Jessica, not ever. The Scientology way of life is all she's known, all her life—she thinks it's great stuff. I used to think so, too—so I've got no ethical grounds to criticize or fuck up her life's path in seeking freedom. A terrifying klaxon blared from my phone's receiver, and I hung up.

I didn't cry, I didn't howl at the moon, I didn't curse the allegedly immortal life of L. Ron Hubbard or any number of other Scientologists who had turned my daughter against me, using Church canon as an excuse. I didn't go online to vent my rage and my grief to the hundreds, if not thousands, of ex-Scientologists who would've cheered me on and supported me. I didn't do anything healthy like that. What I did was walk calmly up the stairs to the bathroom of my little townhouse in Seattle. I reached up to the top of my medicine cabinet and took down the smooth black leather case that held my assortment of blades, alcohol swabs, and needles. I chose a number 10 surgical scalpel—it's always been my favorite. I opened my shirt and looked up into the mirror. My ribs were clearly defined beneath my skin, and that made my anorexic little heart smile. Just above my heart—that's where I cut a valentine heart into my skin.

The place where the blade first breaks skin, that's what hurts the most. It's only for a split second. The next thing you feel is warmth, lots of it. The blood follows the blade, welling up through the surgically smooth tear in your body. Your blood is the payoff. Your blood is proof that you're open and you're alive. Your blood says you have the power to kill yourself if that's what you really want to do.

Cutting has always been orgasmic for me, and I came the way cutters do: orgasm as total relief. Genitals have nothing to do with it. After you've cut yourself, you don't feel the sadness or the anger anymore. After you've cut, you can put your heartache aside, and that's what I did. I put Jessica aside. I moved on to the next item on my do-before-I-die list: I went blonde.

It was a dozen years after my gender change, and I'd never gone blonde. All my life, blonde had called to me, like some people are called into the service of the Lord. I wanted to be a kickass blonde, like Geena Davis in *The Long Kiss Goodnight*. I wanted hair like hers—I wanted eyes like hers and a mouth like hers. But I'd spent most of my life as a ruggedly handsome Jewish guy of Russian heritage, and I was afraid that too much of the rugged guy-ness would leak through the blonde and I'd be a yellow-haired guy in a dress. I'd be a towheaded freak, a platinum clown. Well, some angel up there must have heard my prayers and taken pity on me, because I ended up a devastatingly cute blonde. That accomplished, I moved on to the next item on my do-before-I-die list: *Become a star.*

Seattle is a great place to live if you're deeply depressed with suicidal longings, but it's no place for a happy-go-lucky blonde with dreams of stardom. Three weeks after I went blonde, I'd rented myself a truck and I was driving east to New York City with an old orange cat named Gideon and a butch dyke who enchantingly resembled nothing less than a gallant young Christopher Walken.

———

That was fourteen years ago. I've been writing this book for the past six years—against the recommendation of three thoroughly reputable psychics. My slowpoke leukemia hasn't killed me yet, and I no longer suspect that it might. It's been fourteen years of some serious chasing after stardom and just as seriously running away from it, but I haven't become a star. I might be on my way, though. As I write this book, I have secured myself a place as a sublebrity in the pantheon of America's queer and postmodern subcultures. That makes me happy.

I wrote this book because I've needed to check off two Herculean tasks on my do-before-I-die list: reconciliation with my daughter's life in Scientology, and coming to terms with the ghost of my dead father. I was still a man when my father died, and at his funeral? The only thing that kept me from spitting on his coffin was the respect I had for how deeply my mother had loved that man. He only ever hit me once, but all my life, my father knew how to scare me. He was my worst bully, and I failed him as a son. I was the dreamer who'd never amount to anything, and he was the bad guy: arrogant, distant, and intimidating. As hard as we both tried, we weren't kind to one another. I stopped living my life as a man, in large part because I never wanted to be a man like him.

Talk about a rock and a hard place: I am now—but never could be then—a daughter to my father. And I have been—but no longer can be—a daddy to my daughter. I've got a father/son story that only a handful of people have been able to tell truthfully and from experience. It's a story I've wanted to tell my daughter since the day I left her, just over thirty years ago. She was nine years old, born on the Fourth of July. And I've waited until now to tell this story, because I've been terrified by almost certain reprisal from the Church of Scientology. It's a brand-new religion in its most fundamental stage of development, in that every aspect of the Church is dependent on the infallibility of its founder, L. Ron Hubbard. Scientologists follow the letter of L. Ron Hubbard's writings as carefully and unquestioningly as fundamentalists of any religion might follow their own texts, word for word.

So, here's what L. Ron Hubbard says Scientologists must do— *must do*—about suppressive persons like me. First, we're publicly declared enemies of the Church, and I have been. You can walk into most any Church of Scientology in the world, and there should be a bright yellow piece of paper that reads, "Al Bornstein is an enemy of the Church." And from the moment I was declared an enemy in 1982, I've been subject to something called *Fair Game*. Scientologists will deny its existence. They'll say I'm making this up, all this nonsense about Fair Game. Well. If I am, there are thousands of other people making it up, too.

Scientologists believe the mantra *If it's not written, it's not true.* Well, L. Ron Hubbard did write down the guidelines for declaring a person Fair Game, and exactly how you're supposed to treat that person. I'd quote that for you here, but I don't want them to sue my ass off for copyright infringement. Plus, within the Church it's what they call a *high crime* to paraphrase the founder's words, and my doing so is further proof that I'm a suppressive person. So be it. Here's roughly what Ron wrote to do about SPs like me, back on October 18, 1967.

As a Scientologist, you are sanctioned—if not ordered—by the founder to do whatever bad thing you might want to do with me. It's your canonical duty. You can steal from me, you can hurt me by any means. No Scientologist will think bad of you for doing that—just the reverse. If you fuck me over bad enough to render me no threat to Scientology and mankind, you'll get the equivalent of a medal. You're allowed to trick me by any means, you can sue me, you can lie to me. Hubbard says you can *destroy* me. That's the word he uses. The bona fide Fair Game policy is easily found on the Internet.

Scientologists will argue that despite the fact that their founder wrote that document, I've got nothing to be afraid of, because one year and three days later—October 21, 1968—Ron clearly wrote (and again, I must paraphrase) that the Church of Scientology must cease declaring people Fair Game. And truly, from that day forward, those words did not appear on any official Church publication. Ron clearly explained, in writing, that *declaring* people Fair Game caused bad public relations—but he was quick to point out that even if you don't *call* people Fair Game, you can still *treat* them like they *are* Fair Game. It's all easily searched and found on the web.

I joined the Church of Scientology in 1970, and left in 1981. Ron died in 1986, just a few months before I had my sex-change surgery, back before the Internet. Now, I can with one google read firsthand accounts of Scientology officials and ministers and those in the employ of the Church who've blackmailed, harassed, and even physically beaten troublesome people like me. These are really scary people, and as I've told you: I'm an easy target when it comes to finding dirt in my life.

On the other hand, I could be lying about all of this. Really, this could be something I've made up with the intention to destroy or at least weaken the Church of Scientology—because there's another thing you need to know about suppressive persons: *we always lie*. And we lie with the purpose of destroying anything that's truly good for humanity—and what could be more truly good for humanity than Scientology? That's the reasoning behind Fair Game. I don't *want* to lie, so before I sat down to write the first full draft of this book, I got five words tattooed onto the back of my right hand. They're done in white ink, with shadowing the color of dried blood. They look like they've been carved into the back of my hand, and healed up as scars:

I must not tell lies.

Ask a Harry Potter fan to explain the full significance of the words, and why I wanted it to look as though it had been carved into the back of my hand. Or you can google the words of the tat and my name. You'll even find a picture of it. *I must not tell lies*. The tat was as painless as the ankh on my left hand. The two tats go well together.

I'm an old lady—or an old whatever—and I've learned a great deal about the power of sex, the wisdom of androgyny, and even the logic of eternal life. That's the most important stuff in my life, and I won't lie to you about any of that. I promise.

For over thirty years, I've been too afraid of the Church of Scientology to even try to mend bridges with my daughter. So now I'm going to try. I'm coming up on the last years of my life, and I don't want to go to my grave carrying with me the one-dimensional bad-guy image of my dad. And if they want to look, I'd like my daughter and grandchildren to see a few more dimensions in their dad and granddad.

Part 1

*

CHAPTER 1

Gio

Disney will never make a movie about my life story, and that's a shame—I'd make a really cute animated creature. But I was born and raised to play the role of young hero boy. I spent my first fourteen years living in Interlaken, New Jersey. It's an upper-middle-class island in the middle of Deal Lake, just one town inland from the summer seaside resort of Asbury Park in its glory days. My family was one of a handful of Jews who lived there. I was four and a half years old when I realized I wasn't a boy, and therefore must be a girl. I still lived the life of a boy. People still saw me as a boy, and later as a man—and I never had the courage to correct them. Instead, I lied to everyone, telling them I was a boy. Day and night, I lied. That's a lot of pressure on a little kid.

———

The *Saturday Evening Post* arrived each week, by mail. Norman Rockwell, craftsman of the American dream, painted most of the covers. I longed to be each and every one of those corn-fed midwestern freckle-faced Rockwell girls—engaging, grinning in the face of adversity, defiant, weeping with the loss of love, dependent on the men in her life. Rockwell girls are especially dependent on daddy. And they were blonde. Oh, how I wanted eyes the color of cornflowers and hair the color of fresh-picked corn.

Well, here's a cover that Norman Rockwell would never have painted: my mother on the delivery table, knocked out from not only the anesthesia, but also the pitcher of martinis she'd drunk over the course of her six hours' labor with me. I was born drunk and loving drugs. The first words I heard were, "Welcome to this world, honey. Welcome." Twenty-four years later, the same doctor—Griff Grimm— would hold newborn Jessica and say those same words. Griff and my dad were resident physicians at Fitkin Memorial in Neptune, New Jersey—a small hospital serving a cluster of small seaside summer towns.

Living on the Jersey Shore, the Atlantic Ocean was our magic, and the boardwalk was our magic carpet. Summertime meant sharing that with the tourists—we all had summer jobs that depended on the tourists. In a summer town, the father-son bonding seasons are autumn, winter, and early spring.

My dad and I bonded over old-school pro wrestling—we shared that fandom. Dad had once been the Indiana State College Middleweight Wrestling Champion. He took me to the pro matches in Asbury Park's Convention Hall.

"Remember, Albert," he'd say to me, "it's all an act. But there's a lot of skill in making it look real." I knew that already. I had a lot of skill in making myself look and act like a real boy.

My father was a doctor, so we could afford to sit ringside. He rarely stayed seated. Dad was up on his feet most of the time—as close to the ring as he could get—shaking his fist and bellowing at the bad guys, or at the referee for a bad call. That was his anger. He showed some of it at home, but ringside he really let go. My dad thought he saw me, his son, caught up in the bloodlust of the sport. Nah. It was plain old lust for me. I watched those matches shivering in sexual turn-on. Pre-match, the wrestlers would strut around the ring. One for one, the good guys always gave me a wink. They gave *everyone* a wink, but I took it personally. When they winked at me, I was a beautiful young girl and I longed to be caught up in their arms. Any bonding my dad and I did over wrestling, or fishing, or baseball was—like everything else in my life—based on the lie that I was a boy.

———

Paul Kenneth Bornstein, MD

That was the name, hand-painted on the pebbled-green-glass office door to my father's medical office on the second floor of the Medical Arts Building in Asbury Park. When I turned thirteen and became a man, I was told that one day my name would be painted right underneath his, and we'd share a practice together. It never occurred to me to question that future, and besides, I never argued with my dad. My big brother and I called him *dad*. Only girls called their fathers *daddy*. Dad's patients called him *Doc*—so did most of the tradespeople and store clerks up and down the shore. To them, I was *Doc's son*, as in "Doc's son is here for the prescription," or "You got those roast beef subs ready for Doc's son?" or "Hey, Doc's son is here delivering Christmas presents." Yes, we were Jews but back then we weren't supposed to shout about it. We celebrated Christmas, not Hanukkah. I was bar mitzvahed but, as I've mentioned and as you may have noted . . . it didn't work.

My dad's parents immigrated from Russia—or Poland—or whatever they were calling that strip of land that drifted back and forth. I don't know my family's town of origin, but growing up, I heard vague references to Minsk and Pinsk. *Minsk, Pinsk,* someone would say, and Uncle Davy would unconsciously rub the camp number tattooed on his forearm. He always wore long sleeves. *Minsk, Pinsk,* someone would say, and invariably someone would recite "The Ballad of Max and Anna Come to America."

Max and Anna, my father's parents, were age fourteen and twelve respectively. They were lovers who together supported the radical Red Russian forces seeking to overthrow the czar. Young Max was captured by the White Russians—forces of the czar, not unlike the Stormtroopers in *Star Wars*. Max was banished to a POW camp in Siberia. Thousands of miles west of Siberia, in Minsk or Pinsk, Anna—twelve years old, remember—set off to rescue her radical lefty lover boy. She was dirt-poor, so she had to walk—but like a heroine in some Disney cartoon, Anna could sing, so that's what she did.

Every night of her journey to rescue Max, she sang for her supper and lodgings in villages and at farmhouses. It took her nearly a year to cross Russia, but she made it to the front gate of the gulag where Max was being held. She'd saved some money from her singing, which she used to bribe the camp guards to look the other way while Max clambered under the wire and rose up into the arms of his dear love. The way the story was told, the guard wiped away a tear and gave them back half the bribery money.

So, Anna and Max escaped into the woods of wildest Siberia. They ran all the way back to Minsk, or Pinsk. Uncle Davy insists ravenous wolves nipped at their heels. Two steamer tickets were waiting for them in Bremerhaven, Germany. There was family in New Jersey, and they were counting on Anna to succeed. The two young lovers emigrated to Paterson, New Jersey, where family members had built and later owned the giant silk mills. Beautiful story, right?

It was all a big fat lie—everything I just told you. But, I swear, that's the story I believed all my life. Until ten years ago, I believed that Grandpa Max and Grandma Angie were badass socialist freedom fighters. My brother corrected me one day when I was visiting him and his wife, Deb, down the Jersey Shore. Deb had never heard the story of Max and Anna's odyssey of love and radical revolution— so I began to recite what I just told you. From the moment I began the story, my brother was shaking his head in disbelief. And by the time I got to the Siberian camp, he was laughing out loud.

"Where did you hear that bullshit?"

"Everyone, Alan. Everyone."

So now, according to my brother—whom you should be more willing to believe than myself on these matters—here's the real story of Max and Anna.

Max was not a Red Russian. He was a big supporter of Czar Nicholas, whose regime was violently anti-Semitic. That made my grandpa a turncoat and a quisling. He was the son of a wealthy Jewish businessman, the owner of a large department store in Minsk, Pinsk. Max belonged to a Youth for Nicholas group, the czar's local bullies. Anna's family was wealthy, too. That's how she could afford the singing lessons that coached the voice that later got her a solo number at Carnegie Hall. Most importantly, though, Max and Anna hated each other. It was an arranged marriage. Max left for America, leaving Anna behind. She followed two years later, her family virtually pushing her onto the ship that would whisk her into the arms of the man she despised. There was no Siberia. Wolves may have nipped at Uncle Davy's heels when he was released from the concentration camp and had nowhere and no one to go home to—he wandered for months, and wolves could have sniffed him out as wounded prey. But no wolves came near Max or Anna, unless Anna was wearing their fur. All of this brings me to the impossible conundrum of writing truth in memoir.

I must not tell lies. *And* I promise you I'll be telling lies in this book—little lies, to make the story more fun. I like to lie, I like to tell tall tales. But this book, after all, is for my daughter and grandchildren, and I want them to know some truth of me if they ever care to look. I'll tell you lies I believed to be true—and then I'll correct them like I did with Max and Anna's story. And no doubt, I'll tell lies that I still believe to be truths. I got real good at lying because of the great big lie I told day and night for nearly twenty years—that I was a boy.

I knew what a boy was—I could see them on television, but they weren't me. Good and decent human beings in 1950s America could look at television and see lots of people just like themselves. When I watched television, I never saw anything quite like myself . . . but I did learn how to make myself look and sound like a boy. Liar, liar me. But now I'm going to do my very, very best *not* to do that.

I must not tell lies.

It's in my skin. I see it every time I look down at my hand.

—

My dad grew up working the silk mills. He would be the first of the family to go to college. His twin sister, Frances, paid most of his tuition—that's what women did for their brothers back then. Frances could never figure out why I wanted to be a woman, and I could never explain it to her. My father worked a number of jobs to pay the rest of his way through medical school. In addition to his college champion wrestling days, my father was a semiprofessional boxer. That's where he earned his cauliflower ear and the first of his three broken noses. I was twelve when I watched my father break his nose the third time. He slipped on some ice. When he stood up, blood was streaming down his face. He cursed and told me that I screamed like a girl.

My dad worked a job speed-testing racecars on the Indianapolis Speedway. And in the summers—this was during Prohibition—my dad would drive rum across the Canadian border into the United States and down to the Jersey Shore. He worked for Dutch Schultz, the notorious Beer Baron of the Bronx. My dad totally looked the part: darkly Russian face with a broken nose, his hair slicked down—and he had a crooked grin that made all the ladies go weak in the knees. My dad was a bad boy *and* the new doctor in town—he was a complete catch. Not that my mother was looking for a catch at the time. She was in college, and she was wearing Leon Goldberg's fraternity pin.

—

My mom was born Mildred Lillian Vandam, the youngest of three children in the home of Albert Herman Vandam and his wife, Esther Cohen Vandam, whom everyone called Essie. She was a downtown Henry Street Jewish good-time girly-girl who liked her gin. Essie was the girl—later the woman, and later still the old woman—who, at a party, would sing and dance on tabletops while shaking her behind. Her husband, Albert, was an orthodox Jew who spent half the year scouring Europe for religious relics and the other half of the year selling them to the Catholic Church. After Al died, Essie tried three times to kill herself. She spent her last years living in our house so my parents could keep an eye on her.

My mom had grown up on New York's Upper West Side, in an apartment not far from Grant's Tomb, overlooking the Hudson River. She'd attended Julia Richmond High, a girls' high school across town on the East Side, where, in her senior year, she read the tragic lesbian pop classic *The Well of Loneliness*. Mildred followed her brother Leroy into Brown University. She was supposed to find a good husband there.

Well, my mom didn't actually attend Brown University. She went to Pembroke College *at* Brown University. That's where the girls went. Boys like me and Uncle Roy, we attended Brown University proper. Boys and girls all took the exact same classes—it was completely coeducational except for the dorms. But Brown back then was part of a deeply rooted New England Baptist old boys' club. No women could hold a diploma from Brown University.

Up until 1970 there were two exceptions to this academically determined gender divide—two women who hold a Brown University diploma prior to 1970: Wendy Carlos, pioneering synthetic music composer who graduated Brown University while she was still Walter. And me, Albert Herman Bornstein. If I asked them to print me a copy of my diploma—and if I paid them for it—Brown University would use the name Katherine Vandam Bornstein. They've already changed it in their records.

———

My mom and dad met when he paid her a house call to cure her tuberculosis.

Paul Bornstein had set up his practice in Belmar, a few blocks from where the Vandam family summered each year. There was no air-conditioning back then, and fans don't cut the miasmic heat that is and was a New York summer—so any New Yorkers who could afford to, fled the city for the beach, the boardwalk, and the deep-sea fishing of the Jersey Shore.

Eighteen-year-old Mildred was lying in bed with what Essie knew to be tuberculosis. Their regular doctor had laughed at Essie's diagnosis, and he'd gone deep-sea fishing with Essie's husband, Al. That left Essie alone in the house—her daughter upstairs, dying of tuberculosis.

Essie placed a phone call to the nice new doctor in the neighborhood—he was a Jew, so that made him even nicer—and in a few minutes Paul came knocking on their door, with a little black doctor bag like you might see in a Norman Rockwell painting. Essie took young Dr. Paul up to her daughter's room. It was perfectly noir: bad boy meets wealthy, young it girl. Paul was rugged and handsome. He was a doctor, but he talked like a mill hand. He walked like a wrestler. Mildred lay there in the bed, propped up with pillows, a thoroughly modern cute-as-a-button flapper. The two of them fell in love at first sight, and they stayed in love with each other until the day they died.

Essie insisted on staying in the room for the medical examination. Paul approached Mildred with his stethoscope. He tapped Leon's fraternity pin fastened to her pajama top, prominently positioned over her heart.

"So, what's this?"

"Absolutely nothing, Doctor."

Mildred casually unpinned Leon's undying love from her heart and tossed it to the floor. Paul laughed and applied the stethoscope to her chest. You just know he heard her breath and heartbeat quicken.

They made a lovely couple, my parents. Mildred was as gracious as she was elegant and beautiful. Paul was as gallant as he was rugged and handsome. My mom thought she was the luckiest girl in the world. My dad never got it, how a class act like Mildred could fall for a palooka like him.

———

Around the time that my teenaged mom-to-be—not in the least tubercular—was making googly eyes at my dad-to-be, L. Ron Hubbard—like my father—was in his early twenties. While my father was setting up a medical practice on the Jersey Shore, Ron Hubbard was reportedly off tramping through Asia, learning Eastern religions and customs. All of us in Scientology believed this about Ron. He was an explorer, an intrepid researcher into the darkest depths and starry heights of the human soul. He engineered and built the Bridge to Total Freedom.

Lafayette Ronald Hubbard was a rugged guy, just like my dad.

He was born on March 13, 1911, in Tilden, Nebraska. My dad was born just a few months later, on May 19. If you believe the authorized biography, Ron grew up out by a tribe of Blackfoot peoples. By the time he was four, he'd already learned all the Blackfoot lore there was to learn, so tribal elders made him a full-fledged blood brother. What's more, at thirteen years old, Ron became the youngest Eagle Scout in the history of Scouting. So goes the authorized biography, and as Scientologists we believed it.

A great deal of that authorized biography has been poked full of holes. There's evidence that many of the outrageous claims about Hubbard's life are out-and-out lies—go ahead, give it a google. As Scientologists, we always figured he stretched the truth a little—to make a good story a little bit better—but we thought most of his reportedly grandiose and holy life was true.

———

After a respectable period of engagement, my mom and dad were married. After another respectable period, Mom gave birth to my big brother, Alan Vandam Bornstein. Yes, we were both Al. He was big Al, I was little Al. For the record, I have a cousin Al, too. Big Al and Cousin Al were prewar babies, I was post.

A year after my brother was born, the Japanese bombed Pearl Harbor. The same day, my dad signed up for military service. He served in MASH units across North Africa. Over the years, he rose to the rank of lieutenant colonel, in command of his own MASH unit outside Paris near the end of the war. I have a photograph of my father in North Africa, in the desert. He's sitting outside at some government-issue table. The sun is blazing, and he's got his shirt off. He's deeply tanned. He's writing a letter. It's got to be a letter to Mildred, because his whole body says *I love you*—his whole body says sexy.

My favorite photo of the two of them together was taken the day he got back from the war. They're out to dinner, sitting together in a booth. The photographer was sitting across the table from them. They've finished their meal. My mom had just turned to my dad and the photographer captured the moment that she's hugging on him with joy and abandon and love—so much so that my dad is shyly overcome with his own happiness. Pretty picture.

—

Seven months after my dad returned home, my mom miscarried a girl-child. A few months later, I was conceived into the same wonderland womb. Now, here's what I think: No one really knows what the previous tenant of my mom's uterus had left behind for me to pick up and use. I'm sure that girl body had been meant for me. I'm sure I was supposed to call my father *daddy*. And that is simply not decent enough material for a Norman Rockwell painting, or a Disney feature-length cartoon.

CHAPTER 2

The He-Man Woman-Hater's Club

I watched *The Little Rascals* on television. It was a weekly show about a gang of preadolescent boys. They were most of them working class. Some were homeless and lived with an old woman they called Granny. They had boy adventures that could almost have been real. In one of the better-known episodes, the little rascals start up what they called the He-Man Woman-Hater's Club. I didn't think it was funny. I wanted to grow up to be Audrey Hepburn: skinny, graceful, charming, delightful, smart, talented, a star, and a lady. I didn't want the Little Rascals to hate me.

Whatever it was that boys did, I couldn't do naturally. I *learned* how to act. I stopped running screaming from spiders and bugs. I joined the Cub Scouts. But when it came time to make my rite of passage into the Boy Scouts, I chickened out. My first Boy Scout meeting was in a firehouse one town away, within bike-riding distance. I wore my Cub Scout uniform—I'd been told it was optional. My uniform with all its merit badges gave me the courage to face the big kids—about thirty of them. I guess they were Boy Scouts but there was no way to tell for sure—they weren't wearing their uniforms. In fact, they were all buck naked. It smelled naked in there. It smelled like naked boys. They were laughing, pointing at me, yelling at me to take my clothes off. Chubby little me, I turned tail and ran for half an hour, all the way home. My brother drove me back the next day to pick up my bike. That was no place for a cub, no place for a beta wolf like me.

You've heard of alpha wolves. They're the ones who own things. They own territory. They own mates. They own their children. There are men who are like that—my father was an alpha wolf, and so was L. Ron Hubbard. Two of my three wives, and every butch dyke I've ever bedded, has been an alpha wolf. All my daddies have been alpha wolves . . . woof.

Beta wolf, that's me. That's always been me. We don't own, we follow. We don't direct, we serve. Alpha and beta wolves survive in symbiosis: one cannot live without the other. As far back as I can remember, I have pined for the love of an alpha wolf.

And of course it's not all about love—that's the wish, that's the fairy tale. Most often, beta wolf is about terror. Not every alpha you're going to meet is going to be your lover, so when you're a beta wolf, you spend a lot of time in service to real jerks—but you learn how to work it. Puppies know how to work an alpha wolf daddy—they're cute. Cute is bottom line for beta wolf behavior. C'mon, puppies are adorable. As soon as they see you, they flip over on their backs, they stretch their four legs until they're impossibly long, they wriggle—they get so excited that they piddle.

This sort of behavior—cute, as a verb—is disarming. Cute is a survival tactic. Cute is life and death. Cute is what puppies and cubs and beta wolves do to keep ourselves alive in the face of . . . well, the big bad wolf. We are saying,

"I don't want your land. I don't want your mate or your children. Look at me, I'm baring my throat and my belly to you. One bite, that's all it would take . . . and I'd probably taste pretty good. I'm no threat to you. You've got me so scared I'm peeing myself." And then, maybe we'd make big liquid love eyes and we'd say, "But aren't I cute? You don't wanna hurt me, daddy. You wanna cuddle me. And if you're real good, I'll let you have more than a taste of my blood."

All my life, I've rolled over for alpha daddies.

But cute is not what boys and men were supposed to do. There was no *use* to being cute, there was no money in it, unless you were in show biz, in which case—despite how gosh-darned cute they are—only a few boys, and fewer men, are going to make a living with cute. What's more, every single element of mass media declared loud and clear: *cute is dumb*. There was no feminist viewpoint in those days, no NPR. Cute was dumb. In '50s mass media, the only people who crawled on their bellies, rolled over, and stretched their throats out as far as they could . . . were girls and women. I watched them, and over and over I said to myself, *that's me*. That's me, always smiling like that. That's me, making everyone happy by just walking down the street being cute. In my young mind, the fact that I identified with cute proved that I wasn't a boy. I'd never grow up to be a man. Neither, it turns out, did my father. Nope, Paul Bornstein wasn't a man.

This is one hell of a family secret I'm about to tell you, but as a member of the oldest living generation of my family, I get to decide what secrets to tell and what secrets to keep. Now, I'm not saying there was anything effeminate about Paul Bornstein. *Au contraire.* But I have been privy to two facts of his life that marred his otherwise flawless manliness: my father had never been bar mitzvahed . . . and my father had breasts.

Bar mitzvah is the only hope a Jewish boy has of becoming a man, so technically speaking, my dad was still a boy like me—and I knew this as a fact, all my life. On his first day of Hebrew school, eleven-year-old Paul got into an argument with his rabbi, and he kicked the guy in the shins. Then he stormed out of class and never returned. According to the letter of Judaic law, my father's temper got him stuck in boyhood all his life. I knew this about my father, but the fact is our family never followed Judaic law, not all that closely anyway. Dad called us secular Jews. So, bar mitzvah or not, my thirteen-year-old dad was a hard-working mill hand, and *that's* what made him a man in the eyes of our family.

My father's breasts, on the other hand, were far more damning. His boobs were body and blood. "Fat-man boobs" doesn't quite describe my father's bosom. It was Jimmy Rubin who first called them to my attention. It was a lovely summer day at the beach.

"Jesus, your dad's got tits!"

"He does not."

"Does too! Look at 'em."

By golly, there they were, sprouting from my father's hairy chest—large, round breasts. They were even sort of perky, with cute little pink nipples. Now, you might think that this was a traumatizing moment in my life, but keep in mind, please, that I was a budding transsexual. My father's tits were reassuring.

I was ten years old, and for six years I'd been beating myself up for wanting to be a girl. Now I knew I wasn't the only one—my own father was part girl. No, really. This was my rationalization: my father had a twin sister—their bodies were entwined, all of their prenatal lives. For nine months he and his girl twin had shared flesh and blood and hormones, and goodness knows what else. What effect might that have? I refuse to google this question, because I want to believe in the magic of it. I'd felt the warmth of that same magic, after all, the moment I slid into my mother's womb, a room still warm from the girl-child who—a few months earlier—hadn't made it to daylight alive.

—

The story about my father kicking his rabbi in the shins on the first day of Hebrew school is documented in an article I wrote for the *New York Times* sometime last century. So it must be true. Well, it's not. It's another damn lie that I believed all my life to be the truth. After my brother read that story in the *Times,* he phoned me and said,

"Hey, where did you get that thing about dad kicking his rabbi in the shins?"

"He told me that. Mom told me that!"

"Well, it's bullshit. He didn't go to Hebrew school, because he was too busy working in the mill. He didn't have time for Hebrew school, and you know he didn't really believe much in that crap anyway."

I like my father's version better. The day I left the Church of Scientology, I thought about my father kicking his rabbi in the shins.

—

In the late '60s, early '70s, the term *male chauvinist pig* replaced *he-man woman-haters*. Bottom line, an MCP was a guy who put more value on men than he did on women. Paradoxically, some MCPs put their women up on a pedestal—a statue of his fantasy—and that's where their women were supposed to stay.

My dad proudly proclaimed himself a male chauvinist pig. He oinked—at home, and out in front of other people—at parties, at work, in restaurants and bars, on the beach. That's what he'd do. Even my brother remembers that. Our dad collected little piggies—it gave him great joy to line them all up on top of the television. He wore ties and shirts with piggy patterns—not at the same time. My mother never would have allowed that. He wore cuff links with snarling pigs, from some college whose mascot was a snarling pig. He kept an adorable stuffed pig on the back shelf of his car, a Buick Riviera with the license plate MCP-1. He charged girls and women twenty-five cents to sit in his red leather recliner. It smelled of Latakia. Sitting in Dad's chair for free was one good thing about being a boy.

"Dad, you really are a sexist pig."

"You're goddamn right I am."

We all laughed. It kept the peace to laugh at my father's little jokes. Gender in our family was simple: real he-men were supposed to hate women, or at least know they're a whole lot better than women. Husbands behaved proprietarily with their wives. From the day they were married until the day he went into the hospital to die, my father bought every article of clothing my mother ever wore, and most of her jewelry as well—gold, every piece of it. He bought her Chanel and Yves St. Laurent. Her summerwear was exclusively Lilly Pulitzer. Please tell me, what was I doing as a boy knowing all this?

Two years after my father died, my mom called me on the phone. I was a brand-new girl then, and given to gushing about clothes. This day, it was my mom who sounded like a teenaged girl.

"I went to the mall today, Kate," she said, excited, "and I bought myself a sweater—cashmere with pearl buttons. Well, the buttons aren't real pearls, but I don't think that matters, does it?"

It was the first article of clothing she'd bought herself in over forty years.

"Fake pearl buttons? They're fabulous, Mom. Oh yay, you!"

"Yes, Albert! Yay, me!"

"Kate."

"Oh, I'm sorry dear—Kate."

———

Ron Hubbard and Paul Bornstein grew up within a sexuality system that required no thought whatsoever. You were a man and you loved women, or you were a woman and you loved men. Anything else was unseemly or perverted. Their sexuality system didn't include—except as freaks—lesbians, gay men, bisexual men and women, or sadomasochists. And as far as gender was concerned, there was no intersex, and *transsexual* was a word that wouldn't be invented until 1963. Their generation's system of sex and gender refused to acknowledge the self-proclaimed genders of hundreds of thousands of she-males, he-shes, dykes, fags, drag queens, drag kings, butches, femmes, cross-dressers, uniform fetishists, or anyone else who danced in the dark funhouse mirrors of my daydreams and nightmares. There were no words for any of that—not in the house that Paul built, and not in the church that Ron built.

———

I was just over eight years old when I found the photograph among my dad's war souvenirs, his naked-lady photograph from France in World War II. She had hair between her legs, and she even had hair under her arms, which you could see because she was being held—arms and legs spread painfully wide—by eight US soldiers. The naked lady had tossed aside her long, wavy hair and you could see her face. She was crying. Or screaming. Behind them about twenty or more US soldiers—I never counted them—were raising their rifles and cheering. When I was a lot older, I asked my father about it.

"She was a Nazi spy. We gave her what she deserved."

My mom sent Dad off to war with a gross of condoms packed carefully into his duffel bag. She knew that boys will be boys, and she wanted my father to be prepared. My mother wasn't prepared for the lady who knocked on our front door some months after the war ended. My mom was going about her wifely chores of managing the house and looking after Alan, my six-year-old brother. She was maybe six months pregnant with a little girl who would never be born. *Ding-dong.* My mother went to the door and there stood a pretty, young woman, wearing clothes from Sears, Roebuck. My mother, telling this story, always stressed the part about Sears, Roebuck. It was the '50s version of Kmart. The young woman at our front door was nervous, but she lifted her chin and spoke.

"I met Paul in France. May I come in, please?"

My mother didn't move from inside the doorway. "My name is Mrs. Paul K. Bornstein. And you are . . . ?"

Know the name of the person who wants to talk with you before you agree to talk with her, that's what my mom taught me. The woman at the door spoke her name, then added that she and Paul had served together for years. My mom didn't respond.

"Mildred, I'm here to tell you that Paul will be divorcing you."

Silence.

"He and I will be getting married, and we'll be taking your son." My mother allowed the fury to flash in her eyes, followed by a snow queen's gaze of ice.

"Young lady, from the little I know of you, I can see you aren't half the woman that Paul needs in his life. I'm that woman. You've had your fun. Now go home and get yourself another man."

The young woman's shoulders sagged.

"He said you'd say something like that." She left and never came back.

That's the way I heard my mother tell it.

CHAPTER 3

What Sex Had to Do with It

My father was driving us out for some soft-serve ice cream. In addition to wrestling, he and I bonded over food. I was watching the boardwalk flash by my window. We were almost there.

"Are you still a virgin?"

"Wh-what?"

"What?"

"What?"

Whenever I needed to stall, or avoid answering a question, I took advantage of my father's deaf cauliflower ear.

I'd had sex, plenty of sex—but I'd never had intercourse with a woman. I had *great* sex, masturbating into a soft sock, hungrily staring at pictures of ladies' and girls' underwear ads in the Sears, Roebuck catalogue—or the naked native ladies of faraway island countries in *National Geographic* magazine. These weren't particularly sexy pictures. This wasn't pornography. These were simply pictures of women standing around in lingerie, or women wearing loincloths, staring into the camera like they'd never seen one before. I stared at those pictures and jerked off, and as soon as I could feel myself to be the girl in the picture, I'd come.

Of course I knew about sex, the kind my father was asking me about—boys and girls, genital intercourse. But I was a fat little Jewish boy, and I dated nice Jewish girls with whom I didn't even talk about sex, which was off the table for nice Jewish girls.

Several times, I'd stroked with wonder the magnificent breasts of Sophia Tranakis—at the movies. She was Greek Orthodox, so it was OK. We never said much to each other. We did climb all over each other, kissing. I was in awe of her breasts and nipples, and Sophia enjoyed my worshipping hands. In turn, she rubbed my cock through my pants. Looking into my eyes, grinning, she ordered me not to come. So what was I supposed to tell my father when he asked me if I was a virgin? My delaying strategy worked—he rephrased the question in specifics I could answer.

"Well, have you gotten laid yet or not?"

"Not yet, no."

Silence hung in the car like a dark cloud.

" . . . But, Dad, I think maybe Sophia might, you know, soon, it could be . . ."

He held up his hand, silencing me. His eyes never left the road ahead of him.

"I've been talking this over with your Uncle Jay."

Uncle Jay wasn't my uncle, he was a close friend of my dad's—and Uncle Jay was a psychiatrist. Oh my god, was I a virgin because I was mentally ill?

"Uncle Jay has a patient who's a prostitute, and he's set up a time for the two of you to get together."

A what, did he say? A prostitute? I mean, thank God I wasn't mentally ill, but omigod, a prostitute!? My mind flipped to Shirley MacLaine as Ginnie Moorhead, the prostitute with a heart of gold and a misogynistic name, opposite Frank Sinatra in *Some Came Running*. I made myself pout like Ginnie. I'd practiced in the mirror. My father wouldn't see me, he never took his eyes off the road, ever. No, my father's prostitute scenario was all wrong—I shouldn't be playing the Frank Sinatra role. And wait a minute, the prostitute was one of Uncle Jay's patients? That would mean she was mentally ill. I was scared.

My father had pulled into Carvel's soft serve, and we were eating our cones in silence. I licked mine, he bit chunks off his. Between bites, he cheerfully told me that not only was I being set up with a prostitute—a mentally unstable prostitute—but that my first erotic encounter would take place in my father's medical office, on the bed where his patients lay as I ran electrocardiograms on them.

Summers, I worked in my father's office. He'd narrowed his specialty to upper chest and respiratory, cardiac cases—so his patients were mostly geriatric. Every day, two or three of them needed a cardiogram. I used suction cups to fix the twelve electrical leads to each of their bodies. Thick saline goo provided conductivity. After several patients, the room got smelly. That was the room, the very bed, I was supposed to have my first ever sex in—with a lady who must have had some good reason for seeing Uncle Jay, the psychiatrist. Then it occurred to me—maybe she was going crazy because she had syphilis. Maybe she'd give me syphilis. And even if I managed to survive the evening, wasn't I breaking some law? Wasn't she breaking some law? And how about Uncle Jay?

"How can Uncle Jay set me up with one of his own patients? Isn't that illegal?"

"I'm paying her for it, you damned fool, not Jay. You're meeting her tonight."

I stared resolutely at my waffle cone.

"Have a ball, Son!"

A ball was not what I had when I stood face to face with Audrey, the woman who was supposed to make a man out of me. She looked like Aunt Frankie, my father's twin sister—and that was wrong on so many levels. I looked away several times and looked back at her—just to make sure—and she still looked like Aunt Frankie. It was summer, it was hot. Both of us were chubby—my skin was clammy and so was hers. I turned on the ceiling fan and watched through the dim light as she struggled to get out of her girdle. At last, she lay down on the electrocardiogram bed, opened her legs, and patted the sheet beside her. I sat down obediently. She didn't smell all that good—I don't think it was hygiene, but rather the heat, and the rubber girdle. I'd taken off my shoes, nothing else. She cocked her head.

"You don't wanna do this, do you, honey?"

"I don't think so, no, not really."

"Why? Do you like other boys?"

"I don't think so. No." She watched me silently flail for words. I couldn't find any.

"C'mere, baby."

Audrey drew me gently down to rest my head against her breasts—which did smell good—and we lay like that, quiet, for about half an hour. Later that night we sat together in a malt shop.

"My name's not really Audrey. It's Alice."

"That's what they would've named me if I was a girl. Why Audrey?"

"Audrey Hepburn," said Alice. "I wanna be skinny and beautiful like her." This is where I should have protested that she was already beautiful. Instead, the truth dropped from my mouth before I could stop it.

"I want to be Holly Golightly."

"Oh? Really?"

"Yeah. Really. You're the first person I've ever told. Please don't tell Uncle Jay."

Audrey patted my hand. I felt entirely too vulnerable and switched gears.

"Why are you seeing Doctor Jay?" I didn't expect to see her grin so broadly.

"I hurt people, then I leave 'em."

"You didn't hurt me."

"You aren't dangerous."

We finished our malts, and walked back through Sunset Lake Park to the Medical Arts Building. The air smelled of lake water, and the trees were in full blossom. I remembered the rules of gallantry and asked if she wanted a ride home.

"You drive?"

"No, no. I'll call my dad and he'll pick us up."

An awkward pause as we both recognized the danger in that.

"No thanks, Al. It's a beautiful night. I'll walk home by the lake." In those days, a woman could safely take a late-night walk, alone, in the park.

"Sleep well, Audrey."

"You too, Holly."

We hugged as I imagined sisters did.

I called my dad from the payphone to please come pick me up.

"Did you do it?"

"It was amazing, Dad."

"That's my man!"

I never told him what really happened. He was proud of me. And if Audrey/Alice said anything to Uncle Jay, I never heard about it.

———

My real first time was with Candy. We met when I was a senior at the Pennington School, an all-boys prep school. It was the day of the senior prom, a week before graduation. I'd invited Bernadette Marlowe, the sister of a classmate and the love of my life. We lived hundreds of miles away from each other, which gave me the courage to profess undying love. I'd written numerous Shakespearean sonnets—in flawless iambic pentameter—to Bernadette. She was Donny Marlowe's sister. He was captain of the wrestling team.

It was a perfect spring day—dappled sunshine and the scent of newly cut grass on the rising and falling breeze. I ambled the grounds of Pennington Prep, reminiscing on my three years at the school. I'd done well—president of my senior class, editor of the yearbook, winner of several trophies for declamation and speech, and—having learned how to starve myself earlier that year—I was fabulously skinny. My eggheadedness had paid off for me. Dad was proud of me, and I was proud of myself. I'd made National Honor Society, I'd earned myself a half dozen year-end trophies, and I'd won early admission to both pre-med and medical school in an accelerated MD degree program at Brown University.

Graduation was to be held in the new gymnasium. It wasn't completely constructed, so no one was allowed on the site. But fuck it, I was a senior. I'd found my way in, and I was standing on the open stage of the new assembly hall. The proscenium was framed by red velvet curtains. I looked out to the rows of empty seats, and I took a bow. And the red velvet curtains moved. There was no wind. There wasn't a sound. Empty theaters are places of great power and possibility, places where just about anything can happen.

I called out, "Hello?"

Nothing.

"Who's there behind the curtain?"

Was that a sniffle?

"Are you OK?"

A sob. Most definitely a sob.

"Hey, it's OK, I'm not going to hurt you or anything."

Out stepped a girl, younger than me or maybe just slightly older. Her face was streaked with tears, and she looked for the world to be Shirley MacLaine in *Some Came Running*—except *this* girl's brassy red hair hung straight down past her shoulders. She wore a short skirt, a really short skirt. It was the shortest skirt I'd ever seen on a girl who wasn't in the movies. I was thinking that my prom date and true love, Bernadette Marlowe, wore all her skirts down below her knees where they should be, when all of a sudden this strange, beautiful girl fell into my arms, held on tight, and sobbed for a good five minutes, by the end of which all thoughts of *Some Came Running* and senior prom had vanished from my mind.

Later, she told me her name was Candy. I swear to you by all that's holy, that was her name. She'd run away from home, to get away from the police. They had a court order to take her to reform school. Shoplifting, she said.

"Not the occasional lipstick, mind you. Why, I've taken so much merchandise, I could've opened my own cosmetics counter," she sniffed, "and I would've if my stepfather hadn't called the cops on me when he found it all piled up in the hall closet."

I'd never known anyone who had a stepfather. I'd walked smack-dab into a teen romance film, and right on cue I fell desperately in love—and right on cue the two of us fell to the stage floor and made out for two hours.

Bernadette Marlowe was at that moment on a train. She wouldn't arrive until early evening. I knew the right thing to do, and I did it.

I called a time-out, right before we were actually going to do it, and good guy that I was, I persuaded Candy to visit the school chaplain with me. Candy and I walked across campus in the early twilight. The chaplain welcomed us into his apartment, and his wife made us tea. The four of us sat down in their living room, and Candy poured out her story of a broken home, a stepfather who beat her, and an alcoholic mom who never tried to stop him. The chaplain, his wife, and I were stunned. Things like that didn't happen in our lives. Things like that only rarely happened on television.

At the end of her story, the chaplain explained how things would only get worse for Candy if she kept running away. With good behavior, she'd be out of reform school in three months. So, phone calls were made. The police from her home town in New Jersey would dispatch a patrol car to pick her up—it could be any time before midnight. Some hours away. Candy held her face in her hands. We hadn't touched each other since we'd come into the chaplain's apartment, but now I reached out and held her hands in mine.

"I'll stay with you until the police get here."

"Oh dear, Al," the chaplain was quick to say, "what about your date for the prom?"

I looked down into Candy's doe eyes, then back up at the chaplain.

"Candy needs me more than Bernadette does. I'm staying here with her."

Then the chaplain did something that adults never do: he and his wife left to chaperone the prom, leaving us alone in their apartment. We made out some more, but we didn't make love, though Candy clearly wanted to.

"I don't have any rubbers."

"That's OK, you can pull out before you come."

I had an idea of what that meant, but I wasn't sure exactly how or when to do it. I didn't want to tell her I was a virgin. Like lightning, my mind came up with a terrific line.

"We'll wait until you're free. We should both be free for that."

"Oh Al, that is so romantic! I love you."

"I love you, Candy."

By the time we saw the police car's flashing lights through the windows, it was past eleven and I'd missed the prom. The chaplain was standing outside the apartment speaking quietly with the police. Candy and I swore we'd write and meet again.

"When we're both free to do it," she breathed in my ear. My boner hadn't quit for over four hours. I'd pay for that in the morning.

The two of us walked out into the light fog and chill of the dark early spring night, holding our hands in front of our eyes to shield them from the beams of police flashlights. A small crowd of students and teachers had gathered to rubberneck the wreck on life's highway that was Candy the runaway and me the senior class president. Candy was led off by the police, and I was escorted to the headmaster's office.

The next morning, Bernadette Marlowe took the train home. I never saw her. Donny, her brother, threatened to beat me up—two guys pulled him off me. My parents arrived midday, and we met in the office of the dean of students. I was suspended for three days for conduct unbecoming a Pennington School gentleman. The dean said I'd be receiving none of the awards or citations I'd earned— not at graduation, not ever. I couldn't argue with that, but my parents did.

"You can't blame Albert for this," my father insisted. "He's a kid!"

"Yes," chimed my mother, "what sort of judgment was your so-called chaplain using when he left them alone in the apartment?" My thoughts went to Nurse in *Romeo and Juliet*. He was using that sort of judgment.

The dean held firm, and my father drove us home. We had nothing to say to each other. I locked myself in my room for three days. That's when I noticed how pasty white my skin was, and that's when I first tried a self-tanning product called Man-Tan. I returned to school three days later for graduation. My face and hands, and even my palms, were toxic orange. No one was mean enough to bring it up.

Candy spent the summer in reform school. We wrote each other two, three, four letters a day, swearing our undying love. I was seventeen years old. It turned out she was eighteen. The day of her release in late August, we met at a motel halfway between where we both lived. We fucked. It was quick, urgent, and uncomfortable. I used three rubbers in just under thirty minutes. It's not like I had the Internet to research technique. We kissed good-bye, promising each other nothing.

CHAPTER 4

Size Matters

I grew up in a touchy-feely family. My mother gave everyone a kiss on the cheek. My brother punched guys in the arm. My dad specialized in bear hugs—he'd growl and hug tightly enough to make most people yelp. But he was tender when he held me, his young son, on his lap. When I was the cub of the family, my father's lap was always there for me. He was a fat man, and he had a big lap. Secretly I promised myself that the day I could reach my arms all the way around my father, that's the day I'd turn into a girl—I tried and tried, but my dad and I were both too chubby to conjure my magical sex change. In contrast, my brother and my mother were slender. We never called my father fat, but that's what he was. We called my father heavyset or stocky, or built like a bull. He liked that last one a lot.

In the '70s my dad discovered astrology and heavenly validation that he was Taurus, the bull. My dad loved being a bull as much as he loved being a male chauvinist pig. He wore turtlenecks with big gold bull medallions on heavy gold chains. The sweaters were always too tight. Didn't he see himself as fat? I'd never let anything like a roll of fat creep over my belt buckle. Since I was a child, I've dressed my best to hide the fat parts of me.

L. Ron Hubbard was fat, fatter even than my father. I met him in 1972, just when he discovered turtleneck sweaters. Why do fat men think they look good in tight clothes—because they can get away with it? Am I fat phobic? I guess I am, because I sure can't stand looking in the mirror and seeing me fat—and that's all I ever manage to see—me, fat. Fat was a big issue in our family, and fat was gendered. My mother explained it this way . . .

"Girls can be solidly built, but it's not at all attractive and it can quickly turn to too-fat. Not boys, though. On boys, a little extra meat is healthy."

My father was a healthy boy, an athlete. There weren't many Jew athletes, but my father was one of them. I hated phys ed. I took after my mom that way. It was a big deal when the dean of women of Pembroke College at Brown University called her on the carpet and informed her that she hadn't taken the requisite number of physical education credits, and until she did, my mother wouldn't graduate. She had one semester to make up for nearly four years of missed athletics. My mom devised a clever plan.

———

The lettering on the door read Phyllis Hadway, Head Coach.

My mother knocked timidly.

"Come on in, I'm not naked."

Coach Hadway was a solidly built woman with short hair who wore sensible shoes. My mother let herself into the office and at once burst into tears. My mother could conjure tears whenever she wanted to. It was something every girl needed to know how to do, she told me, after she finally began to accept me as a daughter. Her tears touched Coach Hadway's heart.

"Hey, what's the matter, honey?"

My mom explained that in order to graduate, she required education in the physical sense. Coach Hadway nodded gravely.

"Let's fix this up, Mildred. We can't have you not graduate, can we?"

We most certainly could not. Coach went to bat for Mildred. The dean agreed that if she could pass the end-of-year phys ed tests, then Mildred could graduate. And so, for her last semester of college, my mother's life revolved around faking physical education. For starters, Coach assigned her to bowl three times a week. There was a bowling alley directly beneath the coach's office, and Coach Hadway satisfied herself that my mother was bowling by the unmistakable sounds of the rolling ball and the falling pins. What the coach didn't know was that my mother was downstairs, sprawled comfortably in an overstuffed armchair, kicking a bowling ball down the alley while a friend at the other end of the alley knocked down the pins—as the two of them sipped martinis.

There was a swimming requirement as well. My mother couldn't swim, but she passed her test by holding onto a long pole, the other end of which was held by Coach Phyllis Hadway. My mother splashed and kicked as the coach slowly walked from one end of the pool to the other, dragging my mother through the lap she needed in order to graduate. And that's the true story of how my mom managed to graduate from Pembroke. My mother taught me that lesbians have kind hearts, which I've found mostly to be the case.

—

My mom was an early civil rights supporter, and to her that meant our family should buy as much as we could from colored people— who wouldn't be called people of color for another thirty years. Their stores lined Springwood Avenue, west of the railroad tracks. Mr. Knuckles, our electrician, and Ray, the dry cleaner, and Mr. Gray, the tailor, and another Ray, the plumber—they all had their storefronts on Springwood Avenue. So did Fisch's Department Store, where my mom shopped for me.

Because it served the colored part of town, the clothes at Fisch's Department Store were different from the clothes sold in the white part of town. Fisch's carried bright colors for men—hipper fashions. I had a sharkskin suit when I was twelve, and a mohair/angora blend V-neck sweater in off-white and moss green. The sweater looked manly on some of the adult men I'd seen wearing that style, but the same sweater made me look like a girl. Oh, I was overjoyed with shopping at Fisch's in support of the civil rights movement—because Fisch's Department Store carried dungarees and sweatshirts just like the kind Tommy Warner wore to school.

Tommy Warner haunted my erotic dreams all through grade school. Tommy was a tough guy, short for a boy, and even though he was white, he lived on the wrong side of the tracks. He was the closest thing to James Dean I'd ever seen in person. He wore sweatshirts and dungarees to school. They weren't called jeans in 1960.

If you used a time machine to transport Tommy Warner as I knew him to, say, the Castro in San Francisco? He'd look like any baby butch dyke I've ever fallen for. So of course I wanted to fuck him. And since I really couldn't do that, I wanted to be him. But I was a pudgy little Jewish boy who lived on the right side of the tracks. I'd been skinny until I turned four or five and realized I wasn't really a boy. Then I started eating in earnest, and I became the fat kid. I got my stretch marks when I was twelve years old. In the early 1950s, fat boys were called husky.

It took several months to convince my parents that all the kids were wearing dungarees and sweatshirts to school so why couldn't I? It was late fall, 1962, when I finally stood in front of a mirror, doing my very best Tommy Warner, including the extra hair tonic for the slicker look. I looked like an alien, setting off to eighth grade wearing my brand-new never-been-washed dark dungarees and an overlarge dove-grey sweatshirt. It was thrilling. I felt tough, like no one could give me any shit. I felt sexy for the first time in my life, and it lasted all of ten minutes into first-period English.

The teacher sent me to the principal's office to discuss my fashion statement. I was a good boy, the principal informed me, and good boys didn't wear such clothes to school.

"But Tommy Warner does," I blurted out.

"Tom Warner is not a good boy," said the principal. "Now go home and change your clothes."

My dungarees and sweatshirt were confiscated and donated, probably to someone who lived on the wrong side of the tracks. Next year, I was shipped off to an all-boys prep school where we all wore wool poplin, five-pocket, flat-front pants in charcoal-grey heather with a black blazer emblazoned with the red school crest (Washington crossing the Delaware, because that's what he did someplace nearby), white shirt, and black tie.

———

My new school required that, each semester, all the boys join some sports team. In my senior year, I tried out for the wrestling team. I was heavier than I'd ever been—200 pounds. Plus I was tall, at five eleven. Who could possibly beat me? As it turns out, anyone could. My first match in the "unlimited" weight class, I was pinned to the mat in less than thirty seconds. My coach didn't mince words.

"You're too damned fat, Al. Drop some weight and let's see what you can do in a lower weight class."

The next weight class down was 179 pounds. So I stopped eating. For three days, I only drank water. Beginning on day four, I ate one hard-boiled egg, three times a day. To keep myself from feeling hungry, I drank a pitcher of water at each meal. And I drank hot Jell-O five times a day, believing it would harden, expand, and fill me up. It worked—every day I went on the scales, there was less of me. I reported my weight loss to my dad on my weekly call home. He was thrilled. He'd had his own tricks to make weight when he was a wrestler in college.

After a lifetime of being the fat kid, I was finally dropping pounds. My own clothes were too big for me, but they were all I had. I'd shave my face smooth as silk. Standing in the mirror, wearing my now-oversize blazer, shirts, and pants, I looked waif-like—a girl wearing her boyfriend's clothes. I was over-the-moon happy. I was down to one egg a day. And Jell-O. Lots of hot, liquid raspberry Jell-O. Bright, tiny stars and flashes of colored lights were passing into and out of my vision, just like they do when a princess is happy in a Disney film. I started passing out a couple of times a day. After three days of that, I got sent to the infirmary.

The nurse called my father—as she always did when I reported in to the infirmary. My father, the wrestling champ, he had to know what was going on, didn't he? He had to know I was starving myself, right? And as a doctor, he would know all the implications that had for my body, wouldn't he? But no. Over the phone, he diagnosed me with anemia and prescribed iron pills.

I plummeted to 179 pounds just in time to wrestle midseason.

I stepped out onto the mat, lean and mean, anemic and unfocused—
and the other guy pinned me in under a minute. I couldn't have
cared less. I knew how to make myself skinny, and skinny equaled
pretty girl. I lost another twenty-four pounds and carried skinny with
me into college.

———

Brown University didn't give me an education so much as it gave me
a place to live where no one told me what to do and no one told
me what to wear. It was my first opportunity to voluntarily come together with others my age and form an extended family. I graduated
college in 1969, and I'm still in touch with friends I made there.

Brown University is where I learned sex—by the end of my fresh-
man year, I'd gotten good at it. The key was love. No matter if it was
gentle and sweet or rough and passionate, there was always love—I
fell in love with every woman I had sex with. Well, it's called making love, so I did. What's more, I only had sex with women I wanted
to be. I wanted to learn how to make sex good for her. Touching her
body, moving with her, I imagined being her, feeling what she was
feeling. I wasn't interested in my own orgasm—I masturbated for
those—so sex with me lasted a long time. Girls really liked that, word
got around, and I was making love with girlfriends of girlfriends. It
was the '60s, and we were all happy about it.

There was one kind of sex that made me feel more like a girl
than anything else: sucking cock. Late nights, I'd walk along the city
streets of Providence, Rhode Island, holding out my thumb, hitching a ride. Guys always picked me up. I was young, cute, and skinny.
They were most always professors—older than I.

They'd drive me to their houses. Most all of them were married
and cautioned me to be quiet so as not to wake up their wives. They'd
pour me a drink, lay a blanket out on the living room floor, and I'd
suck them off—quietly. In my mind, I was Holly Golightly or Ginnie Moorhead. I never asked for money, but most times I got twenty
bucks, twenty-five if I could make 'em love me. Very few of those
guys were rats—they were mostly sad, closeted gay men. The gay

rights movement hadn't yet begun, so there was no one to encourage them, no one to tell them they weren't freaks. Every one of my evening professors was a gentleman—just before dawn, they insisted on driving me home. I didn't want them to know the name of my dormitory, so I always gave them the wrong address. There was no kiss goodnight. There was no kissing ever. Kissing would have meant I was falling in love with them, and I wasn't out for love—I was out for cock, and the feel of being girl while I sucked them.

Finally, it got too painful—doing sex just for sex. I wanted romance, and there was no romance in skulking around. Periodically, I stopped hitching, fell in love with a wonderful girl, and knuckled down to being a real guy—sometimes for months or even a year at a time. Inevitably, I'd reach the point where I couldn't take it, being a man any longer—but there was no way to bring it up to my girlfriends—so I dove into weed and alcohol, way too much of both. That would trigger the breakup, and I'd be back out on the streets, hitching rides for blowjobs. There was one memorable ride . . . and one kiss.

He was in his late twenties. I never learned his name. I was nineteen, and I was stoned. He was driving a kelly-green MG convertible sports car with soft camel-color leather seats. He slowed down and pulled to a stop alongside me   he was boyish, a young Robert Redford. The top was down, so it was easy to look down and take him all in. His eyes bored into mine—I felt skewered. I smiled and nodded. He laughed out loud, hopped out of the car, and came around to open the door for me—the first guy who ever did that for me. I wondered how his moustache might feel against my lips.

I slipped into the low-slung seat; I could stretch my long legs out all the way, the soles of my feet on the firewall separating me from the engine. In one smooth motion, he slid in behind the wheel, shifted into gear, and we were on the road. I sniffed, then took a deep inhale of leather, motor oil, and English Leather cologne. I was so happy, I squealed. He chuckled.

"Have a drink."

Without taking his eyes off the road, he reached into the glove box and pulled out a bottle of crème de menthe liqueur. I sipped slowly. The green sweetness made my teeth ache, and I savored the pain of that. We passed the bottle back and forth. Each time I took it from him, he stroked my hand—only he stroked it like he was stroking my cock. Soon we were out of town; he found us a dark wooded road. Several other cars were pulled over on the shoulder—I guess it was a lovers' lane, I'd never been there before. We pulled over and stopped. The engine was still running, my camel leather bucket seat was still vibrating, and I quickly finished swallowing my drink. He leaned over and kissed me on the mouth. He tasted like a guy. I wondered if I tasted like that to girls.

"Your moustache tickles."

His eyes actually twinkled in the moonlight. I kept pulling at the green syrupy liqueur. He pulled the car back out onto the road. A warm comforting crème de menthe fog was coming over me. The tingle from his moustache stayed on my lips. I wondered what subject he taught. My guess was art, sculpture maybe. He had well-defined hands. My guess was Rhode Island School of Design. The MG came to a stop. My eyes flew open. I did a lot of blackout drinking in those days. We were parked in the middle of a cornfield. Full moon. I was scared and I covered that up with cockiness.

"Come here often?"

He laughed, reached over, and pulled me into his arms. We made out for a long time. We sucked each other's cock. It was him sucking mine that made me ask him to please drive me home. He was a gentleman and didn't question me. He put the car in gear and we crept out of the cornfield onto the highway. I slept or blacked out until he pulled over to let me off in front of the dorm I told him I lived in. After his car disappeared around the corner, I walked the four blocks to where I really lived. I smelled like English Leather, motor oil, and boy. I tasted like semen. I didn't shower or brush my teeth. I went right to bed and jerked off, imagining myself to be that guy's girlfriend. Then I was asleep. I jerked off again when I woke up.

Two weeks later, I received a small box in the mail, wrapped in brown paper. Cool! The last time I got one of those, it was a huge wedge of hashish from a friend of mine who was tramping through India. There was no return address. Inside the brown paper was a wooden box, the kind English Leather used to pack their cologne bottles in. I slid open the lid and saw, nestled in pink wrapping paper, a small green mini bottle of creme de mènthe.

My first thought was, how could I ever run for president of the United States with this as a skeleton in my closet? I ripped my name off the wrapping paper and dumped the box and bottle in the trash. If there was a note, I never read it. He never tried to contact me again. I never found out how he got my address. Maybe he'd taken a look through my wallet while I was passed out on those soft camel bucket seats. Or maybe I told him in my blackout. I often was chatty in my blackouts, which were growing more and more frequent as I drank more and smoked more weed.

———

My being skinny had a lot to do with how much I enjoyed sex. I liked the way I looked when I was skinny, and that's a big deal— liking the way you look. I was still comparing my body to women's bodies in magazines, but I'd moved beyond Sears catalogues and *National Geographic*. I was into *Playboy*, and not at all for the articles: I combed that magazine for women I could possibly become. But more than *Playboy*, there was tranny porn.

I am talking seriously beautiful boys who made themselves into seriously beautiful girls. Even when they wore dungarees and sweatshirts, they were achingly beautiful as not boy/not girl—a little bit of both, with fabulous names like International Chrysis, Candy Darling, and Holly Woodlawn. There was no Internet, but I found their pictures. That's who I wanted to be. *And* that's the kind of freak I was so afraid of becoming.

But I couldn't resist them, those beautiful boy/girls. They posed saucily in magazines with names like *Female Mimics, Chicks with Dicks,* and *Real Transvestite Beauties.* Tranny porn came in several genres. In addition to the mags, there were homemade zine-like books of tranny porn novels—mostly about men being forcibly turned into women. They had titles like *My Brother No More* and *Teased, Tormented & Transformed* and *Transvestite in Bondage*. You could buy this stuff in Times Square, where you could also see movies like *She-Males in Action, A Boy/Girl Night Out,* and *Olga's White Slaves*. As long as I kept myself skinny, I could see myself becoming the kind of girl in tranny porn who always made me wanna come, just looking at her—and it scared the hell out of me.

CHAPTER 5

A SciFi Writer, an Actor, and God Walk into a Bar

After I found out I was a girl and I began to eat a whole lot more and I got fat, I dove into reading books. Most kids can see themselves in books without having to switch genders in their mind—never mind that it's a complicated thing for a little kid to have to learn. *The Hardy Boys* didn't do it for me. I went straight for my brother's collection of classic science fiction. I read Robert Heinlein, Isaac Asimov, Fredric Brown, Ray Bradbury, E. E. "Doc" Smith, A. E. van Vogt, and more. I read them all. I never read any of L. Ron Hubbard's science fiction. When I first joined up with Scientology, it was a surprise to me that he'd written any. In my search to find people like me—outsiders—and worlds other than mine, I'd never come across anything by Hubbard.

I read *Superman* comics. My parents wouldn't let me read *Batman*, saying it was far too adult for me—so of course I bought every issue and read them sitting on the curb outside the corner store across the street from junior high, memorizing each page before I threw it away on the way home. *Batman* was all about freaks—and *Batman* was too adult because each and every freak had a storyline that revealed their innermost hearts. *Batman* told stories about real freaks—the level of freak I considered myself to be. There were lots of freaks in *Batman*—over-the-top evil freaks, comic freaks, tragic freaks. They were all freaky because of some superpower, dark obsession, uncontrollable hunger, or need to be perfect, the best, the one in charge, the one who owned everything. Some of the freaks tried to use their freaky gift as a means to do some good in the world. Some of the freaks yielded deliriously to their evil natures and wanted to destroy everything. But good guy or bad guy, all of the freaky characters in *Batman* lied about themselves. It made me feel a little bit better about my own lies.

I read a comic called *Plastic Man,* about a guy who could shape himself into anything he wanted to be. I imagined being *Plastic Man,* shaping myself into girl and never shaping back to boy. More than a few SciFi and fantasy authors had begun writing about men who were magically or technologically turned into women, women who rightly assumed themselves to be men, alien races that have more than two genders, otherworldly sexual adventures.

I was reading two or three SciFi books at a time, searching for characters like myself. It wasn't long before I wanted to create my own worlds, in my own words. In my early teens I became a storyteller. At summer camp, and among my friends, I was the kid who told good stories long into the night. I was ten years old when I started writing my own science fiction. Most of my stories were *Twilight Zone* rip-offs. I wrote on a teal Olivetti portable typewriter. There were no copy machines back then—I used carbon paper. If I hit the keys hard enough, I'd end up with my original and two copies. I proudly gave one of my first books to Aunt Frankie, my father's twin sister. Big mistake—that's when I learned a cardinal rule of writing: know your audience. I watched Aunt Frankie's face contort in horror as she read. Finished, she looked up at me and fairly shrieked.

"Death! All you can write about is death? At your age? Does your father know you write these terrible stories?"

"Ummmm."

She waved me silent. "I'm going to tell your father to take you to a psychiatrist."

And I hadn't even written the part about wanting to be a girl.

So I was off to see Uncle Jay, the psychiatrist. I was ten years old. He gave me ink-blot tests and word-association tests. I drew pictures of a house, a family, and the world. He watched me pick out toys to play with. There were wooden blocks, tin trucks, rubber soldiers, Barbie dolls, and a doll-sized tea set made of real china. I knew better than to pick up the girls' toys. The evaluation went on for three hours, and then Uncle Jay called my parents into the room to out me to them.

"Paul, Mildred, I have news for you. Albert is an artist."

My mother gasped. My father muttered, "Oh, crap."

I was thrilled with the diagnosis. It explained a lot. Being a certified artist, I had more leeway in my interpretation of the world. I didn't yet know that in our family, *artist* was another word for beatnik and/or homosexual. I wasn't allowed to read any beat authors— I didn't know there were any. My parents thought it was a big deal to let me read *The Catcher in the Rye*—I found I had nothing in common with Holden Caulfield.

Seven years after Uncle Jay pronounced me an artist, I was sitting across the desk from my academic counselor—it was my first day starting premed at Brown University. I looked down with dismay at my required courses: statistics, algebra, trigonometry, calculus. *Fuck that*, I thought. I'm a fucking artist, and I'm not doing the kind of art that needs much math. So I dropped out of premed and signed up for liberal arts.

"Way to go, Albert," said my brother on the phone, "you really kicked Dad in the teeth." It'd be the first of many times I'd kick my dad in the teeth. Walking back to my dorm that night, I felt dizzy and feverish. I stumbled into the infirmary and collapsed on the floor in front of the reception desk. I woke up a day later in a hospital bed. They told me I had mononucleosis, and I'd have to stay in the infirmary for my first three weeks of college.

When you're brand-new anywhere—especially at a new school— you look for people like yourself. You look for the people who want to play the sport or games you like to play. I'd been a theater geek in my all-boy's prep school, and I was released from the infirmary just in time to audition for a campus production of Shakespeare's *Richard III*. I was cast as the Duke of Norfolk—I had one line. I don't remember it. But I was onstage. With twenty or more other people my age who were all intent on acting. We shared four weeks of rehearsal time together. I doubled in crowd scenes. That did it for me—I was going to do theater for the rest of my life.

In acting, as in science fiction, you get to play with gender. Indeed, actors *must* play with gender, because every role you get in every play is a different kind of man or woman than you've ever played before. The key word is *play*, and I've always enjoyed playing at being someone who isn't me. And that's exactly what has always made actors untrustworthy: people can never be sure we are who we say we are. We're *great* liars.

My college years amounted to running away to join the circus. I wasn't a student, I was an actor. There was no theater department at Brown in the late 1960s, but for decades, the university catered to student productions the way another college might cater to its football team. We had terrific facilities, including a proscenium theater—with no wings, but loads of fly space. The theater engaged Mr. Leslie "Les" Jones to build and paint the sets. He was in his early sixties when I arrived—he'd been a legendary scene painter during the heyday of vaudeville.

The theater boasted four large dressing rooms, one for men, one for women, one for male leads, and another for female leads. There was a large green room to hang out in before and during the show. And there was a well-stocked costume room. In my second year at Brown, I'd moved up high enough in the theater hierarchy to warrant me the trust of carrying a full set of theater keys. Over the next three years, I learned to dress myself as a woman in that magnificent costume room. Theater people work late, so I had to wait until two or three in the morning to let myself in. Tall as I was, I was skinny, so I was only somewhat limited by the sizes. I became peasant girl, three kinds of princess, and half a dozen kinds of whore. One night I was a fairy in white tulle—I took my own breath away.

I was an artist, they'd told me, and I dove into art. There were a

few acting classes hidden deep within the English Department, and
there were courses in most every department that were applicable to
theater—and there were a sufficient number of student productions
on campus to keep me in rehearsal the whole school year, four years
in a row. Summers, I worked in summer theaters, taking jobs as a
stage carpenter, scene painter, and set designer. On top of that, I
managed to step into two or three fun character roles each summer.
On top of *that*, it was the '60s, and—shy of skirts and dresses—I got
to wear whatever I wanted to wear. I made myself over into a fabulous
hippie boy. I had one summer-long affair with a Cape Cod beach
boy. He looked like Michael York in *Cabaret,* he was that pretty. But
because I looked rugged, even manly, and because I loved women so
deeply, no one thought I was gay, let alone transgender.

I was never a leading man, more of a character actor, playing
villains, clowns, old men, and criminals—character actors can play
leading roles as long as they're in one of those categories. Professors James O. Barnhill and John Emigh mentored me for four years
through more than a dozen roles, capped off with my senior-year
performances as the Marquis de Sade and King Lear. I got hooked
on the applause. It helped my self-esteem to know that people liked
something about me, and that I had a good use for my razor-sharp
skills in lying.

At Brown, I found true love with actress JoBeth Williams. We
were Richard Burton and Liz Taylor, the stars of Brown University
Theater. After a year of mad love, I was deep into marijuana and
scotch. JoBeth wisely broke my heart and went on to become a great
actor. I was back out on the street, hitching rides with my evening
professors.

———

I was still deep into my anorexia in 1969 when I arrived at graduate school at Brandeis, just outside Boston. It wasn't called anorexia
then, not for boys. Anorexia was for girls. For me, the doctors kept
calling it anemia, and it kept me in and out of the hospital. It also
kept me out of the army. I'd grown my hair long, and I wore sandal-

wood beads over flowered shirts, suede vests, and striped purple bell-bottoms over groovy Frye boots. I wore a flowered headband around my shoulder-length hair. Skinny as I was, when I looked into the mirror, I could almost see girl.

I'd just begun my postgraduate studies in acting when the draft notice arrived. I didn't know much about the politics of the Vietnam War. I was too busy rehearsing, fucking, or getting stoned. I knew it was fucked of the United States to be overseas, meddling in someone else's country, burning it to the ground. I was expecting my draft notice, and I wasn't scared when I got it. I had a plan: I was an actor. I knew I could lie my way out of it, and I knew I could get a lot of help doing that.

Theater people help each other out, and my acting teachers helped me devise a subtle act of madness. The night before my draft physical, some girlfriends of mine helped me shave off all my body hair—there was a lot, so it took a long time. We invited other theater people; we all got stoned and called it a happening. My skin was red and raw when we finished, and my lady friends rubbed me head to toe with a homemade patchouli-scented lotion. I couldn't stop touching myself, I was so soft.

The next morning, I brushed my shoulder-length hair all shiny. I pulled on my tight purple pinstripe bells and my brightest paisley shirt. I smelled like a girl. Skinny me, that's who I was at 8:00 a.m., when I was standing in the boys' locker room of a local high school gym with about a hundred other young guys who'd been called in for their draft physical.

A sergeant ordered all of us to strip down to our skivvies, leave the locker room, and line up on the basketball court in alphabetical order. I took off my shirt and pants like everyone else, and took my alphabetically correct place in line.

"You there, naked boy!"

I smiled dreamily at the red-faced sergeant, just the way I'd been coached. I wasn't wearing any underwear.

"Get your skivvies on, boy!"

"I don't wear underwear," I explained patiently in a soft voice. "It chafes."

The entire draft physical process ground to a halt for the five or six minutes it took for the US Army to decide what to do with me. They ordered me to walk through my physical wearing my low-slung unisex striped purple bells. All the soldiers and other draftees wore some version of white underpants or olive-drab army uniforms. I alone was colorful. In this avatar, I strolled from station to station, where I was poked, prodded, quizzed, measured, and queried—every square inch of soft-skinned, sweet-smelling me.

At the last stop, I told the psychiatrist about the dream I'd had all my life—the one where I get turned into a girl against my wishes.

"In this dream," I told him truthfully, "I live in a country of all men." I told him that in my dream, there was a country of all women, and the two countries/genders had been at war with each other for an awfully long time—as long as anyone could remember. I wasn't lying. It was a recurring dream.

"For the first time in years," I told the psychiatrist, "a truce has been called. I'm being sent over to the women's side. They've tied me down to a roughly hewn wooden cart."

"And why is that, young man?"

"I'm a peace offering," I breathed. "They're gonna make me into a girl."

The doctor glanced down with what seemed to me to be a wistful look at the waistband of the girly jeans hugging my flat, hairless boy hips. A cloud of patchouli encircled us.

"I'm worried," I told the doctor.

"Why are you worried?"

"Am I going to be able to eat my macrobiotic diet while I'm in the army?"

My medical records were filled with bouts of anemia, which would support my macrobiotic-lifestyle claim if he were to ask for proof. But instead, this doctor looked me in the eye—like he was good daddy—and said,

"Son, the army doesn't want you."

He gave me a psychiatric draft deferment, designation I-Y.

I asked him for his name and address, and my father sent him a box of cigars.

———

Toward the end of my first year of graduate school, I was cast as Prince Hal to Morris Carnovsky's Falstaff in Shakespeare's *Henry IV, Part I*. It was a role that should have gone to a second-year student. Mr. Carnovsky was a legendary actor, and a complete gentleman. I was fortunate to get the chance to act with him. Kevin Kelly—the hard-to-please theater critic of the *Boston Globe*—thought we did a good job with the show. He called me out as "lanky Al Bornstein." My father was so pleased to read that. Lanky—it made me feel sexy. But the role nearly killed me.

Prince Hal as Shakespeare wrote him is a do-nothing, lazy, artsy, smart-ass drunk and womanizer who couldn't care less about the throne. He wasn't a particularly good swordsman. Hal's arch-rival, Hotspur, is a warrior, a patriot, and the finest swordsman in all of England. Well, there's a scene in the play where Prince Hal has to fight Hotspur to the death—and the script calls for Hal to beat Hotspur. The director reasoned that the only way Hal could win was if he cheated. So he brought in a professional fight director to stage our breathtaking sword-and-dagger fight. At the end of the fight, Hotspur disarms me. There I am, lying on the ground waiting for his death stroke, when my buddy Poins hands me a spiked club. I whack Hotspur over the head and win the fight. The director wanted our production to be an antiwar statement, so it worked just fine that Hal was a cheat.

At one point, I'm supposed to miss my footing, drop my sword, toss the dagger away from my body, and fall to the ground. We rehearsed it dozens of times. Three nights before opening, I hadn't eaten for a few days. We were deep in the fight scene. On cue, I lost my footing and tossed the sword from my body. Then I fell to the ground before I realized that I hadn't let go of the dagger, which was now buried an inch or so into my neck, just a hair's breadth from my jugular vein. My mom's big brother, Uncle Roy, lived nearby. He was one of the world's leading anesthesiologists, chief of the department at Peter Bent Brigham Hospital. He drove over immediately to pick me up and rush me through the emergency room. Once again, I was diagnosed with anemia. I sweet-talked the doctors into letting me get back to rehearsal. I still have the scar on my neck.

———

Doing acting isn't all that much different from doing cute, or even doing sexy. It's all *look at me, look at the parts of me I want you to see.* So, now I was good at doing that, but it all seemed selfish—the sin side of vanity, the obsessive side of Narcissus. I was raised with a Russian immigrant work ethic that said I had to be useful or I might as well be dead. So the question became: why act? I could make audiences laugh, and I could make audiences cry—in service to whose good works could I contribute my talent?

In the spring of 1970 I finished my first year of graduate school and—in the spirit of my favorite book at the time, Herman Hesse's *Siddhartha*—I set off across country to find something of spiritual value that would open me like a ripe fruit and find me delicious. I was driving a VW camper, the model that came complete with a cute little icebox and tiny gas stovetop, a nice fold-down bed, and even a hammock in the pop-top. I loved that little camper. I set off with a sack of fresh fruit, a box of veggies, dried seaweed, and a big bag each of brown rice and oatmeal.

My first stop was a huge old rambling house in western Pennsylvania—Amish country. I was driving down the highway when I saw the group of maybe fifty guys. They were raising a barn. I pulled up, offered to help, and was welcomed with big smiles and a counter-offer to stay a few days to finish things off and celebrate with a church service on Sunday. I'd sleep in my camper, and they'd feed me. Truly kind, lovely people.

I'd been a stagehand and stage carpenter for years, so working on the barn and a couple of sheds was a pleasure. The food was delicious. Freaky as I looked, I turned heads throughout the community, but they turned my head during Sunday service. The Amish youth were called up front to read from the Bible. Seventeen, nineteen years old maybe, and they stumbled over nearly every word. All of them.

Elitist me, reading was my touchstone to spirituality. In addition to all my science fiction, I was daily reading from Zen Buddhist texts, tomes of pagan witchcraft, and several books about the history of the Jews. I read my tarot cards daily. I left the Amish community the next morning and continued my journey west.

I was equally dissatisfied in my sojourns with the Baha'i, the Kabbalists, and several genuine salt-of-the-earth hippie communes. How do you reconcile spiritual whoopee with being pretty, that's what I was looking for.

The Baha'is were too Sears, Roebuck. The Kabbalists were even more dowdy. The communes tempted me. I traded one of my flowered shirts—the heliotrope, with lime-green leaves and milk-white blossoms—for a sweet, embroidered linen and flax peasant blouse that smelled faintly of sex. I left after only a few days' stay. Indoor plumbing is one of the few things in my life that has always trumped fashion.

—

July 1970. I was climbing a mountain in Colorado. I'd been reading up on the Essenes. Most people have heard about the Pharisees and Sadducees. They were the two main factions of Jews in the days Jesus walked the earth, and they were as clearly divided as early twenty-first-century Democrats and Republicans in the USA. But there was a third large faction of Jews who lived up in the desert mountains. Some scholars suggest that Jesus spent considerable time with this highly disciplined sect of ascetics.

The Essenes believed that the body is the temple for the spirit, and—unlike the warring Pharisees and Sadducees—the Essenes were advocates for peace. These were Jews who made sense to me. The Essene way of life resonated with every hippie-chick bone in my body. I decided to begin my holy journey in the Essene manner: seated on a mountaintop, fasting one day for every year of my body's life.

I was twenty-two and anorexic, so three weeks of starvation seemed fine to me. I fasted for two days, driving as fast as I could across the flatlands of Kansas. I needed a mountain soon, and I was dizzy with hunger when I finally drove up into the Rockies and pulled my camper over to the side of the road. With not a moment's hesitation, I began to climb. Mind you, I'd never climbed a mountain before. But I kept climbing, in search of a nice place to sit, where I would meditate on the world and its problems for the next nineteen days. I was about thirty feet up the side of the icy rock when I fell off. I landed in a big, soft snowdrift. That's the truth. I took my safe fall as a sign that the spirits of the Essenes wanted me alive so I could finish my quest. Lying on my back in the snowdrift, I looked up at the mountain—clouds obscured its peak. I got up, dusted myself off, got into my van, and drove into Denver to buy myself a pair of proper hiking boots.

It never occurred to me to take lessons in mountain climbing—I didn't know there was any particular skill to it. I was convinced I'd fallen off the mountain because the soles of my Frye boots were too slippery for climbing. I reached Denver just after six in the evening. The shoe store was closed, but next door was Scientology, and they were open. They were wide open and waiting for a guy like me who'd been acting his way through life. The sign on the door of the Scientology center was a picture of a hooded monk-like person, holding up a torch to illuminate a treasure chest, which cast off rays like the sun. The words underneath the picture said:

Abandon your tedious search!
The answers have been found!
Join Scientology, an applied religious philosophy.

I was an Essene-in-training, but I was intrigued. Cautiously, I walked in. Half a dozen people were sitting around the reception area, and they were all eating pizza. It smelled so good, and I was suddenly aware of how hungry I was. Was it possible, I wondered, to achieve enlightenment while eating? Eating *pizza*? The ladies were dressed neatly and fashionably. The guys all wore jeans and cowboy shirts. They welcomed me in and offered me a slice. I accepted gratefully, nibbling gingerly at my first food in days—my first processed food in over a month.

"So what do you do here?" I asked. "What are you all about?"

The young woman behind the receptionist desk smiled and pointed to a large sign on the wall, clearly labeled "The Aims of Scientology." In the interest of keeping my publisher's lawyers happy and actually getting this book published, I'll paraphrase.

Scientology wants a sane civilization. They'd have a world where *no one* was insane. Scientology wants to change planet Earth into a world with no criminals and no war. They want to accomplish that by making everyone a Scientologist. They'd focus on the most able people first, making them *more* able and prosperous. Honest people would have rights in Scientology's world. I wondered what would happen to liars like me—because according to their aims, it would only be honest people who would be free to rise to greater and greater heights.

I chewed my pizza carefully. I hadn't eaten dairy in over a month, and the cheese was already knotting my stomach up something fierce. I asked for and got directions to the bathroom, where I threw up my few bites of pizza and fainted. I fell to the floor in slow motion and couldn't get up for about three minutes. I finally pulled myself up to the sink. I washed my face and hands, rinsed out my mouth, and rejoined the people in the front room. Talk about a classy entrance.

I needed a break before climbing any more mountains. I figured I might as well find out what piece of the *Great Big Spiritual Puzzle* Scientology had figured out—then I'd fast for twenty-one days and welcome my spirit into the temple that was my body. None of that happened. Instead, I joined up with Scientology. Two years later, I married the young woman at the reception desk—at sea, aboard L. Ron Hubbard's private yacht. A year after that, she and I brought Jessica into the world.

———

Prior to my life in Scientology I'd been trying to learn boy at the same time I was secretly trying to learn girl. I was successful as a boy, and

I never showed anyone the girl I believed myself to be. The battle of the sexes raged in my mind, day and night. I was twenty-two years old when Scientology told me that life was much simpler than that.

My gender was a ship without sails, tempest-tossed. I needed an anchor. I needed a life preserver. Here's what the Church of Scientology threw me: they said I'm not my body, and I'm not even my mind. They told me that I am a spiritual being called a *thetan*—from the Greek letter *theta*, which we were told meant *perfect thought*. Male and female is for bodies, they told me. Thetans have no gender.

Can you imagine a more appealing theology for someone like me?

Part 2
*

CHAPTER 6

There's Nothing Funny about Any of This

BBC JOURNALIST: I wondered, Mr. Hubbard, if you could explain simply to a layman what Scientology is?

L. RON HUBBARD: I think that would be a relatively easy idea, because it is actually a subject which is designed for the layman and if you couldn't explain it to the layman you would have a very difficult time on it. The subject, the name means "scio," which means knowing how to know in the fullest sense of the word, "ology" which is study of, so it is actually study of knowingness. That is what the word itself means. The . . .

BBC JOURNALIST: To me that doesn't mean very much. I didn't understand that. I mean, what does it do for you—in theory?

L. RON HUBBARD: It increases one's knowingness. But if a man were totally aware of what was going on around him, he would find it relatively simple to handle any outnesses in that.

(vo): After three hours of talking we never got an explanation from him that we could understand.

—from "The Shrinking World of L. Ron Hubbard,"
World in Action, BBC Television, 1967,
filmed just three years before I joined Scientology.

"So, what's Scientology?"

Molly, the young woman sitting at the reception desk in Denver, grinned up at me. She had shoulder-length chestnut hair. Her eyes were deep caramel brown and they bored into me. It was my first contact with a Scientologist's focused gaze—I thought it was hot.

"Well, Scientology is an applied religious philosophy."

"It's a religion?"

She smiled and took another bite of pizza, and offered me another slice. Given my stomach's earlier disagreement, I declined.

"Scientology is an applied religious philosophy," she repeated, speaking slowly, enunciating each word. "We're nothing like a religion."

I turned away from her frank, unblinking gaze, which was giving me a boner. To distract myself, I flipped through some books they had on display. They were all written by L. Ron Hubbard, with titles such as *Mission into Time, A History of Man, The Science of Survival,* and *The Creation of Human Ability.* There was a small pamphlet with the unlikely title *Brainwashing*—not by L. Ron Hubbard.

"What's the difference between you and a religion?"

Molly finished chewing and answered me. "Well, Scientology *works,*" she said. "It's not about prayers that might or might not get answered. Religions are all about rescuing your soul or some such thing. Scientology says you *are* your own immortal soul. We have a technology that makes the able more able. Take you, for example—are you gonna wander all your life? Never settle down or accomplish anything? Scientology can handle that."

It wasn't hard to judge me an itinerant hippy. I still had mud on my jeans from scrambling up out of a snowbank after I fell off the mountain. But technology? Scientology had a technology? I picked up the little pamphlet.

"So, you use brainwashing technology?"

Molly laughed—at the idea, not at me. "It's proof we found," she said, "that psychiatry uses brainwashing techniques, and psychiatrists are actually in league with Soviet Communism."

"Ah." I thought of my Uncle Jay, the psychiatrist and a staunch conservative.

"Scientology is very much against psychiatry. Have you ever been to a psychiatrist?"

"Some tests when I was a little kid. Ink blots, that sort of thing."

"No treatment?"

"Nope."

"You're lucky. Psychiatry can really mess up your mind."

A vaguely prehistoric caveman gnawing on a joint of raw meat dominated the cover of *A History of Man*. Holy crap! It was all about past lives! I flipped through the pages and learned that we live in a deadly serious universe—and with humanity in the woebegone shape we were in, it was all going to crash one day. Only the strong and the ruthless would survive to inherit the planet. I'd never tried *ruthless* before. I'd tried pretty much everything else. All I knew is that I wanted to stop *wanting* to be a girl. Maybe ruthless would help.

I turned the book over to read the back jacket, which claimed that Scientology could make the blind see, the lame walk, and bring sanity to the insane. If you were already sane, it said, Scientology would make you more sane. I mentally threw my lot in with the insane in need of some sanity. And . . . past lives?!

"Who's Elron Hubbard?"

"It's the letter *L*, for Lafayette, and Ron—it's not one word, Elron. He's the founder. He built mankind the Bridge to Total Freedom, and now we get to cross it and go totally free!"

"By using Scientology?"

"Yep! Wanna try a Communication Course and see for yourself?"

"L. Ron Hubbard can cure sick people?"

From behind me, a cheerful male voice boomed, "Sure he can! It says he can on that book cover, doesn't it? That means it's true. If it isn't written, it isn't true! Keep that in mind while you're finding out who we are and what we're about. Scientology works, but it has to work for you. Hey there, I'm Larry!" He extended his hand—we pressed palms and pumped once in that time-honored American guy/guy ritual.

I asked Larry did he remember any of his past lives.

"Sure I do!" Scientologists use a great many exclamation points when they talk.

"So, who were you?"

"Well, I can't tell you details until you're further across Ron's Bridge to Total Freedom, but I'll give you a hint. Have a look at this book right here!"

He held out a copy of *Mission into Time*. The cover illustration was crudely painted—men in space suits loading boxes into a spaceship. I was confused. Did that mean he used to be a cargo hand at some spaceport?

"So, L. Ron Hubbard went back in time? That's what this book is about? And what's it got to do with who you used to be in a past life?"

Larry laughed, but he didn't make me feel stupid. He laughed like what I said was funny.

"That book right there? That's going to tell you how L. Ron Hubbard tested and proved that we have all lived past lives."

"And Larry worked with Ron on his mission into time," affirmed Molly.

"So, he really proved he'd lived past lives?" I asked. "He could remember stuff?"

"Well, I wouldn't be standing here trying to sell you this book if it was going to say he couldn't remember squat about his past lives, would I?"

I asked Molly if she and I had shared any past lives together. She smiled and told me I wasn't ready to hear the answer to that question, then she took another bite of pizza. A few hours earlier, I'd been making myself ready to fast for twenty-one days on top of a mountain. These people were eating pizza, most likely sleeping in comfortable beds, and casually talking about their past lives. I was sure Molly was flirting with me, and I was flirting back. An applied religious philosophy with pizza and wicked good flirting was sounding a whole lot better than starving myself for twenty-one days.

Larry was still talking—I hadn't been listening.

"Now *this* book cover is really cool! Don't you think?"

He was holding up *The Creation of Human Ability.* On the cover, a woman in a bear suit sat on a wooden chair in front of a red curtain, gnawing on a vaguely poultry-like thighbone. What was it with the eating from bones?

"Can't stop staring, can you?"

"Ummm . . ."

"That's because Ron designed these covers himself, based on images everyone has stored in their minds."

"*Those* images are in my brain?"

"Mind, not brain. *Brain* is part of the body. Your *mind* is a storage facility for millions of mental-image pictures that you carry around with you. And yep, everyone has these particular images stored in their minds." He tapped the book cover. "These are incidents from past lives that we all have in common—only they're hidden from our conscious minds, so it's a surprise when they effect our day-to-day lives."

"We were all bear ladies?"

Larry frowned for the first time, and switched tactics. "What do you think when you see Jesus on a cross?"

"I feel sorry for the guy?"

"How about a great big gold statue of the Buddha?"

"I'd feel inspired."

"That's because you're *supposed* to feel inspired. All the world's big religions are mental implants, and your mind thinks they're real. What really happened is that the bad guys reprogrammed your mind like you'd reprogram a computer."

"Ah."

I had no idea what he was talking about. This was 1970, back when no one outside of MIT talked about computers. The only computers that existed were something called mainframes, whose memory banks took up entire buildings.

"So whenever you see Buddha," Larry concluded, "you feel inspired. Jesus, Muhammad, all those guys."

"I am so confused."

"Your *mind* is confused, but your mind isn't *you*. I just told you enough truth to shake up your memory banks," Larry was saying. "*You* are not your memories. *You* are the guy who gets to look through all those memories. *You* are a spirit! You're not your body, your brain, or your mind! You are an immortal spiritual being, completely free from the physical universe of matter, energy, space, and time!"

"You think I have a soul?"

"I know you don't *have* a soul—I know you *are* a soul! We call that soul a thetan, from the Greek letter theta, which means *pure thought*." He pronounced *thetan* to rhyme with Satan.

"You're saying I have past lives . . . why can't I remember them?"

"With Scientology, you can!"

God help me, but this was making sense. I clasped my hands to my chest.

"This body is not who I am?"

"Nope, not in the least."

I took a deep breath and asked the million-dollar question: "Are there male thetans and female thetans?"

Larry and Molly both laughed. I'd asked a funny—not stupid— question.

"No, no, no. Sex is for meat bodies, not for thetans."

"So, in past lives, we've all been . . . ?"

"Men and women? Oh, sure! Me, I've been a man more often than I've been a woman."

"Me, too!" Molly laughed.

I had visions of Molly as a guy—maybe one of those hunky space- men who were loading up the spaceship on the cover of the book. Or maybe she'd been a gladiator and I was a slave girl—like the *Gor* series of fantasy novels I was reading at the time. My boner was back and raging.

So . . . *thetans have no gender?* These people were talking about a possible answer to the conundrum that had been ruining my life. I casually turned over the book so I didn't have to look any more at the lady in the bear suit. I figured the bad guys had programmed it to make me feel grossed out.

"Do you teach any courses in past lives?"

Molly and Larry told me that the Communication Course, or Comm Course, was a prerequisite for every other course they taught, and it would only cost ten dollars. I had a couple of hundred dollars with me—money I'd made in public parks, painting flowers on children and hippies for fifty cents apiece. I had maybe five hundred more in the bank back East. I wasn't broke, but I was being thrifty. Larry sidled up to me.

"So tell me," he said conspiratorially, "what is it you think is going to happen to you at the moment of your death?"

That did it. I forked over the ten bucks for the Comm Course.

—

As a doctor's child, I grew up believing that death is what happens when some doctor didn't do their job right. Death was losing a patient. It would happen every couple of months. My father would phone that he wouldn't be home for dinner and we should eat without him—that he'd be up, sitting with a patient, maybe old man Schlivik, who might not last the night. "Nonsense, Paul," was my mother's standard rejoinder. "You won't lose him, and we'll all eat when you get home."

Then we'd wait for old man Schlivik to die. I was a chubby little boy who didn't like to wait for dinner. So there was a system—if Dad hadn't lost him by nine o'clock, we could eat anyway. That's what happened. We were finishing dessert when the phone rang. My mother wiped her lips with her dinner napkin, rose gracefully from the dinner table, and walked in silence to the phone in the hallway.

"Dad lost old man Schlivik," whispered my brother.

"I know, I know."

My mother picked up the phone and listened to my father.

"All right, Paul. Take your time, I'll wait up."

I missed what they said next, because the cuckoo clock sang out ten o'clock—it was a loud little bird, and it always startled me. Following the last coo-coo, another set of chimes sounded the hour, followed by three more chiming clocks. They'd coo-coo or bong, one after the next. My father had set them up that way, including two Westminsters. Four times an hour, he stopped whatever he was doing and allowed himself to be transfixed by the pronouncement of time.

"Paul, I'm waiting up for you and that's all there is to it. Tell Sylvia I'm so sorry. I love you." Telephones were heavy objects back then. Even when you tried to hang one up quietly, it made a clunk you could hear across the room.

"Boys, your father lost poor old Mr. Schlivik."

"We know," we answered in unison.

"You go sit, Mom. Albert and I'll clear the table and do the dishes."

"Thank you, boys. Yes, maybe I'll have a glass of wine." Alan poured Mom a glass of white wine. He did that when Dad wasn't home.

"Can Albert and I watch *The Twilight Zone?*" It was the first season, and it was Alan's and my favorite show.

"No, it'll give you bad dreams."

I chimed in with *Pleeeeeease?* When Alan and I teamed up on either of our parents, it was my job to be so darned cute that they couldn't say no. So the night my dad lost old man Schlivik, we watched "Time Enough at Last," the scariest episode of *The Twilight Zone* I've ever seen—it still gives me bad dreams. Burgess Meredith is a librarian—the only thing that gives him joy is reading, but he works too hard and has no time to read. Spoiler alert—if you don't want to know the ending, skip to the next paragraph. OK . . . so the world blows up in a nuclear war and Burgess Meredith is the only guy left— he spends months collecting up every book he'd ever wanted to read, and now he's got all the time in the world to read them. Happy ending? Nope. He steps on his triple-thick reading glasses and crushes them beyond repair, so he can't read a word. We watched that episode of *The Twilight Zone,* and then we went to bed. I was still awake, worrying about the bomb falling and me not being able to read anymore, when the back door slammed shut—my father was angry.

"Damn, damn, damn."

He never took it easily, losing a patient. None of us used the words *dead, die,* or *death.* Patients got lost, and it was doctors who lost them.

No more was said. I was the only one in the family who wanted to know more about death. I'd bring up the question at the dinner table, and my dad would only scowl and talk about the difference between heart-dead and brain-dead.

"Do you *know* it when your heart dies?" I asked him. "Do you *know* it when your brain dies?"

My dad's face crumpled up the way it did the afternoon he heard that some doctor had lost his father.

"I've seen patients sit up in bed after heart death, Albert—they just come back to life. Some of them are changed, some of them don't remember anything about it. Brain dead means our instruments can't measure your consciousness anymore—God help you, you still might be conscious and we wouldn't know it. I can't imagine how frightened that patient would be."

"And what if the bomb drops, Dad, what about then? Is there a heaven? Is there a hell?"

Jews never talk about heaven or hell, but my dad kneeled down in front of me, so we were eye to eye. He spoke softly.

"There's a heaven, Albert, and there's a hell—but only if you want them to be there."

My mom knelt down beside my father.

"You want to know about death, Albert? Start with trying to feel the exact moment you fall asleep. Once you've felt that in-between place that isn't awake and isn't asleep, I bet that's when you're going to know a lot more about death."

Neither of their words made sense to me, but decades later I believe now what they both told me then. Over the years, I asked them to tell me more—what did they knew about death? But I learned not to ask. Death went back to being when a doctor lost you.

———

As a newbie, it was jarring to hear how nonchalantly Scientologists talked about death—even though they only spoke about it via the terms and conditions written down by L. Ron Hubbard, the B-list SciFi writer. Hubbard acknowledged great thinkers and freedom fighters who preceded him, but ultimately any ideas about life, death, and the nature of humanity other than his own were considered wrong, or at best incomplete. Anything that Ron hadn't written—or anything that Ron wrote but someone had altered—was called *squirrel technology*. It's a high crime in Scientology to alter any of Ron's words—but if you want to read the Church canon I read when I was a Scientologist, you're going to have to go digging for original copies of the books. There aren't many left around. It's a fact that while David Miscavige, the leader of today's Church, has been in charge, at least eighteen of L. Ron Hubbard's books have been edited and reissued. I'm saying this to make the point that the Scientology I subscribed to then isn't the Scientology you'd find today if you were to walk into a Church of Scientology. But one thing has remained unchanged: Hubbard's notion of the great big secret to humanity's suffering—his SciFi vision of the dawn of humanity, which would be revealed decades later in 2005 when the TV show *South Park* aired an episode called "Trapped in the Closet."

Here's the gist of it. Seventy-six million years ago, the evil overlord Xenu had to solve the problem of an interstellar baby boom in the Galactic Federation, the likes of which had never been seen before. As his final solution, Xenu captured billions of thetans, then froze each of them into their own block of ice and had them flown to planet Earth, which was then called Teegeeack. Xenu's troops dumped the iced thetans into volcanoes, which he then ordered exploded with hydrogen bombs. Completely disoriented, the thetans flew up out of the volcanoes, where Xenu had positioned thetan catchers—huge funnels in the sky. When all the dazed and confused thetans were rounded up again, they were implanted with images that would enslave them—images like Jesus Christ, Buddha, and (I can only presume) ladies in bear suits seated on a stage and gnawing on a bone. After all the violence done to them, the thetans' sentience was nearly completely degraded. That's when Xenu let the thetans loose here on Teegeeack, where these "degraded" thetans attached themselves to early cave dwellers, believing themselves to be part of the cave dwellers' bodies. They became what Ron calls *body thetans* or BTs.

This explains why you're not always in complete control of your body, because thousands of decayed body thetans are controlling minute parts of your body and your mind, and their existence is blocking you from total freedom.

South Park ran a cartoon version of Hubbard's version of the story of creation, overlaid with the words, "This Is What Scientologists Really Believe." It's true, we did. We thought Darth Vader was small change compared to the evil that was Xenu. We believed in Xenu, but we thought he was laughably pathetic in the face of our superior technology.

The Church of Scientology to this day is grounded in principles expressed in metaphors and language rooted in mediocre SciFi and pulp fiction, and there's some pretty wacky stuff in those stories. But that's nothing new—lots of religions use wacky metaphors to get their points across, and most religions don't take kindly to you laughing at their wacky metaphors. Scientology's wackiness isn't laughable to Scientologists because they understand that their success or failure in the world is a matter of intergalactic life and death. If you laugh at *that*, it simply proves you aren't a real Scientologist, you are a squirrel. When you laugh because you didn't know any better, you are what Scientologists call a *wog*—a nasty racist slur first used by British colonials to refer to native Asians.

———

I was raised to believe some pretty wacky stuff. I *believed* that Abraham, the Patriarch of Judaism, was visited by God, who, doubting Abraham's devotion, ordered him to lay his beloved son, Isaac, on an altar, and kill him with a knife. Sure, Abraham agonized over what life would be like without his dear son . . . but finally he decided he loved God first and above all beings—and God the Father wanted proof of that.

So Abraham laid his son down on an altar. Isaac was fully conscious, and he agreed to do this. Why? Because Abraham said, "I love you, Son. You're a good boy, and I want you to make me proud of you in the eyes of my father, God, who's up there watching us right now." And Isaac bought it, because Abraham had first dibs on Isaac's heart. Then Abraham raised the blade. Was Isaac smiling, do you think? The Bible never tells us what's going on in Isaac's mind. Might he have *wanted* to die under his daddy's blade? He did, after all, just lie there. Might he have been the world's first goth kid with a death wish, looking up at the blade in his daddy's hand and thinking, *Yeah, cut me, daddy. Wanna bleed for you, daddy.* Well, that's how I've always read it.

So Abraham brought the blade down with all his might—and only then did God step in. He had an angel stop the blade a hair's breadth from Isaac's neck. Then God said, "OK, I believe you, Abraham. Go, be a patriarch of all Jewish people everywhere and forever—and you, Isaac, do what your father tells you to do, or next time I won't stop the blade." The end.

Talk about wacky metaphors, do Jewish fathers know how badly they're traumatizing their sons each time they tell them this story??

———

Most all people laugh at one wacky religious myth or another—it's all fodder for comedy. But back when I was a member of the Church of Scientology, and someone laughed at us? We'd smile to ourselves and think, *Wait till we take over the planet. Then we'll see who's laughing.*

CHAPTER 7

Where Have All the Flowers Gone?

The swinging seventies swept across the USA on a wave of free love. Out in the wog world, hippies lived communally—they shared each other sexually. They said *I love you* to everyone and they pretty much meant it. In the suburbs, husbands swapped wives and wives swapped husbands. Singles prowled city bars in hopes of a quickie. Orgies were readily available for little more than the price of admission and a couple of drinks. Sex was everywhere in Scientology too, except for between me and Molly—we were best friends, not lovers.

I was getting laid . . . a lot. I'd been living in Denver just over a month, and I was still the artsy hippie boy. Anorexic me, I looked hot in the bright bell-bottoms and flowered shirts I'd brought with me from back East—people didn't dress like that in Denver yet. Depending on who was assessing my fashion statement, I was eye candy or a brightly colored target. To keep myself unmistakably manly, I sported my manly moustache. My red-black hair curled down to just above my shoulders—I wore an embroidered headband to keep it out of my eyes. No, that's a lie. I wore the headband because it looked pretty and it made me feel like a girl. I think it's true that ladies dress for other ladies, and the ladies of Scientology liked my taste. They liked the taste of me, and I wore the taste of each of them on my moustache. Before you start thinking I'm being all misogynist here, please understand that it was me who was the sex object. I was passed from woman to woman like a good book. For me the sex was still less about me having an orgasm and more about *how on earth could I please a woman?* Sex was imagining myself as the woman I was having sex with.

I'd stopped smoking grass. Scientologists aren't permitted to use recreational drugs—it messes with the pictures in your mind. The pictures that are bad for you are called *engrams*, and they're the mental images that hold the memories and sensations of pain, suffering, and any degree of unconsciousness. So no drugs for me beyond the two packs of cigarettes I smoked a day, and getting rip-roaring drunk on my rare moments of time off.

I'd found part-time work as a scene designer and set builder at Denver's Third Eye Theatre. Days, we built sets and rehearsed shows. Nights, we performed. Theater people rarely get to see much sunlight. I was the only Scientologist in Denver who was acting on the stage, and that earned me even more points with the ladies. Given Scientology's ill will toward homos, I politely turned down several very sweet offers by some very handsome guys—the kind of butch gay men who've always been able to make me feel like a woman.

To remove myself from homosexual temptation—and to make enough money to pay the rent and take more courses in Scientology—I left the theater and found myself a job as a night watchman. I worked the graveyard shift with Rex, a wouldn't-hurt-a-fly German shepherd. I slept days and took classes in Scientology five nights a week and all day Saturday and Sunday. In Scientology, there are no teachers—no one can teach you anything better than Ron himself. Instead, there are *course supervisors*, whose job it is to watch that you read and listen to the words of L. Ron Hubbard correctly.

Between class periods, I'd hang out with Molly, Larry the franchise holder, and whichever girl I was sleeping with at the time. Molly knew all about my promiscuity—she found it amusing. She told me that the women at the center had a nickname for me. My name was Al, and they called me Alley Cat. Life in Denver was good. I enjoyed being a boy toy to the ladies of Scientology.

During course breaks, all of us would swap past-life stories—I don't think they let you do that anymore, but we spent hours speculating on the abilities of OTs (*operating thetans*—spiritual beings who live exterior to their bodies, with full perception and ability). Larry was the only OT we'd ever met, and we were in awe of him. Back then, as now, the Church discouraged OTs from showing off their superpowers—but this was Denver, the Wild West. So when I asked Larry if he could move a piece of furniture without touching it, he just laughed.

"Sure I can," he said. "But let's make it interesting. If I can move that chair without touching it, you'll buy two more books tonight. If I can't do that, your next course is on me."

"Deal." Holy shit, we were finally going to get to see some OT action!

"OK, bear with me. I'm only OT III, not OT VIII. I can't do this anywhere, anytime."

He climbed up onto a desk, where he stood with his fingertips to his forehead. He closed his eyes. I looked over to Molly, who looked back to me and shrugged her shoulders. Larry frowned and opened his eyes.

"The chair's too close to the window, and there's too much interference from the street outside," he said to me. His fingertips were still pressed to his forehead. It was clear that this position had a lot to do with the powers of telekinesis. "Could you please drag the chair into the center of the room?"

I did. He closed his eyes again, frowned, and said, "It's just too far away. Just drag it a couple of feet closer to the desk, will you?" When I did that, Larry opened his eyes and grinned at me.

"OK, I made the chair move without touching it . . . twice! Now, go buy those books."

I was liking Scientology. Slapstick wins me over every time. There's not much slapstick left in today's Church, though, if that's what you're looking for. But when I was traveling across the USA, I was looking for a God to believe in. Talk about slapstick, I was born with a God whose whim ended up with me being a boy who didn't believe I was a boy—and I was *commanded* to love Him. How do you love a God who does something like that to you? Well, as a young, conservative Jew in the 1950s, I learned that loving God meant you obeyed Him and you feared Him. In the Old Testament, someone's always on their knees, begging Our Father's forgiveness, promising to be better next time, swearing to be more obedient or love Him above all others. My little-kid brain turned that into *That's how daddy wants you to love him, or he'll get angry.*

In 1960 I was twelve years old, teetering on the edge of my bar mitzvah and life as a born-again Catholic. A nun, that's what I *wanted* to be. A year earlier I'd watched the film *The Nun's Story,* six days in a row, all for free because my big brother managed the movie theater. Audrey Hepburn is Sister Luke. She marries Jesus and fucks it up totally with God, who's now her father-in-law. Free spirit that she is, Sister Luke divorces Jesus because he can't or won't stop his dad from bossing her around. The last scene of the film is one long take of Audrey Hepburn leaving the nunnery to pursue her life's calling as a doctor and to help fight the Nazis. That's who I wanted to be! I wanted to be that girl—join a nunnery, fail miserably at obeying God, and go off to follow my heart's desire. I owned a rosary and a missal. I bought them in a Catholic bookstore, conveniently *en route* to Hebrew School. I kept all these sacred objects hidden behind a loose panel in my bedroom. That's where I'd later hide all my girl clothes and tranny porn. When I felt afraid of God, I said Hail Marys over and over and over and over. I studied *The Book of Saints* more thoroughly than I studied the portion of the Torah I eventually read from the pulpit on the day of my bar mitzvah—and despite the fact that I became a man in the eyes of my synagogue, I never gave up my dreams of becoming a renegade nun. To this day, I invoke Sister Luke's spirit of disobedience.

I grew up on evening-prayer terms with God, but as a hippie, I came to believe the Beatles when they told me that *all you need is love.* Scientology overlaps Judeo-Christian fundamentalism on the understanding that *to love is to obey.* I've lived with *that* equation all my life, and the only way I've managed to make it work for me has been by finding someone to obey who (a) won't be mean to me and (b) makes me shiver with desire—but that wouldn't come for decades after my twelve years of service to the Church.

—

Molly and I fiercely believed in Scientology's attitude of all-or-nothing. We left Denver together and traveled to California to join the Sea Organization—*sea*, because we would live and work on ships. Ron said that life aboard ship would make men out of us mice, alpha wolves out of us betas. In August 1970 Molly and I each contracted with the Sea Org for a period of one billion years—all or nothing—dilettantes not welcome. The Sea Org fleet was three strong when I joined: a ship in Copenhagen harbor, a boat in Long Beach, and the Flagship, whereabouts classified.

In the 1970s, the Sea Org was topmost management for all of Scientology. We were the elite corps. Sometimes, we were the shock troops. We wore naval uniforms. We had ranks and insignia. We saluted each other. Depending on our rank, we called each other *sir* or *mister*—it didn't matter whether you were a man or a woman, right? Thetans have no gender.

Molly and I still hadn't made love. We were beginning to flirt with the idea, but any chance of a private space together disappeared when we signed on as Sea Org crew of the *Bolivar*, a souped-up subchaser from World War II. The *Bolivar* wasn't big enough to be called a ship—she was a boat. Captain Bob Young was ex–British merchant marine. He was one of the very few people in the Sea Org who knew anything at all about ships. And we wouldn't know it until much later, but Captain Bob was one of the very few Sea Org officers who was fun to work for. Molly was assigned to the galley; I went to the Deck Force.

We crewed the *Bolivar* for less than two months before we were reassigned to the flagship of the fleet, the twin-screw motor yacht *Apollo*—home of L. Ron Hubbard, who had appointed himself Commodore. At 340 feet from stem to stern, the *Apollo* was one of the largest private yachts in the world, second only to Queen Elizabeth's—and hers was only a foot longer. The *Apollo* was a beautiful ship. She'd been a channel ferry that had crossed the Irish Sea with cargo and cattle belowdecks, and cabins for about a hundred passengers. During World War II, she became a troop carrier. I get it now how all those *Star Trek* characters fall in love with their ships.

The Commodore often hinted that all Sea Org members were reincarnated officers of the old Galactic Federation millions and millions of years ago. Hey, we knew we were immortal, so it was no big deal to sign a contract for a billion years. The Sea Org motto is *We Come Back*. It was all very *Star Wars*—way before *Star Wars* came out—and we loved it. Sure, L. Ron Hubbard had been a so-so science fiction writer back in the forties. So what? He was good at painting the big picture and making it all real for us.

In his SciFi, Ron Hubbard wrote about good and evil—and so, we lived it. He wrote about folksy space jockeys who saved the universe in the nick of time—that was us. He wrote about the great hardships they had to face and how long it would take to get the job done. Life in the Sea Org was hard, and we knew it would take us well over a billion years to clear out this sector of the cosmos. There were good guys and there were bad guys, and we were the good guys out to save the universe. It was all a great and noble adventure for the love of humanity. That's how it started, anyway.

———

Winter 1971. The *Apollo* was tied up to the dock in Agadir, Morocco. I was pounding hemp and pouring tar into the seams between the long planks of teakwood, one laid next to another. Ships, however subtly, corkscrew through the sea—there has to be space between the planks for give and take. That space is filled with long, sticky ropes of hemp, which are covered with tar. Eventually the hemp dries out and the tar cracks—it was a full-time job to maintain the decks with pliant hemp and tar. That's where I came in—I was posted to the Deck Force with the job title Decks In Charge.

The work was routine, just a few steps. I roped off a section of deck to make myself a work area of roughly eight feet by twelve feet. The first phase was to pry up the cracked tar and dried-out rope—I used an old twelve-inch steel marlinspike. From a large spool of fresh tacky hemp, I cut one-foot lengths. Using a mallet and chisel, I tapped the thick, sharp-smelling stuff down into the cracks.

The next phase was to seal the hemp with hot liquid tar. Off in one corner of the deck, I'd set myself up a cast-iron pot to hang over a propane flame for melting the chunks of hard rubbery tar. The cauldron bubbled sensuously, giving off the unique scent of hot tar. To this day, recalling the smell can calm me down.

Then came the tricky part of the job: I had to fill a long-handled cast-iron ladle with thick bubbling tar and carry it to the patch of deck I'd prepared with hemp—without spilling a single black drop. Then I'd ladle the tar down into the wide cracks between the planks so that my bead of tar completely filled—but didn't overflow the crack. Depending on how much you spilled, it could take up to half an hour to remove the stain from sun-bleached bone-dry teak. My year as Decks In Charge taught me grace. I got so good at that job, I could lay a straight bead of tar, six feet long, on a rolling sea.

The sundeck was the topmost deck of the ship. The Hubbard family lived below—his wife and children to starboard, and the Commodore himself to port. For quiet's sake, I'd work the entire deck barefoot, because the Commodore was most always somewhere beneath me, working or sleeping. In either case he wasn't to be disturbed. The hot deck seared the soles of my bare feet, but I was stretching my ability to take whatever the sun wanted to dish out. When I was a fat little kid in the 1950s, the sun scared me and burned me red as any steamed lobster. But when I finally came to understand that I was a thetan? Ha! I laughed in the face of sunburn! It took months to burnish my skin to a mellow deep red-bronze—it made me feel sexy, hot to the touch. I felt fine about pretending to be a guy. According to Hubbard's theories, that's what all thetans were doing anyway— we're all pretending to be human.

—

I enjoyed my life as a knuckle-dragging deckie—and like all Scientologists everywhere, I kept a statistic of my production. My stat was "number of square feet of leak-free decking." In Scientology, a person's worth was measured by production, and production was measured by stats. How you were treated by the officers and your crewmates was determined by the line of your statistic on a graph: how steep up, how steep down.

"Al's stats are up. He's a good guy." And they treated me like a good guy. Yay, upstats—boo, downstats.

If your stats were down, friends tended to shun you, sneer at you, or pick on you. According to Church doctrine, statistics determined your *condition of existence,* i.e., how effectively were you helping Ron and the Sea Org take over the planet. Everyone's stats were to be truthfully told and openly posted. Lies are anathema to Scientologists, especially lies about the Church and lies about production. All Scientologists in good standing are trying to produce something— anything—that helps the Church of Scientology take over the planet. Those are their words: *take over the planet.* In the Sea Org, there was no relaxing, no goofing off, no leisure time. We were on duty or on call for duty 24-7, for every day of our billion-year-long contract. Well, it was rumored you'd get twenty-one years' furlough between lives— but I never saw that written. Judging by the increasing number of young teens in the Sea Org—my two grandchildren now among them—time off between lives is likely to be a whole lot less than twenty-one years.

———

Sea Org members were allowed two weeks' leave of absence every year, if you could find your own replacement and if there was no important work to be done. Deckhands were considered easy to replace, so the Deck Force became the principal replacement pool, and we'd work belowdecks at some administrative job that would measurably help Ron take over the planet.

Belowdecks was another world—a messy one. Workspaces were assigned along the narrow passageways of the lower decks. Maybe five or six Sea Org members could afford real desks at antiques shops ashore, but most desks were made from four- by four-foot sheets of plywood, hung from the deckheads by any combination of rope, string, wires, and chains. Filing cabinets and bookcases jutted out into the walkway at crazy angles to the bulkheads. And paper—there was so much paper.

Everyone—from L. Ron Hubbard himself to the lowest deckhand on the ship—was issued an in-basket and an out-basket. There were no pending baskets, ever. Nothing was to be kept pending. If you picked up a piece of paper, you were by Church canon supposed to deal with it then and there. Most all of us learned how to stash our pending dispatches and orders out of sight, but even then most everyone's in-basket overflowed to their desktops. If your stats were up, inspectors might overlook your overflowing in-basket. If your stats were down, inspectors searched for, found, and announced your forbidden stash of unanswered memos and orders.

At sea, 'tween decks was not only messy, it was dangerous. The pitch and yaw of the ship caused the hanging desks to sway dangerously on their ropes, chains, wires, and strings. Despite "readiness for sea" drills, there was always a bookcase or filing cabinet falling on someone because it hadn't been tied up correctly. Everyone aboard was responsible for making their areas seaworthy—we usually sailed on twenty-four hours' notice. Every couple of months, though, we might only get a one- or two-hour heads-up before we set sail—usually caused by a public relations flap onshore. Over time, most of us learned how to quickly pack up and make ourselves safe and ready to travel.

My first transfer to an administrative post arrived in my in-basket a few months after I'd come aboard the Flagship. On any ship, the bosun is in charge of the Deck Force. He's the guy who knows the most about ships and boats. George, our bosun, wanted me to keep on tarring decks, but he had no choice but to sign off on my two-week leave from the Deck Force as Temporary Director of Promotion. Joan, off to visit her family, briefed me on the job in one sentence.

"We don't sell anything here on Flag, so there's really nothing to do." She waved her passport in front of my face gleefully. "I'm all ready to leave. They passed me on all my security checks."

Our passports—crew and passengers alike—were kept in a safe in the Port Captain's office. To get your passport back with permission to leave the ship for any extended period of time, a Sea Org member was subjected to rigorous security-clearance checks—sec checks—by inspectors of the Church whose job it was to ensure that you hadn't committed any crimes and that your intentions were aligned with Command Intention. In a pre-leave security check, you'd get hooked up to an e-meter, the Church's tool for spiritual counseling. You picked up the electrodes—we called them cans, because Ron's earlier model of e-meter used tin cans to pass the small current through a person's body. Mental mass, he said, would register on the meter. One of his earlier versions of electrodes were alligator clips, but he only used those on tomatoes. Truth.

The press likes to call the e-meter an inaccurate lie detector, but we knew better. In the right hands, the e-meter could locate and uncover our deepest thoughts, our hidden secrets, even the ones we weren't consciously thinking. These are the sort of questions you might be asked in a sec check. (I'm paraphrasing.)

> Is it your intention to leave the Sea Org?
> Do you have ties to any criminal organizations?
> Are you planning to speak with a psychiatrist or psychologist?
> Do you have plans to contact any known suppressive persons?
> On your leave, are you planning to engage in any sexual
> perversions?

Questions like that, for hours. If the meter registered any mental charge on any of the questions, you were obligated to confess your crimes. If you had mental charge and no crimes this lifetime, you had to look at your past lives and confess *those* crimes. Then, your mental charge would be gone and you wouldn't be tempted to commit that crime again. You were security checked for however long it took for the e-meter to read clean on everything you were asked. We all had our own tricks that could—most of the time—manipulate the reactions that might show up on the meter.

Joan had passed her sec checks and was off to visit her family. I had myself a desk, an empty filing cabinet, and not a lick of work to do.

I spent my time studying Ron's scale of emotions. As early as 1955, Ron had laid out all human emotions on a hierarchal scale.

He assigned each emotion a numerical value—some emotions being only decimals away from others. For example, wogs might say that someone is angry. We Scientologists would say that that person is 1.5. It was all about the precision with which we could predict human emotion and reaction, and thus control it. I was closing in on a theory: what better tool for sales and marketing than a mathematically precise way to get people to listen to what you want them to hear? All you had to do was find out where they were on the tone scale, and talk to them a half to a full tone higher, and presto! They'd feel better.

No matter that there was no promotional work to do, there was plenty of other work for me. At sea, all ship's crew—administrators included—did bridge duty at one of several posts: helm, lookout, navigation, radio. I was a lookout. In port, we all took turns standing watch a two-to-four-hour shift as Quartermaster (QM) of the Gangway. During the day, it's a busy job: writing down the names of people as they came aboard or left the ship—logging whatever supplies were loaded aboard—and keeping an eye on what was going on in the rest of the harbor. In predawn hours, QM is a piece of cake. But it was during predawn hours that I got the Y-shaped scar you can still see on the palm of my right hand.

The scar is nearly three-quarters of an inch long, and it cuts across both my heart line and my life line, causing more than one old gypsy lady to glance up at me with varying degrees of pity and horror. I got that scar when I caught a chunk of teakwood as I skidded across the poop deck while I was trying to single-handedly save the Flagship *Apollo.*

We were tied up at the Portuguese island port of Funchal, hundreds of miles west of mainland Europe, out in the North Atlantic Ocean. It was a quiet morning, chilly and damp. I was leaning against the ship's rail, daydreaming about a past life I'd led as a lady pirate. Every ten minutes or so, I'd pace the deck from dockside to harbor side, peering into the harbor's darknesses for agents of suppression.

The sun had risen above the island's tallest mountain, warming up the harbor air into a mélange of delicious smells: low tide, freshbaked bread, and tar. The morning fog swirled itself away under the early-morning heat, and I could see across the harbor to where a rusty old Russian freighter maybe a hundred yards off our port beam was inexorably, almost dreamily, steaming dead at us. Holy crap! The Russians were coming. *The Russians were coming!* Ron always said it'd be the goddamn Communists.

Moored as we were, we couldn't get out of the vessel's way—and the silent freighter didn't have time to stop. Ships and boats don't come to a dead stop in the water. There's no brakes. Some deep-sea oil tankers can take up to two miles before they come to a full stop, and that's with their propellers in full reverse. Seasoned sailor that I was, I realized in the blink of an eye that the freighter wasn't able to stop short of ramming us, and I was running across the deck when I skidded and fell. A teakwood splinter half the size of my thumb ripped open the palm of my hand. Nevertheless, I scrambled to my feet and sounded the Damage Control alarm.

Horns, bells, and sirens sounded out on every deck of the ship. My palm ached. Damage Control Teams sprang awake and raced to their stations along the ship's rails. We'd had drills for damage control, but none of us ever thought we'd actually be doing what we'd drilled to do: lowering mattresses and truck tires suspended on thick hemp ropes down over the side of the ship at varying heights, in the hopes of cushioning some of the inevitable impact. Dark red blood dripped from my palm to the bright white decks—not that I noticed, because the Russian freighter was now sounding her own horns and whistles. They'd run signal flags up their mast, undoubtedly in some naval language that bridged English and Russian. But none of us on board the *Apollo* could read those flags. To our credit and using a book, we managed to run up some flags on our own foremast that pretty much said, "We're tied up at dock. You have to turn."

The first sound of Damage Control woke up the Commodore, who had burst out of his office and now stood at the rail two decks above me. He was swearing a blue streak at the hapless officers and crew of the Russian freighter. I finally noticed the pain in my hand and stared down dumbly at the chunk of wood sticking out of my palm.

"You goddamn Commies and your goddamn rust-bucket!" Ron yelled. His booming voice bounced off the mountains that ringed the port. Early-morning dockworkers craned their heads to see an old man scream in vain at certain destiny. I pulled the splinter out of my hand—gobbets of my blood burned bright red blossoms into the bone-white splinter-dry wood. Time had slowed to the point where I could reflect on that. And that's when the Commodore leaned out over the rail and roared across the harbor in the loudest, angriest voice I'd ever heard.

"*Turn*, you jackass *Commies! Turn!*" The echoes of his command bounced off sea walls and jetties: *Commies turn. . . Commies turn. . . Commies turn.*

Windows flew open in the town across the harbor. We all braced for the impact, the squeal of steel ripping steel. And then the freighter turned. She did. Impossibly, that rusty old Russian freighter turned on a dime and steamed her way out of the harbor without slamming into us. Isn't that the damnedest thing?

The Commodore laughed, waved at us, and went back to sleep. He was never really angry in the first place—he only *sounded* angry. The Old Man had mastered human emotion and reaction decades ago—he was miles above Anger, 1.5 on the tone scale. He alone lived in Tone 40, Serenity of Beingness. It's the emotional tone at which a sentient being can do anything. The Old Man had obviously assessed the Russians at an emotional tone of Fear, 1.0. The Commodore acted out No Sympathy (1.2), and when he had their attention, he upped his emotional communication to 1.5, Anger—well, rage, but rage isn't listed on his scale of emotions. It sure looked like rage—it looked a lot like my father's rage—but all the while, Ron was really using the power of Tone 40.

———

I spent two weeks as Temporary Director of Promotion, poring over Hubbard's theories of controlling human emotion and reaction. Emotions weren't the only phenomenon that Hubbard had jimmied into a hierarchal scale. In Scientology, there are mathematically precise scales for every human perception. There are scales for justice and scales for your very condition of existence. There are scales by which you can assess entire nations and predict their behavior. This was great stuff! But I was due to return to the Deck Force in a couple of days, so I wrote down my ideas for the Commodore.

Staff members at any level of employment in the Church of Scientology are encouraged to write daily reports to the Commodore. Aboard Flag, there was a better chance he'd read yours. His messengers combed reports for anything he might find interesting, and if you were lucky, you'd wake up to find an answer from Ron in your in-basket—in his own handwriting. The night before I left my sweet soft job, I wrote a daily report to Ron that went something like this:

> Dear Sir,
>
> I've come to the end of my time as Temporary Director of Promotion, and I'm glad to report, Sir, that I've learned a great deal about the value of your research as it applies to the fields of promotion and public relations.
>
> Your emotional tone scale is indispensable if you want people to listen to what you're promoting, or if you want them to buy what you're selling—do I have that right, Sir? It wouldn't matter if you're selling goods, services, or Scientology to an unsuspecting wog world—all it takes is to bring them uptone, make them happier with who we are and what we've got.
>
> Using your scale of emotions, Sir, I've developed a system by which I can theoretically get anyone excited about anything, just by talking higher and higher on the emotional scale. I tested this out, Sir. I stood off to the side of the line at the ship's canteen and snack bar, and I'd strike up a conversation with the people on line. After a few moments, I could assess their emotional tone. I asked them what they were going to buy, and then I'd sell them on buying something else—a particular piece of candy, for example—using an emotional tone a few notches higher than their own. It worked every

damned time, Sir. People walked away happy with what I told them to buy.

So, Sir, theoretically all a PR officer would have to do is send out surveyors to take emotional tone scale assessments of a demographic to determine their emotional tone level as numerical values. Then you'd add up those numbers and divide by the number of people who were surveyed. The resulting number is the tone level of the target population. Plan your PR campaign half a tone to a tone higher, and it's gonna be a winner every time. Right? Sir?

Well, I head back to the Deck Force in the morning. I'm looking forward to it. I miss the sun. I hope this line of thought is helpful to you in some way, Sir. It's been a privilege having the kind of job that gave me the time to figure this out.

Thanks again.

Al Bornstein, AB

Seaman AB was my rating—it means *able-bodied seaman*. A rating is like rank, but the word *rank* applies only to officers—below officer were three levels of petty officers. That would be my next step: one day I'd be promoted to Petty Officer and down the road, I'd make Chief Petty Officer. Crew would call me Chief. One day I'd be ready for that. But for now I felt proud to sign "AB" after my name—it meant I knew the basics of keeping a ship afloat. A few hours after I'd sent my daily report up to the Old Man, I was stowing my administrative paperwork, smiling to myself, when a snappily dressed Commodore's Messenger appeared at my desk. I looked up, prepared to be dressed down for the Russian freighter incident—the Old Man must have just found out it was me on watch that day.

"Sir," said the messenger, "the Commodore sends you his best regards and says he's promoting you to Warrant Officer." She saluted me.

"I . . . why?"

"Your daily report, sir. He read it and couldn't stop laughing."

And then she laughed the Old Man's laugh—well, a soprano cover of his laugh, but it may as well have been the Commodore himself standing in front of me, laughing his ass off.

The six to twelve crew assigned to the Commodore's Messengers unit were always—with one or two exceptions over the years I served in the Sea Org—the youngest crew members on the ship, female, and beautiful beyond words. There's been lurid speculation regarding the Old Man's messengers. From what I remember, and from what I've been told by ex-messengers, I'm pretty damned sure there was nothing sexual going on. But they were handmaidens in every other sense of the word—trimming his nails, powdering his feet, holding his ashtray—but no sex. The messengers were the toughest, most no-nonsense officers and ratings on the ship because they were the Commodore's avatars in the game that he was playing with us. Commodore's Messengers, each one of them, had been trained to—*mimic* isn't the right word—*duplicate* his emotional tone, his inflection, his rage, and his laughter. So this girl standing in front of me was laughing just like the Old Man. Then she spoke like him.

"Great job, Al! Great job! You're not going anywhere but Public Relations! And I'm gonna work your ass off!"

Oh. My. God. L. Ron Hubbard was gonna work my ass off!

Ron used a lot of exclamation points when he talked—he was more restrained in his writing—and we followed his example. There wasn't much calm, reasoning discussion in the Sea Org—it was all about orders and how to follow them.

The next day, L. Ron Hubbard issued a new policy letter—a canonical decree for the administration of the Church, printed in green ink on white paper. He proclaimed that public relations had finally become a simple-to-do step-by-step technology which—if you did it just the way he told you to do it—would get invariable results. The problem worldwide was low production, as measured by the statistics Gross Income and Paid Completions. The reason for low production, he wrote, was that staff members were too low-toned. At best they were Bored (2.5), but most likely they were Scared (1.0) or Apathetic (0.1). The function of public relations in the administration of the

Church, he wrote, was to manage the emotions of staff members, so they'd all be Enthusiastic (4.0) and produce lots more income and paid completions of services. In the policy letter, LRH muses on the effectiveness of a public relations officer assigned to the executive director of every church with the job of making us all Cheerful (3.5) and productive.

I don't begrudge the Old Man claiming credit for that—not then, not now. It was my idea to use emotional manipulation for the sales and marketing of Scientology—to get more people paying tolls as they crossed Ron's Bridge to Total Freedom. It never would have occurred to me to use the tone scale to manipulate staff. No, my grudge with L. Ron Hubbard only revealed itself with the benefit of hindsight. He twisted the use of my idea into something that ended up being mean to people. Sea Org officers, and Church executives in the field, had been verbally abusing staff for years—they'd never needed a policy letter to do that. But the new policy letter, based on my idea, gave officers and executives of the Church the explicit right and duty to scream at, berate, and otherwise abuse staff, all in the name of saving the planet *now, now, now.*

The next day, I was summoned to the Commodore's office on the topmost passenger deck of the ship. It had originally been the ship's gentlemen's parlor for first-class passengers. The office, ironically enough, was oval, with burled-wood paneling on the walls. LRH spent all his administrative time behind a massive oak executive desk that occupied fully a quarter of the room. His in-basket was empty. Always. His out-basket was full. Always.

"Al, come on in! Sit down! You know Sylvia?"

Ensign Sylvia Calhoun was the Commodore's personal public relations officer—in the old sense of the word. She managed the Old Man's image. Her own image was disarming—she was a pixie brunette with large green eyes that either sparkled or flashed. Sylvia was one of the few crew who questioned the Old Man's orders and got away with it. I was crushed out on Sylvia, but she was way out of my league, so our relationship was purely on the playing field of production in service to LRH.

"Hey, Sylvia," I said, forgetting to call her *sir* and grinning like an idiot.

"Hey, Al," Sylvia said, grinning back at me. "Officer Al," she teased. "Flag Director of Public Relations Al."

The Old Man was chuckling—it was more of a rumble.

"Upstat Al," Sylvia concluded.

Remembering where I was, what I was, I saluted LRH and then Sylvia. They saluted back. If I'd been a puppy, I'd have fallen on my back at their feet, wriggling and peeing myself.

We talked surveys for about half an hour. As Flag PRO, it was going to be my job to measure, establish, and maintain the pulse of all Scientology staff worldwide. Flag was in the business of sending orders out to the field, so it became my job to remove any emotional barriers staff might have to complying with those orders. I had one week to complete and tabulate the first international survey.

"You up to this, Al?"

"Yes, sir!" A snappy salute to Sylvia, another to the Commodore. Broad steps led up to the Commodore's office, and I faux tap-danced down them like I was James Cagney as George M. Cohan in the film *Yankee Doodle Dandy*—my second-favorite film of all time. Now that should have told L. Ron Hubbard something about me. But Ron already knew my whole story. He knew I wanted nothing more than to be a pretty girl.

L. Ron Hubbard pored over the confidential counseling files of everyone aboard ship. So the Commodore knew me for the sicko pervert I truly was, and knowing this I did what I'd done all my life: I lied. I played at being manly Warrant Officer Al Bornstein. I completed my staff work as diligently as I could—all in the hopes that maybe next lifetime I could be a pretty girl, daddy's girl, like Mary Badham as Jean Louise "Scout" Finch in *To Kill a Mockingbird*. As a Scientologist, I believed that would be me, one lifetime soon.

———

Daily visits to the Commodore's office continued for a couple of weeks. I completed the international survey on time. On the subject of taking over the planet, Scientology staff worldwide were at an emotional tone of 3.75, between Strong Interest and Enthusiasm. On the subject of doing their own jobs, however, the international tone level dropped to 0.95, smack-dab in the middle of Numbness and Terror.

"Gotcha!" exclaimed the Old Man, pounding his desk for emphasis. He outlined his plan to bring worldwide Scientology staff upscale to where their feelings about their jobs matched their feelings about taking over planet Earth. Because staff were so low-toned emotionally, we had to pitch the first campaign at a level of Anger (1.5). We watched the statistics as they came in at the next week-ending. Damned stats went up, pretty near one for one. There was much celebration aboard the Flagship that night. LRH's breakthrough in public relations had worked like a charm, which, in a way, it was.

Ron was so excited by the fantastic international results of his new PR breakthrough that he began to use it aboard ship. My days became casual strolls between decks, above decks, down in the engine room, aft in the galley and laundry, deep down in the lower holds of the dorms, missions management, and course rooms. I strolled every foot of that lovely old ship, secretly conducting surveys of crew members to find their emotional tones. I was under orders from the Old Man to hide the survey questions beneath casual conversation, and by golly it worked. One by one, every area of the Flagship became more productive the following week. Hot damn!

These were good days. I was an officer and a gentleman. I was learning how to be a guy in an entirely new way, but the rules for *this* kind of guy were crystal clear and written down in detail by L. Ron Hubbard himself. The promotion in rank bought me my own tiny cabin in the passenger quarters of the ship. I was a ladies' man like my father and L. Ron Hubbard before me, and I rarely spent a night alone in my bunk.

For over six months, my life aboard ship went well. And then LRH blew it—he bragged to the crew how successful he'd been in assessing their tone levels and manipulating them into more and more production. And from that point on, staff emotional-tone-level surveys stopped working. Everyone knew what was coming when they saw me. No one wanted to be seen as low toned, so everyone got good at faking it. Word of what he'd done spread out into the field.

The Commodore and I launched the second international survey two months after he'd bragged of its success. The results came in considerably higher on the emotional scale. Ron took that to mean that his breakthrough was successful beyond his wildest dreams. He pounded me on the back. I wasn't so happy, and neither was Sylvia. We knew it was padded but neither of us felt we could tell the Commodore that staff were wise and the numbers were fake.

Sure enough, the next campaign failed miserably. Stats went down. The Old Man was furious that I'd fucked up as badly as I had. I was summarily removed from post and transferred back to the Deck Force. I was happy to go. I'd had my fill of paperwork. I wanted to get back to the solitude of my bone-white decks beneath the burning sun. The Commodore let me keep my rank. It turned out to be more of a curse than a blessing.

CHAPTER 8

Love Was Never Free

The outdoor work revitalized me. I lost my private cabin, and I was back berthing up in the fo'c's'le, on the port side of the bow, in a cabin built to hold six deckies in bunk beds. We had much more room than the students or admin crew, who slept tightly crammed in triple bunk beds in the ship's holds where thirty years earlier, cattle had suffered their voyage across the Irish Sea. There was no sex in the deckhands' cabin. The bunks were too narrow, and none of us was liberated enough to have sex with a woman a couple of feet away from four or five other guys. So each of us either crept off to have sex with a woman who had her own cabin, or we learned how to jerk off in silence. By morning, the room smelled like a movie booth in an oceanfront porn shop. I enjoyed that life, until the morning a Commodore's Messenger woke me from a deep sleep. She had her hand on my chest in the manner prescribed by LRH, so we wouldn't sit up suddenly and slam our heads on the bunk bed above us. I opened my eyes—the messenger must have felt my heart pounding.

"The Commodore wants you to know that the First Mate has been transferred off the ship, and as ranking officer in the Deck Force, you're the new First Mate."

And then she was gone.

George the bosun should have gotten the job, we all knew it. But as an officer, I was expected to make it go right. This was the catch-phrase we used in the Sea Org whenever something looked too diffi-cult: *make it go right*. So me—the nice Jewish boy and closet queen—I was going to make it go right as a senior nautical officer aboard the Flagship, second only to the ship's captain. I'd been aboard the Flagship less than two years, and I was in charge of the seaworthiness of an entire ship and its crew. Beyond tarring the decks and tying some fancy knots, I knew nothing about seamanship and navigation. *Make it go right!* they told me. More importantly, I had to turn myself into a serious alpha wolf. First Mate was a big-deal job—people's lives would depend on my decisions. For weeks, I was a watched and scared thing, fumbling my way through ship's paperwork and staying up late nights trying to learn celestial navigation.

The good news was that the post of First Mate came with a roomy private cabin, up on the starboard side of the fo'c's'le—and that meant that Marion and I could move in together. She was a smart, beautiful, slender young woman, seventeen years old. I was twenty-four. Marion worked in the Data Bureau, keeping track of every statistic of every staff member around the world. She was both a woman I wanted to be and a woman I wanted to fuck. We loved each other like puppies.

Knock, knock at my cabin door.

"Al? Sir?" It was George the bosun. It was dark. Beyond an emergency, there was no reason he should be waking me. Oh god, trouble?

"Yah, George. What's up?" I sat up in bed. Marion wrapped herself around me, still sleeping. We were both naked.

"Can I come in?"

"I'll come out." I slid out of the double-bed-sized bunk and into my jeans. Marion sat up and cocked her head questioningly.

"I'll be right back." I slipped out the door into the companionway. George the bosun was doing a poor job of pretending he wasn't grinning.

"Charlie jammed a signal flag up into the sheave on the top yardarm."

I knew enough about boats to know that he meant a signal flag had been hoisted too high and had gotten itself stuck in a pulley over three-quarters up the sixty-foot mast. I knew enough about ships to know that the flag had to be unjammed, which could only be accomplished by someone climbing way the fuck up the foremast, then shimmying way out to the end of the pole of wood that crossed the mast, to unjam the fucking signal flag. The yardarm was a good twenty feet farther up the mast than the crow's nest, where I'd spent some time at sea as a lookout. I looked at George expectantly, and knew from his silence that it was up to me to figure out who was going up there.

"So if Charlie got it jammed, why isn't Charlie up the mast getting it unjammed?" I asked reasonably.

"He's too scared. He won't do it."

"Ah."

Another long silence.

"You've asked all the guys, have you?" George nodded, indeed he had.

"And none of you wants to go up there, do you?" Another nod.

I didn't blame them. The yardarm was a piece of wood as old as the ship. We all knew it was held to the mast by a few skinny bars of rusted iron.

"OK," I said. "When the sun's up, I'll get the fucking thing unjammed."

I walked back to my cabin and told Marion what I had to do. She asked me about the part where I might end up falling off the mast and going splat onto the deck. I just shook my head. Then we fucked like it was going to be the last sex we'd ever have together.

Ten minutes after sunrise, I stood out on the forward deck, looking up the mast through a pair of binoculars. Yep, way out on the tip of the yardarm the blue signal flag was crumpled up into the pulley. It was a pretty flag, one the Old Man was proud to fly. It signaled that the Commodore was aboard. I handed the binoculars over to George and—fool that I was—walked over to the ladder and began to climb. The first ten or twenty feet were easy-peasy.

I was the kind of person who didn't like to look down from heights—I'd always known that about myself. I enjoy climbing, always have—I just didn't like looking down. When I was growing up on the Jersey Shore, there were small forests on every block—vacant lots filled with trees, brambles, and vines. A lone tall birch stood high above the woods, and I taught myself to climb it. Springtime and summer I'd spend hours in the top branches and I'd be a princess locked away in a tower waiting for another princess to come rescue me. But all the time up in that tree, I never looked down at the ground—scared the hell out of me to do that.

Knowing this about myself, I looked down at the deck. All the guys were gathered around the mast, looking up at me. Aw, damn. I kept climbing. Masts on ships never rise perpendicular to the deck, they always tilt back for better aerodynamics. Well, the aftward tilt of the mast put more and more weight on my right arm. Soon, I was climbing slowly and deliberately. It took me a full minute or so for every two rungs of the ladder. I looked up to see the yardarm another twelve to fifteen feet higher. *Don't look down,* I told myself—and again, I looked down. A crowd had gathered on the deck, and it was getting larger as I watched. Word had gotten around. Everyone wanted to get a look at Bornstein climbing the foremast. Fuck fuck fuck.

It took another fifteen minutes of climbing to get myself level with the twelve-foot-long yardarm. I couldn't simply hold on to the ladder and reach out to unjam the sheave—the damned thing was strapped to the yardarm a good five feet out from where I was clinging on for dear life. I'd have to reach around the mast with one arm, and propel myself off the mast into an upside-down hanging position on the yardarm. There was going to be a moment when I wouldn't be holding on to anything. *Make it go right,* I thought to myself—and jumped. Fifty feet below me, a girl screamed.

I made it—I hung on the yardarm like a tree sloth. It would be easy as pie to let go with my arms and legs—and that made it the third time in my life I thought seriously about killing myself.

———

The first time I thought about killing myself was in sixth grade—it too was a possible jump scenario. The teacher, Miss Rickards, had divided the class into boys on one side, girls on the other. Not all the teachers did that. The boys knew I wasn't one of them, and I was the target of spitballs, sudden punches in the belly, and anti-

Semitism. My plan was to climb the drawbridge over Shark River Inlet—there were no sharks anymore, but no kids believed that. The bridge opened to let taller boats into the harbor. At its highest point the bridge was a good forty or fifty feet up in the air. I'd ask my classmate Arthur Mayer to come with me. He was a nerdy Jewish closet case like me, and didn't like his life any more than I liked mine. We'd climb up together. At the top, he would smooth my hair, kiss me gently, and we'd jump, holding hands in death. I knew he'd go for it, but I never had the guts to bring it up.

———

Still hanging upside down on the yardarm, I'd inched myself out about four feet. As I started my outward climb, the yardarm gave a jerk and began to creakily tilt out of perpendicular with the mast. I kept inching my way out, sure as I could be that the rusty braces that supported the yardarm would hold up. And even if they gave way, so what?

———

The second time I thought about killing myself was my first year away from home at Pennington Prep, the all-boys school owned and run by the Methodist Church. It was a Methodist school, and there were only a handful of Catholics and Jews. Roly-poly me, I was walking to lunch. It was a Wednesday, the cafeteria would be serving their delicious good 'n' greasy shepherd's pie.

"Out of my way, you fucking Jew."

I stopped, turned, and looked up . . . and up . . . and up some more . . . into the sneering face of the biggest guy in our class. Without a moment's hesitation, I punched him in the mouth, and he beat the crap out of me. Later, in the dean's office, it was all my fault because I hit him first. It was hard being a Jew at that school. My room was three doors down the hall from a guy who'd nailed a three-foot-by-four-foot Nazi flag to his wall. We weren't allowed to lock our doors at night, but that night I was so afraid, I did anyway—and every night after that. That's when I realized how easy it would be to simply cut my wrists. I knew how. My dad was a doctor, I knew enough to cut the length of the veins and arteries, not across them. I'd go out into the woods and cut my wrists. Yeah they'd find me but they wouldn't have to clean up much after me. Night after night, my plan grew more and more clear. President Kennedy was assassinated the day I bought the packet of razor blades, and we were all sent home for a week to mourn with our families. After a week, I didn't want to kill myself anymore.

———

All I had to do was let go—I could make it look like it was an accident. Instead, I inched myself farther out on the yardarm—and the goddamn pulley was finally within my grasp. Hanging from my legs and one arm, I stretched out my fingers and yanked the goddamn blue signal flag, which instantly came unjammed. The iron strap groaned as the yardarm jerked itself more and more out of plumb. A cheer rang up from the deck forty to fifty feet below me. That's when I should have done it. But applause has always been for me a heady antidote to suicidal ideation.

My decision to live was quickly followed by the realization that I had no idea how to get down. But damn me if I didn't act like a Sea Org officer, and with no hesitation I inched my way back to the mast. The yardarm was tilting precariously by the time I managed to reverse-jump myself to the ladder. The fifty-foot journey down the ladder to the deck was a piece of cake. People were cheering, thumping me on the back. I stepped away from the group.

"Bosun, step for'ard," I barked. George looked around nervously but came up to me.

"Bosun," I said, "that yardarm and its fasteners are in terrible shape. Assign one of your guys to have it fixed by tomorrow. Whoever it is that goes up there gets an extra day shore leave."

"Aye, aye, sir!" snapped George with a big grin on his face. "Right away, sir!"

I turned and walked back toward the fo'c's'le. Officers and crew alike gave me a hip, hip hoo-ray. I was the man. I got to my cabin, walked into the head, closed the door, and threw up.

—

January 2, 1972. In everyone's in-basket there was an order from the Commodore: 1972 is a leap year, he wrote, and according to tradition, women have the right to propose to men. What's more, he wrote, any woman who proposes to a man and actually marries him will be promoted one rank. There were some power-hungry single women aboard the Flagship, so we knew there'd be a lot of marriage ceremonies in the coming year.

His announcement didn't come totally out of the blue. We all knew what this was about. Two nights earlier, the crew had one hell of a New Year's Eve party. It was a movable, drunken orgy. Maybe a hundred Sea Org members were having sex everywhere from the topside boatdecks to the lowest holds of the ship. A lot of us were late to work the next day, and my guess is that's what brought it to the Old Man's attention: all that free love had impacted statistics. I was still living with Marion, who'd turned eighteen. She and I still loved each other like puppies.

Molly had worked her way up to the rank of Midshipman, one rank below me. If she proposed to me and we got married, she'd be promoted to Warrant Officer, and she'd be on her way to Scientology stardom. Molly was a creature of ambition, and I thought that was sexy.

It wasn't even twenty-four hours after the Old Man's leap-year announcement. It was 2:00 a.m., and the ship was at sea. I was coming off a four-hour shift on the bridge. When you're a lookout, you spend all of that time outside—either up in the crow's nest or, more usually, on the roof of the wheelhouse, which is called the flying bridge. The stewards had their own duties at sea, which included baking bread, timed to come out of the oven as we got off watch. There were always platters filled with hot, fresh-baked bread, big bowls of sweet butter, and an endless supply of strong, dark coffee. I was chewing on my completely delicious bread and butter when Molly asked me to marry her.

Marion. All I could think of was Marion—we'd been lovers for the better part of a year. I loved her. We had terrific sex with each other. Molly was looking at me, waiting for an answer. I ran my tongue lightly across my moustache, tasting Marion. She'd be in bed. I was going to bring her some hot bread and butter.

"I, uh . . . well, I'm living with Marion, y'know."

"The whole ship knows that, Al. So are you going to marry her?"

Marion and I were happy just the way we were, damnit. And why was Molly asking me to marry her? She and I had never even had sex with each other.

"She is not the right wife for you, Al. You're a Warrant Officer, for Christ's sake. What is she, a Petty Officer Third Class?"

"Second Class, Molly."

Molly snorted.

"The two of you hardly make an optimum Sea Org couple."

She had me there. L. Ron Hubbard defines sex, marriage, and children as a vector along which all beings survive, a unit that generates more power than the sum of its parts. It was our duty to marry optimally, so we'd generate more power for the Sea Org. Molly took hold of my shirtfront and pulled me across the table, close to her face.

"You need someone stronger and smarter than you are," she whispered. "You need me. Now, will you marry me?"

I couldn't control the shiver that ran through my body. Only girls got to hear the question *Will you marry me?* Girl was part of who I was to Molly. She and I had shared a past life in ancient Rome. Molly had indeed been a big, hunky Roman gladiator and I was a helpless, slender sex slave. And oh, how he used me! Oh, how he'd throw me down to the straw matting and ravish me over and over again. I still get starry-eyed, thinking about me and Molly back in ancient Rome. We *believed* that. When you've had an alternate sex-and-gender relationship with someone, you remember it. Molly knew that I'd been girl. She knew how much I liked it, and she played to it. That was our delicious flirtation: we exchanged cultural rules of gender, and she got the power. And now she was asking me to marry her. The stakes of our game had just skyrocketed. She/he wanted to marry me. I let myself swoon, the tiniest bit. I bit my lower lip, then stammered . . .

"OK. Sure. Good idea."

Molly reserves a great smile for people who do exactly what she wants them to do. It was the smile I'd always wanted from my father. I felt like a Disney princess. Molly was still talking. Ceremony? What?

"We'll have it right away," she was saying, "The Captain already said he'd perform it for us."

Oh, Molly was a confident woman. She knew what she wanted out of life. She had beautiful brown eyes, and long, soft chestnut hair, and she was a best friend, but we still hadn't had sex with each other. So *why* the fuck did I just say yes?

An hour or so later, maybe three in the morning—we were still at sea. I'd just come from telling Molly I'd marry her, and now I was standing over my bunk, looking down at Marion, fast asleep, her hair upon the pillow like a sleepy golden storm. I didn't write that last bit, it's from a song by Leonard Cohen.

"Honey, wake up." She stirred under the covers. Even in the dark, I saw she was smiling. I wasn't smiling much. I was way too sad.

"C'mon, hon. I have to tell you something."

Marion rolled over onto her back, and hunkered up on her elbows. Sleepy face.

"C'mere," she mumbled, scrunching over to make room for me on the bunk. I didn't answer, and there was a long silence. Great pauses are like great words: you never forget them. This was a great pause. It said *I love you*, it said *you're so beautiful*, and it said *goodbye*.

Marion had stopped smiling. She patted the bunk beside her one more time. I could still taste her on my moustache from the sex we'd had hours earlier. I first grew my soup-catcher when I played Mack the Knife in *The Threepenny Opera*, summer of 1967. I'd kept it, because it stopped me from seeing myself as a woman. I was a man, tasting Marion, who wanted me to come to bed with her.

"I can't," I mumbled.

She sat up, her back against the cool steel bulkhead. She was naked, and she pulled the sheet up to cover herself. The breeze from her movement blew across the bunk. Suddenly, I was inhaling Marion's scent. Any longer, and I wouldn't be able to say what I had to say. Words poured out of my mouth.

"Molly asked me to marry her, and I said yes and she asked me if I was still seeing you and I told her yes I am and she told me to come down here and tell you that I've got to break it off with you, and so here I am and so it's over between you and me and I'm so sorry." Oh boy, I meant it. I was truly sorry.

Wordlessly, she swung her feet onto the deck, stood up, and gathered up her belongings. She paused in the doorway and turned back to look at me. It was another great pause. You can see this kind of pause in all the great romance films. My eyes dropped to the deck in shame, and I jammed my hands deep down into my pockets. When I looked back up, she was gone. I made my way aft to the crew's galley. Molly was waiting for me. I was such a rat.

"Well," she asked me, around a mouthful of coffee and bread and butter, "is she gone?"

"She is, indeed."

"Good, then I'm moving in with you."

The next day, I helped Molly carry her belongs up to my cabin. She stopped just inside the door and wrinkled up her nose. It smelled like great sex. Great sex with Marion. First thing Molly did was strip the bunk. From the bag she'd brought, she pulled clean sheets and blankets. I hadn't had a clean blanket for nearly a year. But Molly was Deputy Chief Steward, and she had access to the laundry. That meant I'd have that access now, as well. Molly watched me as I made the bunk up with the crisp, clean linens. She quickly undressed herself and slid beneath the covers. It was a cold morning. I wasn't hard. I found myself longing for Molly the gladiator—not boy necessarily, but powerful. I wanted her to take me. I wanted to be the one who was firm and curvy. Standing in the cold cabin, I slowly got naked. Stripping for her made me feel sexy, and that's what finally made me hard, and we finally had our first-ever sex together. It was terrible. I'm pretty sure Molly thought so too, because we never spoke a word about it. The wedding ceremony would be in early March, two months away. We both began to eat . . . a lot. We were both substantially chubby when two months later, Molly and I were married in a Scientology ceremony performed by Captain Bill Robertson.

Captain Bill gifted us with a bottle of aguardiente—Portuguese firewater, made from the fermenting skins of pressed grapes. It's like vodka, only a whole lot stronger. I drank most of it and went into a blackout sometime during the reception. I woke up early the next afternoon. Molly was lying next to me in the narrow bed, awake and looking down at me. If I was reading her expression right, the sex hadn't been any better on our wedding night than on any night before.

"We're going to make a baby, Al."

"Oh yeah?"

"Aw, think about it: a little bitty body for the world's most super-powerful thetan—that's who'd pick us as parents, you know that's the truth."

She was right—OTs are able to pick their next bodies, and it would have to be one hell of a thetan to pick the two of us as parents.

I looked into Molly's eyes and saw not so much love as burning dedication and determination. We dressed in silence and walked aft for lunch. Officers and crew congratulated us on our marriage and Molly's promotion. Molly and I were all smiles to everyone except each other.

CHAPTER 9

Beached

It was a gorgeous summer day in the Moroccan port city of Casablanca—hardly any dust or smog in the air. The sun was high in the sky, and the sky was everywhere—not a tall building in sight. The Casbah squatted low on the horizon, just across the harbor and inland maybe half a mile. The view made me grin ear to ear. Hey, I was dangling off the side of a ship, maybe thirty feet above the harbor water, painting the ship white—*and* I was casually looking over my shoulder at the fucking Casbah—how cool was that? I closed my eyes and thought, I could be a man like this. Fuck it—I *was* a man and maybe that wasn't such a bad thing after all. It was a few weeks after Molly and I were married. I looked down at the harbor water lapping against the dock—peaceful. I could do that now, look down from heights.

"Sir?"

I looked up to see a young messenger from the Action Bureau peering over the fo'c's'le railing. He was waving a sheet of paper at me.

"Warrant Officer Bornstein, sir! I have orders here that you're to turn over your post as First Mate to the Bosun, George Charnas. Once you've done that, report to Lower Hold Three for briefing, per Confidential Flag Garrison Mission Order Number 102." He waved the paper as proof of his chain of command. All Flag Mission Orders had to be approved by the Commodore personally. "Report no later than 1900 hours. Acknowledged?"

Molly was pregnant with Jessica, which was both good and scary news. The two of us wanted to bring a strong thetan into the world, but there was a rule that no infants were allowed to live aboard any ship in the fleet. We had to transfer to any of several Sea Org land bases around the planet. Molly and I had been transferred to New York City with a step-by-step plan (Mission Orders) to set up and run a Sea Org land base (garrison). We'd been hearing about it for days, and now it was official. She was going to be my boss—I was to be her second-in-command. We'd recruit new staff as part of our Mission Orders. Hanging there as I was off the side of the ship, I squirmed at the thought of Molly as my commander.

"Acknowledged!" I hollered. The messenger disappeared from over the railing.

Molly and I had until 7:00 p.m. (1900 hours) to report to the Action Bureau, in the bottommost hold of the ship (Lower Hold Three) where all of Flag's confidential materials were stored to study our Mission Orders (No. 102 is literal—we were the 102nd Flag garrison mission). We'd study for three full days—fifteen-minute meal breaks and six hours for sleep, less if necessary. This was Mission Briefing. Missions were the heart—the glamorous work—of the Sea Org. Missions were sent ("fired") by Flag for any number of reasons: to handle an emergency, remove someone from post, or—most rarely—to reward a hardworking executive. That sort of mission is short range, anywhere from seventy-two hours to three weeks. Garrison missions are measured in years.

I stowed my painting gear in a bucket and hauled myself up the twenty feet to the fo'c's'le to make my way aft as quickly as I could. Molly was supervising the galley staff. She looked up and waved her own copy of our Garrison MOs. We hugged lovingly for the first time in months. I imagined our child in her belly, pressed so tightly against my own—and for the first time in months, we kissed long and deep.

We were going to *New York City*—the center of the world for almost everything that really matters. The Sea Org hadn't yet established a presence there, and that made us pioneers. It was a romantic dream come true for both of us. We'd be working side by side, out on the front lines of the only movement that could and would bring sanity to planet Earth. Work is where Molly and I truly loved each other. We set off together at a brisk pace to Lower Hold Three, where we were quickly shown to our briefing materials, all laid out for us on a table in a room curtained off from the rest of the Action Bureau. There was a lot to do before we'd be ready to fire.

For three days, we studied our step-by-step plan for setting up our multifunction garrison. First, we'd simply be a relay office for all communications and supplies going to and from Flag. The second step was to establish a Sea Org outpost that would serve as Flag's administrative avatar in the field for all orgs within the eastern United States and Canada. Flag would give orders, we'd make sure the orgs would comply. Back then, the word for Scientology churches was *org*, short for organization. The only time we called them churches was for PR, legal, or finance. They were orgs. Our orgs, mine and Molly's. We'd be in charge.

Each step on your Mission Orders is called a *target*, something you had to shoot at and hit bull's-eye, nothing less. During our briefing Molly and I sat across from each other, making a little clay demo (model) of each and every target on our MOs. There were over a hundred targets on our thirty-page-long orders—and per LRH, we had to know the definition of every single word on every single page. For three days, Molly and I routinely quizzed each other on the precise definition of words like *berthing, establishment, compliance*—even the small words, like *the* and *if.* This is based on LRH study technology: if a reader passes any word they don't understand completely—any word at all—everything after that word becomes confusing.

Life aboard Flag had lost most of its charm for me, and Molly seemed to agree. Sure there were fabulous moments, but she had washed too many dirty linens, and I'd poured too much tar. And there were some mean officers aboard that ship—including the Old Man, sometimes. I'd seen him scream at people, demote them from high-level executive posts down to the most menial of jobs, and humiliate them in front of other officers and crew. It didn't look to me like he was using the emotional tone scale on us—it looked to me like the Old Man was often simply a mean old man. Molly's pregnancy had come at a perfect time in our lives—we wanted the baby, and we were both ready to leave the flagship in order to bring our child into the world.

Before they fired us out on mission, we had to prove to the Action Chief that we knew precisely where our mission fit into Ron's plan to take over the planet. Only when he was satisfied that we'd duplicated Command Intention—and that we couldn't possibly fail—would he escort us down the gangplank to the waiting taxi that would drive us down the concrete dock and out of Casablanca's harbor to the airport. If all went well, that would be tomorrow afternoon.

"In New York, we're gonna be the big fish in the little pond," Molly whispered to me in bed that night. Her eyes were sparkling. "That continent is ours." I fell asleep with her arm around me, my head on her chest.

The next day, we easily convinced the Action Chief that we were one hundred and ten percent behind Command Intention. We'd packed all our belongings into three duffle bags and said our good-byes to friends all over the ship—we didn't know if we'd see any of them again. In fact, I haven't seen many of my crewmates for over forty years. But that was life in the Sea Org, lots of goodbyes. Duty came first, and besides, we had a billion years ahead of us, we'd catch up with one another sooner or later.

We'd been given our plane tickets and they'd released our passports. Molly and I were ready to fire—we were a pair of perfectly trained theologically guided missiles.

Officers and crew came to the ship's rails on three decks to wish us well. For a good five minutes, we all cheered, waved to one another, hugged and blew kisses. And then it got quiet—we all stopped what we were doing and looked up. At the rail of the uppermost deck, just outside his office, stood the Commodore. He didn't always show up at mission firings. But he was there for us!

"You two give me New York for Christmas, OK?"

"Yes, *sir!!*"

The Old Man returned our salutes with a wink and a wave, then turned and disappeared into his office to uncover more secrets of the human mind. Molly and I strode down the gangplank feeling like a million bucks.

That was all a lie—everything I just wrote about how we left the ship. That's what *should* have happened—it was the fantasy of every Sea Org member. There were some Sea Org stars who actually did get a send-off like that, including the Old Man's blessings, but neither Molly nor I was that much of a big shot.

Molly and I fired during dinner hour—everyone was eating, and no one showed up except the Action Chief, who *had* to be there to sign us off the ship. The Old Man didn't show. But there was the taxi, waiting for us at the foot of the gangway, and we were beginning one hell of an adventure together. That's how it happened, and the rest was all lies, except the part about the Sea Org being a whole lot of goodbye.

———

At airport after airport, officials nodded and waved us through whatever gate it was they were guarding. We wore our full dress naval uniforms, and people treated us with respect because Ron designed our emblems and insignia to trigger a certain unconscious response from wogs. Not that our uniforms were uniformly alike—we were responsible for buying our own, so no one's uniform looked exactly like anyone else's. But when you were a Sea Org officer out on a mission, you walked with an attitude that garnered respect.

———

Molly and I arrived in New York the next day, still wearing our dress blues. It was obvious that Molly was pregnant—an angle she never failed to work. And the fact that we were both tall and fat gave us even more stature. We stood together out on the sidewalk in front of the Martinique Hotel at Herald Square. The New York org occupied the entire second floor of the hotel—including a grand ballroom with a ceiling two stories high and eight perfect crystal chandeliers. The org used the ballroom as its *academy*—the canonical word for a Scientology classroom.

Molly and I took in our surroundings. Across the street stood a statue of George M. Cohan, the original Yankee Doodle Dandy, who sang the words, *Remember me to Herald Square,* because back in the days of George M. Cohan, Herald Square was a swanky place and the Martinique Hotel was a ritzy establishment for guys and dolls lookin' for a good time. But by the time we moved in, the hotel had been carved up into low-rent housing. Floors were designated as homeless shelters for men, women, and families. The top two stories of the hotel housed a mental asylum.

Mental asylum?!? Psychiatrists!!? That wasn't in our Mission Orders. We'd have to report that right away and be on extra special guard. Yes, we were nutty about psychiatry, but think about it: who puts a mental asylum on the top floor of a fourteen-story building in a run-down part of the city? Every spring, we had jumpers. They'd fall past our windows, which were usually open so we'd hear them land—either on the sidewalk or on the hotel marquis. If they jumped from the other side of the asylum, they landed on the roof of the grand ballroom. Old-time New York org staff later informed us that there'd once been a day when three jumpers landed in rapid succession on the classroom ceiling. Can you imagine? Buh-*dam! Thwump! Crrrr-rack!* So it was a bad part of town. But we were Sea Org officers and we'd make it go right. We gave each other a long hug and walked into the hotel. Molly walked ahead of me, and I carried our three duffel bags. Per our MOs, we marched into the office of the Executive Director of the New York org. He wasn't expecting us—no one expects a Sea Org mission. That was part of our glamour as missionaires (not missionaries).

We informed the org's ED that we were moving into a suite of offices upstairs, and wouldn't that be great for the New York org because they'd be so close to us that naturally they'd do a better job of running their org and make lots more money, right? None of that was true, and all three of us knew it—which is why I felt like a mafia capo setting up a protection scam when we told him his org had to tithe 10 percent of their gross income to us each week from that day forward.

The ED's office faced out to the ballroom through a pair of mir-
rored French doors. Molly continued to explain our MOs and all the
New York org's obligations to us. I had my back to them, gazing out
across the magnificent old ballroom. I was imagining back four or
five decades to when I'd have been a flapper, or maybe a taxi dancer.
The ED was still speaking.

"We have to tithe you ten percent of our income?"

"Your gross income, yes."

"And we still have to pay Flag *their* ten percent?"

"That's also correct."

I'd definitely be a taxi dancer—Shirley MacLaine as Charity Hope
Valentine in Bob Fosse's film version of *Sweet Charity*.

Long, crudely constructed workbenches stretched along the
walls behind the columns, holding dozens of reel-to-reel tape record-
ers. Students listened to L. Ron Hubbard's taped lectures. L. Ron
Hubbard's words—in writing, on tape, or on film—were all we ever
studied—all we ever *needed* to study.

"Sign here that you've read and understood our MOs and the
org's responsibilities and benefits."

The ED snorted at the word *benefits*. Molly's nostrils flared, and
her fists went to her hips.

"Listen here, mister. I'm here on a mission from Ron himself. It's
my job to build an East US that he can be proud of. *You*"—she jabbed
a finger into his chest—"have the benefit of our expertise. Warrant
Officer Al Bornstein will be your direct superior, and he answers to
me. Al?"

I was looking up at the ceiling—an overarching tin roof. It was
raining now, and the sound of it was dreamy. Hailstorms had to be
nothing short of spectacular. On the floor, buckets collected the rain-
water from over a dozen leaks, lending the place a seedy aspect. Just
right for a dime-a-dance gal like me.

"Mister Bornstein, I'm talking to you."

"Yes, *sir!*" I barked to my wife and commander.

"Explain to Barry here just how much more money he's going to
make because we're here."

I blinked my eyes to put a stop to my cross-gendered daydreams, and sat down to convince Barry that he'd be doubling his gross income within the first year. Half an hour later, Barry and I were laughing and slapping each other on the back. Target 14: Use tone-scale tech to handle any and all counter-intention from the ED. Done.

"All right, then," Molly said to Barry, pumping his arm in her killer-grip handshake. "We'll see you bright and early tomorrow morning. Go, go, go!"

We turned and left the org. We were killing our MOs, and it felt great.

——

Two days after we arrived, we held a confidential Flag briefing for NYO staff only—that's what our Mission Orders said to call it. The objective was to recruit four NYO staff members into the Sea Org to staff our new office. Attendance was mandatory in the academy that night. It was after hours, maybe ten thirty. Molly and I wore our full dress uniforms, including gold braid and campaign ribbons. The two-story tin ceiling of the ballroom made for great acoustics.

Molly spoke first. She modeled her talk on George C. Scott's Patton, using the monologue of the great general, standing in front of a flag fully three stories tall, addressing the troops about to go into battle. Molly lit the fire—then I fanned the flames.

I spoke from the heart about the Sea Org, how we'd once been a fellowship of officers of the Galactic Federation, 76 million years ago—and how we were just now getting back together again, and how this time we'd succeed. Molly led the applause. I told them I'd just come from two years' life on the rolling seas with L. Ron Hubbard. He wants you to know, I said, that he's been researching the uppermost levels of OT abilities . . . and . . . he is now ready to release them! I waited for the applause to die down. But here's the trouble, I said—Scientology needs more of a foothold on planet Earth before it's safe enough to give mankind these new abilities. Staff gasped audibly. But Ron has a solution! We cued the audio guy to play the Vangelis soundtrack from *Chariots of Fire*. I'd timed the windup of my talk to follow the rise and fall of the inspirational music. I told them that from this moment forward, New York City would be home to the Flag Operations Liaison Office, Eastern United States (FOLO EUS). People cheered without Molly having to prompt them. I told them that Ron had developed a new, precise management system that really works—and that our mission here was to give Ron the foothold he needed in the eastern United States and Canada. If we do that, Ron says he can release his upper levels in a matter of two years. When the cheers finally subsided, I said simply *Join up,* just in time to trigger a crescendo in the music. "The planet is ours," I said, "and we're looking for thetans who are ready to make it go right for Ron for the next ... billion ... years." The music fell to a hushed simple note. "We're looking for pioneers. We're looking for loyal officers." The music ended. I walked around from behind the podium and got all folksy. "Join up. Come work with us. It'll be hard, but who knows ... after you've worked a couple of years at FOLO EUS, you might get a promotion. And where would that promotion be? Bingo—Flag, and you'd be working side by side with the Old Man. Yeah, that's what we call the Commodore. So, have you got anything better to do with your life for the next billion years? Who's with us?"

We had our pick of over twenty volunteers—the cream of the crop of the New York org. Our Mission Orders said we could steal four staff. We were on a mission from Flag—the ED was powerless to stop us.

———

We wouldn't be living in the Martinique. We'd rented ourselves the top floor and penthouse of the Wolcott Hotel—long ago, a charming weekend's stay for the crowd who lived forty-five minutes from Broadway. The guest log at the Wolcott in the Roaring Twenties was filled with big names. The hotel booked top headliners for their lounge. That was then. Now the Wolcott rented by the day or by the hour. They were delighted to have a regular paying customer for the corrugated tin shack on the roof that they called a penthouse.

"Pardon my asking," asked the old desk clerk, "but what's up with the uniforms?"

I stared at him, unblinking. Scientologists believe that you must *always* look into the eyes of the person you're speaking with. We were taught how to do that without blinking. So, I looked at him with my funny, staring eyes until *he* blinked and ducked his head.

"I'm not at liberty to say," I finally said. And no one on the hotel staff or management ever asked any of us again. Target 18—Done.

The Wolcott is thirteen stories high—bad luck was built into the place. So were rats, and roaches the size of your thumb. Six of us in blue naval uniforms moved into the hotel with drag queens, junkies, and hookers. One floor was given over to the severely depressed homeless. This was the Sea Org presence in New York City.

———

I called my parents about three months after arriving in New York.

"Can we come up and visit you, Albert?"

"Not yet, Mom. We just got here a couple of weeks ago, and we're still settling in." It had become so easy to lie for the greater good.

"Do you have enough money to live on?"

"Ummm, not really, no."

That's why I'd called them—we were so broke. Our weekly allowance fluctuated between $12.50 and $14.00—it barely covered cigarettes and vodka. I was chain-smoking two-plus packs of cigarettes a day. Going out for dinner meant McDonald's, or Gray's Papaya, where they sold two hot dogs for fifty cents with a small drink included. The New York org never made much money, so their 10 percent tithing didn't go very far. Instead of buying food for the crew, an important part of the cook's job was daily dumpster diving down in Chinatown.

For the next two years, my parents sent me twenty-five dollars a week—sometimes more. Molly's mom could afford to send us fifty dollars a month. We were so broke without that money. There was Molly's prenatal care, and the expenses of getting our hotel room set up for the baby's arrival. The Sea Org and Church of Scientology has never provided an insurance plan for members and staff. It was rare, but some Sea Org units had a nurse on staff—we didn't. When we needed health care, we hopped emergency rooms around the city, under assumed names and false addresses. People weren't as manic about identification and paperwork back then as they are today. You just never went to the same hospital two times in a row. Before you were allowed to go to an emergency room, you sat down at the e-meter while a member of the clergy relentlessly quizzed you for up to two hours about the presence of any suppressive persons in your life. That's really why you got sick in the first place. Find the SP in your life, disconnect from the SP, you get better and you don't need a trip to the ER. But that doesn't work with prenatal care. You didn't get pregnant because there was an SP in your life—well, Molly did, but none of us knew that yet. Once a month, Molly and I drove the two hours down to the Jersey Shore, where Griff Grimm—the same doctor who'd delivered me—saw to Molly's prenatal care.

—

Two she-male working girls lived on the floor below our penthouse. We often spent silent time with each other in the phone-booth-sized elevator—a slow and creaky ride. Lulu, Carmen, and I tended to fill the tiny space—Lulu in particular, depending on the size of her breasts that evening. They wore '50s retro-streetwalker anti-chic that was cheap, slutty, and absolutely delightful. David Bowie would have sung anthems for them. *I* wanted to wear that kind of outfit. Their perfume enveloped us, made me dizzy. Carmen was combing out the finishing touches of her Farrah Fawcett do. We'd never spoken beyond introducing ourselves the first time we met. I finally got up the courage to talk.

"You're looking very nice this evening, ladies." I meant it. They were totally cute.

"Are you Navy?" asked Carmen. I'd complimented them on their drag, so now they wanted to know the nature of mine. Her skin shone smoothly in the amber glow of the elevator's single bulb. The five o'clock shadow wouldn't poke its way through her pancake makeup for another four or five hours, and she was confident in her beauty.

"I'm sorry, ma'am . . . I'm not at liberty to say." They both giggled at "ma'am." I was getting a boner. I couldn't remember the last time Molly and I had good sex, and she sure wasn't telling me that I was the world's best lover. We slept in the same bed but we didn't touch each other much. I figured it was because I wasn't a real man—it was more likely we'd never been attracted to each other in the first place. The elevator stopped at the lobby.

"May I escort you ladies anywhere?" Lulu and Carmen beamed warmly at me, said they appreciated the offer but they'd be fine—and off we walked in opposite directions. All three of us worked the night shift. I'd head uptown six blocks to the Martinique. The girls always headed south to Union Square and Max's Kansas City—still a hangout of Andy Warhol's inner circle. I couldn't afford to eat at Max's, but living in the city, my hippie-chick dreams had shifted into fierce fantasies of being a Factory girl. I wanted to be Edie Sedgwick. Of course, I was four times her petite anorexic size, which depressed me so I ate more junk food and I kept getting fatter, which depressed me further. I ate whatever I could, whenever I could. I ate candy bars and doughnuts, rice and beans, pasta, pizza, falafel on pita, all this on top of whatever showed up on our plates from that morning's dive into the dumpsters behind the Chinese dumpling shops. I watched Lulu and Carmen turn the corner three blocks away. I turned my head . . . and in a pool of streetlight I saw some guy slit another guy's throat.

The victim wasn't expecting it. His eyes and mouth were wide open in surprise. He didn't even get his hand up high enough to deflect the blade. Blood squirted out in an arc, just like they make it do on television and in the movies. The guy with the knife took off running east. The other guy clutched at his throat and fell back against the brick wall. Using the wall to keep himself standing, and making horrible gurgling noises, he staggered a couple of yards—and that's when a cop turned the corner and saw the guy fall dead to the sidewalk beneath a long smear of blood across the brick wall. The cop jerked his head away from the dead body and looked wildly up and down the street. I pointed east. It was a genuine he-went-thataway moment. And the cop took off after the perp.

I kept walking to work, thinking to myself, *Oh, you poor deranged earthlings! You are so fortunate we've come to rescue you!*

———

My daughter Jessica was born on the Fourth of July in Neptune, New Jersey. Growing up, we told her that the fireworks were to wish her happy birthday, because only the most important people in the world were born on the Fourth of July. George M. Cohan bragged he was born on the Fourth, but he wasn't. He was a vaudevillian, born into a fiercely patriotic Irish American family, and it made for a better story to say "born on the Fourth of July." But it was the third—just like Jessica. I like saying she was born on the Fourth, and that's a lie, but that's show biz.

Molly's contractions began as she was seated behind her desk, sorting out the problem of the runaway boa constrictor. The snake had climbed into an electrical circuit box, wrapping itself around the wiring for warmth. Now she was stuck, a Gordian knot. It was Sunday afternoon, July 2, 1973. It was a perfect after-the-storm sunny day—not too muggy. Contraction One.

When Molly recovered her breath, she instructed Mia, the boa's keeper, "Get yourself a baby white feeder rat. Build a corral in front of the circuit box, and throw the rat in." Our bags were packed and by the front door. I helped Molly to her feet.

Mia looked puzzled. Molly and I paused at the doorway. Molly looked back at her, exasperated.

"The snake's gonna get hungry. She got herself into the damned box, she'll get herself out of it." Molly was Commanding Officer because she could figure out problems like that.

———

A new recruit carried our bags to the curb, and we climbed into the FOLO's staff clunker, the decade-old midnight-blue first-generation

Ford Falcon with three-speed manual transmission. Traffic lanes heading south were fairly clear.

"Drive faster, goddamnit," Molly hissed at me. Contraction Two.

"Nope, my father taught me to drive a steady seven miles over the speed limit."

"Fuck your goddamn father!"

"In his dreams." I rolled down the window. It was so nice, the low humidity. I wondered how my mother and father talked about me to their friends. My parents hadn't told many people that their youngest son had joined a cult—that's what they called it, they never called it Scientology. I don't know how they explained our occasional visits, dressed as we were in varying ragtag combinations of naval uniforms. *My God! We were having a baby!*

I pulled into the driveway I'd known all my life. Mom and Dad ran out the back door, fast as they could—which was considerably slower than I remember them being capable of. They were out of their wits with joy. To my Jewish family, grandchild trumps anything. Contraction Three. Molly allowed my mother to rush her into the house, where she had a room prepared for Molly to lie down. My mother didn't like Molly, but she was doing her motherly duty—and there was the excitement of grandchild in every move she made.

My father slapped me on the back.

"Sorry, Son," he said, disappointment in his voice, "it's gonna be a girl. I can tell by the way she's carrying." He pulled me aside, put his arm around my shoulder, and lowered his voice. "You keep trying, you'll have sons." But grandchild even trumped grandson, and my father was grinning ear to ear. We all were grinning that night, except for Molly, who was grimacing. Her contractions weren't all that frequent yet, but they were steady and predictable. So there we were in the house, all together with nothing to say to each other. My parents were wogs, and Scientologists have little to say to wogs, beyond *Would you like to take a personality test?*

Ticktock, ticktock went the grandfather clock of my childhood insomnia. It was a gift from old man Schlivik, the Christmas before my father lost him. The clock was too tall for the dropped ceiling of the living room, so my father had my brother saw a hole in the ceiling tiles. The top of the clock now disappeared eerily into the ceiling, right under my bedroom. The damned thing chimed on the quarter hour, Westminster-style. At some point, when I was away at college, the chimes had begun to play themselves in the wrong sequence. Now, each hour, the clock tolled a quarter past. At fifteen minutes before the hour, the maddening clock tolled the hour with all four Westminster chimes out of sequence, followed by a series of loud, long, deep *bonnnnnnnnnngs*—one *bong* for every hour. Growing up, I went to bed at ten and I always heard the sound of ten, eleven, and twelve bongs. The floor shook.

—

Now, this would be the place where my brother would break in and correct me, claiming that the chime was muffled and you could barely hear it in the bedroom—he'd lived in that same room before me. I moved in when he moved out. He'd be right. But you should know that my big brother died two years ago, as I was halfway through writing this part of the book. I took it badly—went back to smoking cigarettes. But Alan's death impacts *you*, in that my fact-checker is gone, and it's important that you keep in mind: *suppressive persons only ever tell lies.*

Well, Alan didn't know much about my life in Scientology anyway... or afterwards either. We'd mostly stopped reaching out to each other from the day I joined Scientology to the week before our mom died. And while he was not a homophobic man, I think it turned his stomach to see his kid brother in a dress. I miss him. I miss having a big brother who beat up the people who picked on me. A doctor lost Alan—misdiagnosed him. He died slowly, painfully, and unexpectedly, and now there's a crater where once there was a family. I'm the last of the Cleavers—Ward, June, and Wally are gone. Beaver never had to deal with death and dying.

Right, now back to the night before Jessica was born. Molly, my parents, and I were sitting in the living room with nothing to say to each other.

Ticktock, ticktock.

The four of us sat silently in the living room, watching *McMillan & Wife* on TV. Molly's mother would fly in from Denver the next day. My mother and father sat with their backs to Molly and me on the couch. The TV droned on until Molly and I couldn't stand it any longer. We told my parents we needed some space with each other where we could check in with the thetan who would be moving in to Jessica's body. My parents stared at us blankly—they had no idea that thetans hang around the prenatal bodies of babies they want to pick up. Wogs. What're you gonna do with 'em? We excused ourselves from the house and went to a movie, *Live and Let Die*, with Roger Moore as James Bond.

Molly, all pregnantly plump, made me feel like a man—and boy howdy, I sure looked like a man. At just under six feet tall, I weighed 220 pounds. I wore my sideburns long and bushy. My moustache ran the length of my upper lip, then dipped down half an inch on each side. I kept myself fat and moustachioed so that when I looked into the mirror, I couldn't possibly see me as girl. I knew I couldn't resist the temptation to dress up if I thought I could look pretty.

Molly's contractions were coming closer together. She and I sat cuddled together in a lounge seat for two in the first row of the balcony of the St. James Theatre—the same theater my brother had managed when I was a kid. Watching the film with my arm around my wife, her head on my chest, our baby in her belly, I nevertheless saw myself as Jane Seymour as Bond girl Solitaire—it was *me* reading those tarot cards. I hadn't read any cards since joining Scientology—that would be squirrel tech. Watching Jane Seymour, I considered starving myself and shaving off my sideburns and moustache.

—

Five o'clock the next morning, we were all gowned and masked in the delivery room of Fitkin Memorial Hospital. I'd explained to everyone in the room the first principle of Scientology birthing rites: no words can be spoken. It's a belief of Scientology—and to some degree a superstition of mine to this day—that words spoken during childbirth have the potential to make more difficult an already physically traumatic event in the lives of both the mom and the babe.

I explained that Scientologists believe that your unconscious mind turns itself on when you're in pain or unconscious, and it records everything that you perceive. Later in life, all of that can come back to haunt you. For example, let's say you look at a newborn child and say, "Wow, look how big she is." Well, theoretically, later in life that could make that child feel fat no matter how much she weighs.

The doctors, nurses, and technicians were surprisingly sweet—even garrulous old Griff Grimm, the OB-GYN who would preside over the birth. He and my mom were good friends—they partied hard together. When I've explained to lovers that Griff brought my mother a pitcher of martinis the night she went into labor with me—and she drank all of it—one for one, my lovers nodded as if that explained everything.

Molly's labor lasted for two nonverbal hours. Then, Jessica was born. Dr. Grimm broke the ecclesiastic silence with the same words he spoke to me when I was born.

"Welcome to the world, baby. Welcome."

Fuck it. If something in her unconscious mind plays words back to my daughter, I'm glad they're words of welcome.

Molly, Jessica, and I spent the following week at my parents' house, along with Molly's mother. Molly and I grew even larger on all my mother's cooking. At the end of the week, we drove north again, to settle back in to life in New York City, where we'd established a Sea Org foothold for the expansion of Scientology. It was our city now—the wogs would find that out soon enough.

CHAPTER 10
Family Man

Summer 1952, or maybe it's 1954. I was lying facedown in the driveway. I was young and still a skinny little kid. My arms were stretched up over my head as far as I could reach. My toes were pointed, making myself as long as I possibly could. The blue gravel was digging into my cheek, my arms, my knees, my palms. I was doing my best to not be abandoned. In the garage, my mom was sitting at the wheel of her robin's-egg-blue 1947 Crosley two-door convertible coupe she'd named Lambie, behind which I lay stretched out on the driveway, a tantrum in still life.

No way my mom could back out of the garage without running me over. My mom adored me. She enjoyed time with me. But my mother was restless, a young beauty with two boys to raise. She rolled down the window and called out to my brother.

"Alan, come get your brother out of the driveway."

I had less than a minute before he'd stomp out of the house and run over to drag me away through the gravel onto the wet, newly mown lawn. I heard the slam of the back door, and his purposefully heavy footsteps down the wooden stairs. He didn't want to do this. He was eleven years old, maybe thirteen, skinny like me and much taller. He had better things to do than drag his baby brother out of the driveway. Now he was running across the lawn. I heard the *crunch crunch crunch* as he crossed the gravel to reach me. My face was in the gravel, and I had only one strategy left. Silence for a moment, and then:

"Mom, he's holding his breath again."

"Tickle him, Alan." She turned the key in the ignition and fired up the Crosley's two-cylinder engine—it sounded like an outboard motor.

"He's turning blue, Ma."

"Tickle him, Alan, I'm late."

Alan went straight for the ribs and all the air burst forth from my lungs in one long scream of pain and delight. I was gulping air. The exhaust from the car made me nauseous, and that was a bad combination with the tickling.

"Aw, Mom, he's gonna throw up."

"Stop tickling him."

I was spent, lying limp. Alan picked up my ankles and dragged me onto the lawn. Mom put the Crosley in gear and slipped out of the driveway. Exhausted from the tickling, the screaming, the kicking, and the sobbing, it felt good to rest my cheek against the cool wet lawn. It was over. She was gone, and I was alone. They could get me—monsters, demons, the Devil himself could all get me now.

"Albert, how ya doin'?" My brother hunkered down next to me. He'd been sitting there, waiting for my tantrum to subside.

"I hate this," was all I knew to say.

"I know. C'mon inside, we'll play with your soldiers. We'll eat potato chips."

"Am I bad?"

"You're the worst. C'mon, kiddo."

So yeah, I've got abandonment issues. Most people with borderline personality disorder do.

—

December 1976, Herald Square, Manhattan. Jessica was two and a half years old, the perfect age for Christmas in New York City.

As Scientologists, we celebrated Christmas in the spirit of a secular holiday—it was an opportunity to give ourselves a lovely time of year, mostly because that's what everyone else wants it to be, too. Christmas was special for the Sea Org in that it was a day free from the fear of doing your job wrong. Christmas was a time to relax without a job title or rank—there was time to explore love, or drink yourself blind, or both. And Christmas was a time to exchange gifts. Presents for everyone, no matter how broke we were. As a child, I learned that giving gifts is how you show your love for someone— and getting gifts showed you how much you're loved.

Growing up, it was my father who amassed the largest pile of gifts—everyone loved him. In the '50s and '60s, Dad's tall stack of gifts covered an entire end of our living room. We began unwrapping his presents right after dinner, and we never finished until it was way past our bedtimes. He got gifts from us, his adoring family, as well as from patients, medical colleagues, and relatives—most of whom we only heard from at Christmas.

Christmas Eve was a drill: my father lay back in his red leather recliner, sipping Wild Turkey bourbon. My brother and I ripped open the packages. My mother wrote on a yellow legal pad the list of who gave Dad what—she would write all his thank-you cards. My dad easily got a hundred presents each year. Lots of love.

L. Ron Hubbard received thousands of gifts.

Within months of having set up our Sea Org base, similar land bases appeared on every continent where there were Scientology orgs. And every Christmas all of us shifted gears—from managing the orgs, our priority became getting the Old Man's Christmas gifts going to the ship. Scientologists around the world knew to send their Christmas gifts for Ron through their nearest continental FOLO, because no one knew the whereabouts of the Flagship—not even us. But we knew who did know. There was a secret relay office in Queens that saw to all the shipping and receiving. Over the month leading up to Christmas, our office received hundreds and hundreds of gifts from all over the eastern United States and Canada. A week before Christmas, it was an all-hands action to package up LRH's gifts into larger packages, which we'd then drive to the secret relay office of New York (RONY).

RONY used all three New York area airports to ship Ron's Christmas gifts. We could have shipped them all from LaGuardia, only half an hour away—but that would mean tying ourselves down to a pattern that spies could easily spot and use to eventually track down

Flag's location—so we drove the extra couple of hours out to the other two airports. It was part of every Sea Org member's job to keep Ron, his wife, Mary Sue, and their four children safe and content.

Oldest to youngest, the Hubbard children were Diana, Quentin, Suzette, and Arthur. All four children and their parents were some shade of redhead. Diana Hubbard—easily as beautiful and charismatic as England's Princess Diana—served as Ron's goodwill ambassador to the non-Scientology public. She never called them wogs. Quentin was a highly trained and skilled spiritual counselor, called an *auditor.* Suzette Hubbard took odd jobs in the Sea Org, even doing a stint off the ship at RONY. Arthur was an artist, a cartoonist. Each member of the family had a list of presents they wanted to buy for the other members of the family, and because we were based in New York City—the city that has everything—our office was tasked with the bulk of the Hubbard family shopping lists.

Their lists sent us down to Greenwich Village for pizza from the shop that claims to be the honest-to-goodness original Ray's Pizza. The Hubbard gift list included clothes from Saks Fifth Avenue, filet mignon from the best butchers in the Meatpacking District, and naval and nautical accessories from Kaufman's Army and Navy on West Forty-Second Street. The Hubbards all lived aboard ship, so there were very few large purchases. Most everything they did order was the best: the best audio equipment, the best diamonds, transistor radios, and pocket calculators.

Christmastime, most New Yorkers make their neighborhoods welcoming—garlands of lights, bells, stars, and Santas festoon the city streets. In the '70s, a New York City street that didn't look good on the holidays was a street you didn't want to walk down without a personal invitation. We lived on the dark streets of Greeley Square, just south and east of the more upper-class Herald Square. Macy's and Gimbels—the two largest department stores in the city—lit up the west side of the street. Both stores sported a two-story Christmas tree mounted on the front wall over the stores' main entrances. Both stores prominently displayed brightly and gaudily lit mangers.

Both Baby Jesuses were white, as were both the Marys and Josephs. All the angels were pink-cheeked blondes. The shepherds and at least one Wise Man were swarthy.

Christmas shopping for the Hubbards got us out of the depressing Martinique Hotel and into the holiday lights and shop windows. Oh! What wonderlands, what siren songs. Jessica rode on my shoulders. One evening, we'd cross the street and walk north two blocks to lose ourselves for an hour or so in the front windows of Macy's and Gimbels fantasy lands. Another night, I'd make sure I carried her up along Fifth Avenue, where all the stores had donned their gayest apparel. My goal was FAO Schwarz, then the largest toy shop in the city at Fifty-Ninth Street and Fifth Avenue, down the street from Tiffany's. Nowadays, people stand impatiently in line behind red velvet ropes just to walk quickly by the fabulous holiday windows of Fifth Avenue. Back in the '70s, there was no crowd control. Mostly, people were patient and polite to one another. Jessica and I could always make it through the crowd to stand up in front of the window, because, after all—I was wearing a naval long coat and cap, and I was carrying a cute-as-a-button two-year-old girl on my shoulders. Crowds parted for us.

It didn't hurt that I was a powerful thetan, and my intention was to make those crowds part for us. Jessica cheered and squealed in delight at the elves, the trains, the Barbies, the princesses. It was just me and Jess. Molly was up the street at Tiffany's, on another Hubbard family gift errand.

"That's what I want, Daddy." She reached around my neck, her little finger in front of my face, pointing at Sleeping Beauty's Tea Party Set. "Tell Santa that's what I want."

"You tell him yourself. We'll walk right into Macy's on the way home, and he'll be there."

"Across the street? Santa's across the street from us?"

"You betcha, punkin. But the Commodore comes first."

With Jessica on my shoulders still, I walked into FAO Schwarz and bought six model car kits for Arthur and six model airplane kits for Quentin—not just any old kits. They'd specified exactly which cars and planes, and it took a while to find them all in the shelves. Jessica was crying by the time we left the store.

"What's up, kiddo?"

"Santa doesn't know I want the tea set, Daddy! He's not going to bring it for me."

"Well, wouldn't Santa be a great big poopy head if he didn't get you what you asked for?"

She was speaking out of Grief, 0.5. So I'd shot back at her with a little mild Anger, 1.5. Through the noise of the Christmas shoppers, I heard Jessica giggle from just behind my right ear. *Scientology works,* I thought to myself.

"Hold on tight, pumpkin," I told her. I had shopping bags in both hands. Jessica leaned forward and hugged my head, clasping her hands tightly around my forehead. We rode the subway back downtown to Herald Square, and we made it onto Santa's line just before they closed it off for the evening. I have a photograph of Jessica on Santa's lap, asking for her Sleeping Beauty's Tea Party Set, which she in fact found under the tree several days later

It was late when I dropped off my bags of Hubbard family Christmas gifts at the office in the Martinique. Someone in the office had made cocoa. Jessica and I each had a hot, steaming cup, and then I carried her home to the Wolcott Hotel. When we got outside, it was snowing. It was Jessica's first snow, and she laughed and laughed. That was our last Christmas on Herald Square. We were about to move the org and the FOLO to the equally rundown Upper West Side.

———

In 1975 New York City was on the brink of bankruptcy. It couldn't pay its trash-disposal bill, so heaps of garbage lay in the street just off the sidewalk. Governor Hugh Carey and Attorney General Louis Lefkowitz were luminaries of the city's dark times, revered then for cracking a Medicaid scam in which Upper West Side landlords were skimming money off the city through cruelty to the elderly infirm who'd been placed in their care.

The controversy centered around a pair of adjoining brownstones, subsidized by the city and state of New York, designated as convalescent homes for the elderly homeless of the city. Conditions were shocking. Patients were sleeping on linoleum tile floors, and staff were feeding them cat food. Many of the patients were incontinent—only occasionally did anyone clean up after them. The landlords were sentenced to jail time. Their buildings went up for auction, and the Church of Scientology leapt at the chance to buy them both. Greeley Square had grown unbearably seedy over the years, and a mission from Flag arrived to help move us to our new digs.

It took about twenty of us just over two weeks to clean out the detritus of the nursing homes. The industrial-strength peppermint room deodorizers couldn't cover the smells of urine, feces, and rotting cat food. It was spring, so we were able to throw open every window in the building. When the smell was finally gone, the building sparkled. A couple of U-Haul trucks later, we were all moved in to our new quarters: berthing and office space for the Sea Org in the eastern building, New York org and New York Guardian's Office (GO) on the west.

The Flag mission had secondary orders to replace Molly as Commanding Officer. She'd been reassigned to Los Angeles for GO training—a senior post was waiting for her. The Guardian's Office was the forerunner of today's Office of Special Affairs, the intelligence branch of the Church. Their job can be more or less summed up as doing whatever it takes to attack, shatter, and destroy psychiatry, psychology, reporters, hostile authors, whistleblowers, and other suppressive persons. Molly had applied for that transfer months earlier. She hadn't told me. It didn't feel like a loss when I found out.

We hadn't had sex with each other for over a year. We'd grown fat—just shy of obesity—and we found each other unattractive. We never talked about this before, but we did talk about it as she packed up to leave for Los Angeles the next day. We weren't quite friends anymore. We respected each other, but there was no romantic or sexual energy between us—we fell into and out of resentment. Jessica would stay in New York with me. Molly's training schedule wouldn't permit her any time to spend with Jessica. Molly and I held hands in the taxi. Despite how far apart we'd grown, we were both crying over the good times. She'd be back in maybe two years.

The cab let us off, and the three of us walked into the airport together—Jessica on my shoulders. We walked Molly out to her gate and sat with her until boarding was announced. You could do that in those days—just walk to the gate in the airport to say goodbye to someone—no security. Imagine that.

Standing at the window, Jessica and I waved at Molly's plane.

Two-year-old Jessica and I rode back to the city. She was crying, and I was in no condition to use the tone scale to help her, because I was crying myself. I told the driver to let us off at Gray's Papaya on Broadway and Seventy-Second Street, a short six-block walk from our new quarters. Hot dogs and coconut drink became a comfort ritual for me and Jessica. For the next two years, rain or shine—if my stats were up—we sat together at the counter of Gray's Papaya for an end-of-business-week dinner.

—

Saturdays were parents' only full day with the kids, and then only if your stats were up. Full days off with Jessica on Manhattan's Upper West Side meant—depending on the season and the weather—some combination of the Museum of Natural History, the Central Park Zoo, the planetarium, and the merry-go-round. Rainy days were for books. *The Wind in the Willows* was Jessica's favorite. Well, I suppose it was *my* favorite—I understood the world from the perspective of mad, mad Toad in his yellow motorcar. I'd read aloud. I've always been able to do a lot of voices. I do a great Goofy, Mickey Mouse's good buddy—it never failed to make Jessica laugh, and that gave me great pleasure.

If your statistics were down, you worked Saturdays while your child was looked after by the nanny. All the children of the FOLO ages two to twelve were watched over in a nursery by Bernadette, the nanny. Parents were permitted only one hour a day with our kids, and only after dinner and before bed.

With those two exceptions—a full day if upstat, or an extra hour if downstat—the children were watched over and raised by Bernadette. Each night, I picked up Jessica from the nursery after dinner, and we'd go read and get ready for bed. Bernadette was teaching the children L. Ron Hubbard's basics of communication and study technology. Jessica gave me progress reports nightly. I sang her to sleep each night with "Frog Went a' Courting." She sang along on the *un-huh, un-huh's* for as long as she could keep her eyes open, then she was off to sleep.

Beautiful child-face on the pillow. I watched her for five or ten minutes every night—trying to envision a better world for her than the one that was envisioned for me. Scientologists call this postulating. A positive postulate is when you make a wish you have no doubts will come true. I did this every night, then I'd make my way quietly out of the room to meet up with Kevin, another officer at FOLO. We were drinking buddies, and that's what we did most nights.

I was still a blackout drinker and rarely remembered coming home. I'd wake up in my own bed, not knowing how I got there. Well, most of the time it was my bed. Sometimes it was Liz's bed. Her husband had been called out West as well. Liz and I spent several nights a week in loving, healing, and comforting sex with each other.

I loved my way through relationships with four other women in the nearly two years Molly was gone. Each one of them loved Jessica, and with each woman, I could play at being a real family man. My role model was Atticus Finch in *To Kill a Mockingbird*. If I couldn't be Scout, then I wanted to be a daddy like him. I did my best for the two years I was a single parent while Molly was off training in Los Angeles.

———

Carousel rides in Central Park, Christmastime on Fifth Avenue, Thursdays at Gray's Papaya. Beyond an overwhelming feeling of love for Jessica whenever I think about her, I've few memories of actual time spent with my daughter. I have fewer than a dozen photographs of her up until she was four years old, and a smaller number of photos of her in her early teens. She'd mailed them to my mom as Christmas presents after I left the Church. I grab for a mental picture of Jessica, and I see her sitting on Santa's lap. I listen for her voice, and I hear a little girl laugh from just behind my right ear.

Here's one memory I've carried for over thirty years—early June 1978. Molly phoned to say she wanted Jessica to come to Los Angeles to celebrate her fourth birthday. I thought that was fair—Molly hadn't seen Jess for nearly two years. I drove with Jessica in the cab to LaGuardia Airport, and walked with her to the gate of her flight to Los Angeles. I knelt down and we hugged goodbye. A smiling stewardess took Jessica's hand and led her aboard. I followed them to Jessica's seat, saw that she was settled in and wearing her seatbelt. I kneeled down and she hugged me tightly around my neck. She smelled of Johnson's Baby Shampoo. I gave her a wave, blew her a kiss, and walked off the plane.

From the gate, I watched the flight take off and disappear into the sky. I rode the bus back to the city. The Mexican divorce papers from Molly arrived on my desk two weeks later. I didn't see Jessica again for another five years.

CHAPTER 11

All Good Things

Fighting the good fight in the Sea Org had made me the good guy I'd always longed to be. After a decade of 24-7 loyal active duty, I was at the top of my game. I was a full Lieutenant. Only fifty people in all of Scientology outranked me. I'd been First Mate of the Flagship; and a few years later, I was working directly with the Commodore, planning public relations strategies for Scientology worldwide. I managed an entire fucking continent for them. Then I crashed and burned on Southern Comfort and Coca-Cola, sex, junk food, and tranny porn—it's what got me through my months-long bone-deep loneliness after Jessica left. My job performance took a nosedive and I was summarily removed from my post in middle management and demoted to sales, where, phoenix-like, I rose from my own ashes brighter and stronger than ever.

I was a terrific salesman, a natural. I'd spent my life trying to make people happy with me, and there's nothing more happy-making than selling someone their dreams-come-true. In Scientology sales, we were taught to find a person's "ruin"—whatever it was that was making a person's life miserable and keeping them from achieving their goals. I could find anyone's ruin in minutes—and in less than an hour, I'd've sold them thousands of dollars worth of Scientology services to handle it. I put together a crack staff, and together the six of us pulled in close to a quarter of a million dollars a week. I was a real man in every aspect of my life—and it all came down to *money money money*. After all, what are your dreams worth to you? How much money would you spend if that's all it took to make your dreams come true? You needed what we had, and we needed your money—most, if not all, of it.

It was common knowledge in the Sea Org that the US government and economy could topple at any moment—splat—end of the world as we know it. That's when we'd march in and take over. We were amassing a war chest for that day, and with that in mind L. Ron Hubbard took very little money from the Church—only the royalties on his books and a small administrative stipend on top of his room and board. Beyond that, every penny went into Church maintenance, defense, and expansion.

In Scientology, we never used the word *sales*. People who sell Scientology services have always gone by the more pleasant euphemism *registrar,* often shortened to *reg*. In the Sea Org, we softened the euphemism even further: I remained posted in New York City as part of the international sales team called Flag Service Consultants. We were among the most highly skilled sales people in all of Scientology, and we sold only the most expensive services—the topmost levels of Scientology, all of which were delivered solely on Flag by the most highly trained Sea Org members in the world. In the late 1970s I was pulling in an average of $20,000 a week for Flag. My personal sales figures often topped out at $50,000 to $70,000, which made me one of the Sea Org's top income makers, which in turn gave me what they call *ethics protection*. In short, no one was allowed to fuck with me. My time was mine to call, and now that Jessica wasn't in my life, there was no reason to be a man. I was a thetan, I reasoned, and as a being with no gender, I was making a rational decision to change my mind. I set off to explore being girl. First, I stopped eating.

The first three days back into anorexia are the most difficult— the hunger is painful at every level of your body, mind, and spirit, but if you can suffer through those three days, you can burst out into the other side to eat yourself one thousand calories a day or less and be damn proud of your resolve, the strength of your decision, and the pounds dropping away daily. Boys lose weight faster than girls, and within two months, I was seeing bones—that meant that my body was as close to being girl as I could be. And for the first time in my life, I had the money and freedom to buy clothes for who might possibly be pretty girl me—and it *was* a possibility, theoretically. For years—consciously and unconsciously—I'd been studying New York women and New York women's fashion. I wouldn't have been able to articulate this back then, but I was learning that no matter what the shape of your body, you can dress it to make yourself look great. That's New York fashion—women here know how to make themselves look great. Knowing that there were people who could master this skill/talent/survival tactic gave me hope that maybe I could learn how to do that for myself—like drag queens, one for one the most beautiful creatures of all humankind.

I had some money. I thanked my parents for the two years of support, and told them I was fine now—and I most certainly was, with 2½ percent commission on all my sales. That netted me some serious cash. All my meals and living expenses were covered. I'd offered to send Molly and her new husband some child support for Jessica, but they declined. I don't know anyone in the Sea Org those days who paid taxes. We were paid well below the poverty line on a weekly allowance of twelve to fifteen dollars. Not me. For the first time in years, I had some spending money.

So—I had the body for girl, and I had the money to dress me up. With Jessica gone, there was nothing to stop me from tracking down Lee G. Brewster's Mardi Gras Boutique, the single largest source of trans porn in the world, as well as a large selection of women's clothes in men's sizes. Before she moved to more spacious floorspace down in the Meatpacking District, Lee ran her store out of a two-room flat on Tenth Avenue, in the mid-Fifties. By then, I was used to walking through urban war zones. I rang the buzzer. A sultry voice purred from the loudspeaker at the front door.

"Who are you lookin' for?"

"Umm . . . Mardi Gras?"

"That's me. Come on in."

She buzzed me in, and I walked up the stone steps to her store. A beautiful boy stood on the landing on the fourth floor. He looked me up and down and gave me a mischievous smile.

"Honey," he drawled, "I've been an FBI agent, a female impersonator, and now I'm a gay rights activist. I thought I'd seen it all, but what on earth are you wearing? That is not the uniform of anything I'm familiar with—and I'm quite familiar with men who wear uniforms."

Gay rights? What was that? The beautiful boy's beautiful eyes bored into mine—and then I realized he was flirting with me. Oh god, oh god, what was I doing here? Eyes cast down, I mumbled something about my uniform being merchant marine. I looked up again, and Lee's face lost its friendliness. He'd become the professional shop boy. He had a lot of customers like me—cross-dressers who were too embarrassed to speak our desire out loud. He gave me a well-rehearsed talk.

"Store policy is if you don't want to talk, you don't have to. I've got pretty much everything you might be looking for. Don't try anything on without asking me first, and if you don't see your size, ask me— I've got girl things crammed into every corner of this place. Call me if you have any questions." He buried his nose in a copy of *Even Cowgirls Get the Blues*. I was reading a copy myself at the time.

Miss Lee worked her shop out of drag. She told me later that it scared the customers. She'd begun her drag career in the '60s, when drag queens were called female impersonators or female mimics. After the Stonewall Rebellion of 1969, Lee had defiantly proclaimed herself a drag queen and gay activist. She set up shop to cater to closet cases like me.

I walked through her shop, all Alice in Wonderland. There was trans porn of every conceivable genre. There were wigs, shoes, and makeup. There was padding for tits, ass, and hips—and there were corsets for bellies. There were racks and racks of women's clothes, most of which fell into two styles: trashy glam and Betty Ford. Closeted cross-dressers of all generations have always modeled their fashion on America's First Lady. The Barbara Bush years were unbearable.

I spent an hour exploring the shop, but I only bought the porn.

I was living in a Sea Org dorm now, and it would be hard enough to hide the books and magazines—there was no place to stash women's clothing, and certainly no place to put it on. So, I had the body, and I had the money to dress it up. All I needed was the space to do it in, away from any uninvited prying eyes. I wasn't a pervert, I kept telling myself. I was a thetan, and thetans have no gender. I was just exploring my options, nothing wrong with that.

—

My good friend Dave Renard managed the Flag Service Consultant network remotely from his office at the Flag Land Base in Clearwater, Florida. By the late 1970s LRH had moved his home and office to a well-hidden, well-guarded desert ranch in Southern California. He'd surrounded himself with a great many more Commodore's Messengers, which had grown from a unit into its own org—young David Miscavige was a member. Sea Org Headquarters—once stationed aboard the Flagship—had moved ashore to a hotel of faded glory in a sleepy town on Florida's Gulf coast.

Dave was a good guy—laid back, unpretentious, and willing to bend the rules as long as it made his divisional statistics go up. He gave us free rein to make money however we best thought we could. Some weeks that meant sitting in my office at the FOLO in New York, but I'd discovered I could make a lot more money on the road, and I quickly became a traveling registrar. I spent two to three weeks at a time living out of hotels in Toronto, Boston, Charlotte, Washington, DC, and Miami. Out of town, my sales strategy was simple: I'd make as much money as possible for the org that was hosting me. If a sale came down to a Scientologist who would pay for services at either Flag or the local org but not both, I'd concede to the org even if that put my stats down for the week. Dave understood the investment. In Scientology management, there's more focus on trends than there is on weekly rises or falls.

I was out in the world on my own terms. It was just me, with no reason I could think of to be a man. Alone and with my own hotel room, I took every opportunity to buy and dress in women's clothing. I was careful to throw everything away before I left town, thus establishing for myself a life pattern of binge-and-purge cross-dressing.

I was averaging $200 to $400 a week with no expenses. *I had money to spend!* I took crewmates and sales prospects out drinking, out to dinner. I once took a sales prospect of mine down to the Meatpacking District to get him laid. He'd said he wouldn't pay me a nickel while he was still a virgin. I paid for a clean hotel room, and I gave the working girl twice the amount she asked for and she smiled what felt like a real smile at me.

I bought boy clothes because I had to. Skinny at last, I had to buy myself uniforms that fit me—and no more ragtag accessories. I had the money to buy a regulation US Navy officer's cap and gold lanyard. I paid the uniform shop to embroider the Sea Org emblem to wear on my cap. I was so well put together that when I looked in the mirror, I saw a girl dressed up in boy Navy clothes. I bought sassy-styled three-piece suits, shirts, and a couple of ties from gay boy boutiques in Greenwich Village. In the mirror, I saw a girl wearing boy clothes.

—

Christmastime in Manhattan, 1977. A knock on my office door.

"Excuse me, sir?"

I looked up from my desk. I was a young Johnny Depp in uniform, my shirtsleeves rolled up high on my arms. Standing in the doorway—halfway in, halfway out—stood a young woman in a Sea Org officer's uniform as tasteful as my own. She was maybe in her early twenties, and she bore a regal resemblance to Princess Diana. I rose to my feet, and the lady in her appreciated the gentleman in me.

"How can I help you?"

"Sir—I'm Petty Officer Third Class Elizabeth Mayweather Reilly the Third. I'm the new Deputy Continental LRH Communicator here, and I'm doing my staff orientation checksheet. You're Lieutenant Al Bronstein?"

"Bornstein," I smiled. WASPS nearly always have a hard time with my name.

"Bornstein," she repeated with no apology, fixing it into her mind.

"Welcome to New York, Petty Officer Third Class Elizabeth Mayweather Reilly the Third. Wonderful name." She blushed charmingly.

"You have a Montblanc pen, sir?"

PO3 Reilly was asking me the question from her orientation checklist. She'd joined the Sea Org a year earlier in Philadelphia, and she'd just been assigned to the FOLO. A new staff orientation check-sheet is a treasure map of sorts written to familiarize yourself with your new office and crewmates. In an orientation checksheet, you're directed to zigzag from one end of the office to another and back again. By the time you've completed, you've met and introduced yourself to every staff member—and for each staff member you're given a question to ask and an obscure object to find.

"I do indeed have a Montblanc pen."

She looked down at her checklist and made a mark, then she looked back up at me. Her eyes like emeralds flashed with delight, and into my office she pranced. Wow.

"The pen, sir?" She glanced around, from my desktop to the bookcase, the top of my filing cabinet. From across the room she couldn't see much. "Where is it?"

"You've got to find it, Mister Reilly. That's part of the fun."

Pointing to my pocket, she tilted her head to one side. She couldn't have been more Tinker Bell. It was all I could do not to gasp.

"Nope."

"May I look around, sir?"

"You may do whatever you wish, Mister Reilly."

She blushed—we both did. She set off to explore my office. I pretended to read a file as she circled the room. Her body was taut as a lean cat's, her thin arms were muscular—like mine. Later, I discovered that we shared eating disorders. Hers was bulimia. She'd reached my desk, and was standing just behind me. I swear by all that's holy to me, she smelled like a meadow on a warm, sunny day. She pointed to my in-basket, empty except for the pen.

"There it is!"

"Bingo! Now you've got a question for me?"

She looked down to her clipboard, then back up at me with the cutest damned frown I'd ever seen and have ever seen since.

"You're not wearing your campaign ribbons, sir."

"Right you are, PO3 Reilly."

"Becky. Sir."

"Becky." Oh, I was hooked. Becky has the same charisma God gave Mary Tyler Moore.

I'd been sitting in my shirtsleeves. I rose, crossed the room, put on my Class A dress blue uniform jacket, and turned to face her. I swam in the attraction that poured from her eyes as she took me in—all Johnny Depp that I was. Wordlessly, she pointed to the array of campaign ribbons on my chest.

"Which one?" I laughed, shrugging my shoulders to invite her touch. She strode over unhesitatingly and laid her index finger on a blue and white ribbon with two stars.

"That's the one."

"And it means what, sir?"

"Al."

"It means what, Al?"

"It means I've been a Flag officer for two years, Becky."

She laughed delightedly and wrote my answer down on her checksheet. Then she came to attention and gave me a proper salute, making to leave. I didn't answer her salute, so she stood there, hand to her forehead.

"Dinner with me, tonight, Becky?"

"I'd be delighted . . . Al."

I took her to Max's Kansas City, where she laughed and pointed at the queens. I told her I thought they were beautiful, but nowhere near as beautiful as she. After dinner, I hailed us a cab and we rode up to the Waldorf Astoria Hotel, where I rented us a room for the evening. Limb for limb, finger for finger, hunger for hunger, we matched each other all night long. We made each other laugh and cry and gasp. Becky was the woman I'd most wanted to become. Sex with Becky gave me a taste of what it might be like to be her.

—

My pal Dave had pulled some strings and successfully secured a transfer for Becky to my office as a Flag Service Consultant, where she and I quickly became a successful sales team. Both of us were charmers, and people kept writing us checks. Because we were technically Flag staff, we didn't have to live in FOLO berthing. We rented ourselves an apartment out in Astoria, Queens, and worked out of our office at the FOLO on West Seventy-Fourth Street in Manhattan. I'd bought us a car for the commute—a 1979 fire-engine-red AMC Pacer. The car was low to the ground, nearly round, and had lots of windows—she was my space shuttle, and I loved her with the same madness as Toad loved his bright yellow motorcar. Becky and I had established the pattern of me going out on tour mostly on my own, while she worked in the city and followed up by phone the sales I'd put into motion weeks earlier. I'd grown my moustache back, and I put on weight—not too much. I was a big guy, but you wouldn't call me fat. When we weren't wearing our uniforms, Becky and I were dressing in more fashionable civvies. We argued that it made sales prospects feel more comfortable when we were out of uniform. Since our stats were up, we were given a green light to wear what we wanted to wear. Well, I wasn't wearing everything I wanted to wear, but I didn't feel much need or desire to cross-dress. Becky and I lived together like a pair of sisters, and that made me feel girl enough and happy.

—

April 1979, City Hall, Philadelphia. The judge glanced down at the divorce papers I handed him—the same ones Molly had sent me years earlier—and burst out laughing.

"Son, this is strictly Mexican—it's not legal in the USA. I'm sorry, but you're not divorced and I can't marry you until you are."

It was a sucker punch from the universe, and I went down. So did Becky, who was instantly on the verge of tears.

"B-b-but the wedding is this weekend," I stuttered.

"It's our big day," she whispered. "Everyone who loves us is coming." She was a waif in the storm, tears welling up in her eyes. And me, I've always defaulted to waif as part of my borderline personality disorder. In any case, the judge looked up from his desk at the two of us, and he caved.

"Aw, you two kids look like you were made for each other." He scribbled something on our marriage application and checked off a couple of boxes. "I'm not going to be the one to stand in the way of your happiness." He stood up and offered each of us a handshake across his desk. "And thank you for your service to the country."

Ha-*ha!* Our uniforms had worked their unconscious glamour, just like the Old Man said they would when he designed them.

—

Becky had lied to the judge when she told him that everyone who loved us would be at the wedding—my parents didn't come. Dad was officially retired from his medical practice—but healers never really retire. He and Mom were spending another month on an Indian reservation in New Mexico, where Dad was volunteering as a doctor. They were living in a house made of clay—my mother and I both enjoyed nature, but we drew the line at indoor plumbing. Mom worked as his receptionist, seeing to all the paperwork. She told me later how warm it made her feel to help those poor people.

"Albert, they were unlike us in so many ways."

"Kate."

"Kate."

My father doctored in the only style he knew: arrogant, irascible curmudgeon.

"They called me Great White Father again," he bragged, "every last one of 'em." He never got the sarcasm of the title.

Mom and Dad were genuinely sorry to be missing the Philadelphia wedding—they adored Becky. My father told me over and over that she was the cutest girl he'd ever known.

"And smart, Albert. You've got a smart one there."

My mother had hugged me close and whispered happily that I'd found a real lady.

"And strong, Albert. She's a strong one."

The wedding was held out on the Philadelphia Main Line, where Becky had grown up. It was a beautiful house—the ceremony would take place in the sculpted garden that was the backyard. Becky's mom died when she was fourteen. She and her older sister had lived alone with her dad. Neither her dad nor her sister became Scientologists, but neither did they laugh at us. They did their best to take us seriously when we talked rapturously of civilizations across the universe and the millennia. Our friend Ron Miscavige—jazz trumpet player of some renown—performed the ceremony. His son, David Miscavige, was nineteen at the time, and according to all the lies on the Internet, he was busy worming his way into the Old Man's good graces.

It was a lovely wedding. Alan was best man. Becky's older sister Andi was maid of honor. We honeymooned on Cape Cod for six days of great sex, which only got better every time we did it.

———

Becky and I returned from our honeymoon to discover we'd been transferred from New York to the Flag Land Base in Clearwater. We were thrilled! We'd been posted as Flag *Tours* Registrars—we'd spend most of our time together on the road, back in the East US for sure, but we'd also be touring cities in Europe! We didn't have that many belongings—it only took us one day to pack everything we owned into a trailer that could hitch onto the back of my little red motorcar. We drove south, a real live Sea Org power team in love.

Molly and her husband, Randy, were already living in Clearwater with Jessica and her baby brother, Christopher—whose name would later live on in my grandson. They'd been transferred from LA a few months earlier. Flag officers berthed in an old Quality Inn motel the Sea Org had bought when they first came ashore in Clearwater. The two-story motel looked like it could be the set for a massacre scene in a Quentin Tarantino film. Jessica and her family lived in adjoining rooms on the first floor. Becky and I built our nest up one flight. No, there was no massacre—well, yes, maybe there was.

Becky and I traveled for months through Rome, London, Berlin, Paris, Copenhagen, and more cities than I can remember. The tour itself was a drill: Geoff, our advance man, would arrive in town two weeks before us. He booked a hall, and promoted my talk to all area Scientologists. Each round of tours had a theme, but it boiled down to *Come hear the officer from Flag tell you about the next amazing new technical breakthrough from L. Ron Hubbard!* I talked to packed houses. Afterwards, I'd meet with the Scientologists for whom Geoff had already made appointments. Over the previous two weeks, he'd met with area registrars and set up the appointments for me—but only with people who would be able to write me a check for at least $5,000 for Flag, and $2,500 for the local org. Life on the road with Becky was nothing but fun for both of us. Well, there was one glitch in our happiness—I'd developed a wry neck. It makes my head tilt to the right and turn to the left. I had to hold my chin to look straight ahead. My father would call it spasmodic torticollis. I thought my neck went that way because of all the time I'd spent on the phone, cradling the receiver in my shoulder for hours at a time, managing orgs at the FOLO. Nope. I learned a few years ago that it's called cervical dystonia, and I've still got it. But the pain in my neck was easy enough to ignore for all the joy we were having together on the road. Becky and I were home in Clearwater for days at a time—rarely as long a stay as a week. That's when I got to drive Jessica to and from school.

My daughter was a tall and slender girl—and beautiful. Everyone said she had my face. Looking back at photographs now, it's true. She did—and she loved my motorcar as much as I did. It was a twenty-minute drive to and from the school, thirty if I took back roads and drove the speed limit. We knew we didn't have much time together, so both of us tried to make each conversation an important one.

"Daddy, what's God?" I was ready for this one. I'd been thinking about it myself.

"Honey, God is the biggest, most good, and most everything of all."

A long silence, then . . .

"Is Jesus God?"

"Where'd you hear that?"

"In school. Is Jesus our Lord?" Jessica was eight, maybe nine years old. She went to public school in Clearwater. Scientology hadn't yet become the town's largest landowner with parochial schools for Scientology children.

"If you want Jesus to be your lord, then sure."

"Is Jesus *your* lord, Daddy?"

"No, punkin. Jesus and I are just good friends."

"You're going to hell, Daddy."

"Yeah, well."

—

In Europe, Scientologists wrote us checks made out to the Religious Research Foundation, a shell company that maintained a Swiss bank account that was in no way linked to the Church of Scientology. Any money we deposited would be used in the service of the Church without having to pass through any country's tax system—it's a common business practice used by many international organizations. Of course, L. Ron Hubbard had no connection with that Swiss account because it was vitally important to keep all his personal finances on the up-and-up so that no enemy of the Church could use any inadvertent financial glitch against him. But that was unthinkable— (a) because he was so powerful, and (b) because he had both the Sea Org and the Guardian's Office to protect him, and we protected him fiercely.

So, life was . . . great. Thanks to my high income, I'd become a Sea Org star. Crew members actually lined up at the doors to send me off on tour, or welcome me home. It all came unraveled on a sunny autumn day in Zurich, 1982. I had just finished making a sizable deposit to the Swiss bank account. I was out on a quickie one-week tour on my own; Becky was back in Clearwater. This was my first time inside the bank's home office. What a beautiful old place it was! The reverence for wealth was manifest in the severe architecture, lightly touched here and there with tasteful elegance.

I was waiting for the teller to return to his window with my receipts when a clerk appeared at my elbow and asked me to step inside the office of the vice president of the bank. Now, this had never happened to anyone else on my staff in all the time we'd been making deposits at this branch, so my antennae went up. I allowed the clerk to usher me in to the huge office of what very well might be a member of some vast international Swiss banking conspiracy.

An older gentleman was seated behind a desk across the room from me. Dignified, tastefully attired. I started to cross the room toward him, but this old guy gave me a big smile, all teeth. He got to his feet, came around the desk, and offered me a handshake. You must understand: for a Swiss banker, that's an expression of true love. For a Swiss banker, that's beta wolf.

"Mr. L. Ron Hubbard," the old guy said to me, "the bank so appreciates your business all these years, and it's such a pleasure to finally meet you in person."

Oops. No, this was much more than an oops—this was a genuine oh fuck! Some SP inside the Swiss banking conspiracy had obviously broken into the files of the Religious Research Foundation and falsely linked them to the Old Man. Fuck, fuck, fuck! I took a deep breath and reminded myself that I was a far superior being to the old man—lying to him came easy.

"I'm so sorry," I say. "But I am not this Mr. El? Hub Hubbard? of whom you speak."

By then, we were both visibly pale. My mind was racing with worst-case scenarios—and the old guy realized that by naming me, he'd violated some strict law of Swiss banking privacy. We froze, our eyes locked in a long awkward silence. Then we each forced a laugh at the silly mistake, we said our goodbyes, and I strolled casually out of the bank.

There was no such thing as a cell phone. I walked across the city square to my hotel, where I placed a call from the pay phone in the lobby. I couldn't trust that the phone in my room wasn't tapped. I called a secret number and reached a telex operator in Denmark. I spoke to her guardedly, but she got what I was saying and fired a message off to Florida that there was some plot afoot that warranted investigation, and I would stand by for orders. The answer came back almost immediately: I was to travel now, now, now to Sussex, England, where the Church owned Saint Hill Manor and an estate of considerable size, with several buildings for advanced classes, as well as UK's FOLO.

My cervical dystonia was in full bloom—my neck was stuck, turned severely to the left and tilted to the right. A bout of dystonia that strong always brought with it a series of searing headaches, the kind where that's all you can pay attention to: the endlessness of the pain. Nevertheless, I took the next flight from Zurich to London, and the first train I could catch from London to Sussex. It was late when I arrived, and I was given a room reserved for visiting officers and missionaires. I took a few tablets of Empirin Compound and slept maybe four hours.

The next morning I reported for debrief to the guy in charge of all the Church's European finances. I told him everything I've just told you, only in much more detail. For three days, I held my chin tightly so I could look at the guy while I was talking with him. Then orders came down for me to come on home on the next available flight. I was going home! I'd done a good job helping to uncover this plot against the Old Man. With the stress release, my bout with dystonia slowly wound down and I slept in fits and starts on the overnight flight back to the States.

As I stepped off the plane in Tampa, I was met at the gate by seven tall, muscular young guys in Sea Org officer uniforms. Heh. I was still the superstar. But it did strike me as odd that I didn't recognize any of these officers, and I knew personally every senior officer in the Sea Org. The young men had serious faces—they told me they were members of the newly formed Financial Police. I'd never heard of that.

"What's going on here . . . sir?"

"You'll find out, and don't speak unless you're spoken to, mister."

"Yessir."

One for one, they outranked me, so there was no questioning their authority. We drove back to Sea Org headquarters in silence. My neck was again throbbing and threatening to wrench itself around to the left. A migraine-like headache was just beginning to break through the surface of my consciousness. All I wanted to do was get in bed with Becky—she knew how to hold my head just so. But straight away, these guys escorted me into a cold, damp hallway in the basement of the Fort Harrison Hotel. Two of the Financial Police sat me down on a metal folding chair, then took up more comfortable chairs for themselves on either side of me. I couldn't say a word—I still hadn't been spoken to.

After three hours, the other five officers showed up—showered, freshly shaven. I smelled sour to myself and I had a five o'clock shadow that rivaled Richard M. Nixon's. The seven officers escorted me down the hall into a room set up with a table and an e-meter. Now, mostly when you're audited, you're in a small room with one other person, the auditor. There's never more than the two of you. But now, one member of the Financial Police sits across from me, operating the meter. Two big guys are standing behind him, two more big guys stand behind me, and one more big guy stands at the door. Years later, I'd find out they call it a *gang-bang sec check.* One of them spoke.

"How long have you been an agent for a foreign government?"

"What the fuck?"

"Thank you," says the big guy across from me.

Now, he didn't say thank you because I'd told him anything he felt grateful for. He said thank you because in Scientology you're supposed to verbally acknowledge anything that anyone says to you. You use words that show you've heard the other person—*Thank you, OK, Good, Very Good,* and so on—words that show you've heard the other person. It's actually quite a civilized way to talk with people, letting them know you heard them. So he says *Thank you,* then a guy behind me says,

"How long have you been a drug addict?"

"What?!" I turned too quickly to face the guy and blinded myself with a bolt of pain.

"Good."

And now I'm going to paraphrase the real honest-to-goodness questions fired at me, over and over for six hours:

Have you ever embezzled money?

I thought to myself, *y'know, I never did*—it never crossed my mind—and even if I'd wanted to, Scientology finance procedures were foolproof and they would've found me out simply by the paperwork. Was my 2½ percent commission embezzlement?

Are you now or have you ever been a drug addict?

Ever? Was I addicted to Empirin Compound? In college, I chain-smoked marijuana and drank beer. But they knew that about me already, and I'd completed my Scientology counseling on drugs—so I was free from their harmful effects, and free from the need to take them. That made me not an addict. I answered no, and the needle on the e-meter agreed with my call.

Have you ever bombed anything?

Goodness gracious no. Skipper Bush and I once threw cherry bombs into a construction site dirt pit late at night. Did that count? No read on the meter.

Have you ever murdered anyone?

Nope. Haven't ever had to.

Have you ever raped anyone?

Nope. Haven't ever had to.

Have you ever had anything to do with a baby farm?

To this day, I'm not sure what they meant by baby farm, and I've been too timid to give it a google.

Do you collect sexual objects?

I answered that no, I don't—which was technically correct. Two days earlier, I'd thrown out my most recent collection of tranny porn before I flew from Zurich to London.

Thank you. Do you have a secret you are afraid I'll find out?

I was beginning to wish I'd kept some of the secrets I'd revealed in counseling sessions over the last twelve years. Once you leave, all that confidential information is fair game for the Church to use against you. Nah, they knew all my secrets. The meter kept verifying that I was clean as a whistle. And then . . .

Are you upset by this security check?

"You're goddamn right I'm upset about this security check."

Thank you.

Well, *that* led to a two-hour trail of related questions only to discover that I was upset by the security check because I'd done nothing wrong.

"Have you ever had unkind thoughts about L. Ron Hubbard?"

"Not a one," I answered. "Ever." But why wasn't he personally pinning a medal on my chest for pulling his ass out of the financial fires? Unless the Swiss account actually did belong to him, in which case . . .

"OK. That read on the meter. I'll repeat the question: Have you ever had unkind thoughts about L. Ron Hubbard?"

"Not unless you're telling me that the Religious Research Foundation is a bank account that funnels money into the Old Man's pockets. Is that what you're telling me?"

"Good. Have you ever had unkind thoughts about L. Ron Hubbard?"

For two more hours, they quizzed me about all the possible unkind thoughts I could ever have had about L. Ron Hubbard, until the meter convinced them I was OK on that score.

"Thank you. How long have you been a spy for a foreign government?"

"I am not a spy, I'm tellin' you. I've been a loyal officer for twelve fucking years."

"OK. What enemy group are you working for?"

And they kept asking me those kinds of questions for a total of six hours, carefully watching the e-meter for any signs that might reveal my evil deeds. Six hours, no evil deeds. Finally, the guy across from me played his ace. He said I've got a choice: I can do three years of hard physical labor, sleeping a maximum of six hours a night on a cold cement floor, eating only table scraps, and talking only with other bad people like me who were relegated to the months-old Rehabilitation Project Force. I could either do that, he said, or I could leave and be excommunicated from the Church of Scientology for the remainder of all my lifetimes ahead of me. The young officer told me that he's going to live into the future as a hero.

"Without Scientology, you are gonna degrade into a mindless

slug of a spiritual being. You're gonna be a body thetan, attached to the toe of some street bum."

So help me, that's what he said. I didn't thank him for saying it. It had been twelve years since I failed to acknowledge something another person said to me. I'd been holding the cans for six hours—you can't ever let go of them. That meant I couldn't hold my head straight, and my dystonia had once again begun to twist my head painfully over my left shoulder—a move that this guy interpreted as my not being able to look him in the eye.

Twelve years.

What was he saying? Sleeping on a cement floor with this neck? And he never answered my question about the Old Man and the Swiss bank account.

Twelve years.

It had to be true. Daddy was a liar and a cheat—I could deal with everything else about Scientology but that. My mind shattered like a plate glass window in a Mack Sennett comedy.

"You excommunicate me," I said, and so they did.

———

I was packed up and gone within four hours. I wasn't allowed to say goodbye to anyone, and if anyone spoke to me, they'd run the risk of being assigned to the Rehabilitation Project Force themselves— even my nine-year-old daughter—because they had a Rehabilitation Project Force set up especially for kids. So I never said goodbye to Jessica. I left her with Molly and Randy. They loved her, and she loved them—they'd give her love, shelter, and food.

I walked across town and a couple of miles down the highway to a truck rental office in a strip mall. I wanted a small van, but the only vehicle available for an interstate one-way trip was a fourteen-foot cargo truck. I pulled into the Quality Inn parking lot just as Becky was leaving our room. I jumped down out of the truck's cab as she ran down the flight of stairs—we stopped just short of touching each other. She was crying. They'd already told her . . . something. I handed her the keys to the Pacer.

"The car's yours."

"Al."

"Shhhh. We can't talk."

She ducked her head and strode quickly away across the parking lot and around the corner, back to work. I loaded all my belongings into the truck in four quick trips, climbed back up into the cab, pulled out of the parking lot, and drove north.

After twelve years of living in a Scientologist's idea of heaven, there I was . . . out here in hell with you. The only difference was I knew for sure it was Hell, and I knew for sure I belonged here.

Part 3
*

CHAPTER 12

The Lost Boys

I've such gaps in my memory of what happened next—though I can recall the most vivid details of what I *do* remember. Most all of us who served back when the Old Man was alive and in charge have had difficulty remembering the days and weeks immediately after we left or got kicked out. I've recently been getting back in touch with friends and shipmates whom I've not seen for thirty-five to forty years, and they've been helping me remember.

A lot of us left before there was an Internet—no listservs or on-line forums. We had telephones, of course, but it was easy to get an unlisted number—some ex-SO members changed their names to avoid retribution by the Mother Church. There were no toll-free hot-lines or phone trees like there are today. Most of us were out on our own, scattering to the darkest corners of our lives and figuring out for ourselves how to reenter the world. Here's what I remember now.

It's a twenty-hour drive from Clearwater, Florida, to the Jersey Shore. I made it in twenty-four hours, sleeping in rest stops because it was drilled into us that *a sailor sleeps when he can*. I pulled up the driveway. My parents and big brother must have heard the truck pulling in—or they were watching out for me—because they were all around me as soon as I jumped down from the cab.

My father stood and walked with a pronounced stoop—some calcification in his spine, he muttered. My mom looked older; no, she looked old—so many more lines in her face. We hugged, and I held her face to my chest. She felt impossibly small and light. My father grasped my shoulder and turned me toward him. He studied my face. His doctor fingers followed the tightly flexed and straining muscles of my dystonic neck. He held my head and pulled me closer to kiss my cheeks. My brother and I gave each other short manly hugs and thumps on the back.

They took me inside, and lay me down on the sofa facing the television set. My mom made my brother and father gather up pillows from all the bedrooms, so she could build and feather a nest for my twisted neck. My father had been watching football, and the game was still on. He maneuvered his own twisted body down into the same red leather recliner he'd had since before I was born, and gave out a loud sigh of comfort and satisfaction. His equally arthritic black Labrador was stretched out on his footstool, and all was right with his world. My dad watched the game—cursing the referees, belittling the players, and grunting at the good plays. Alan had left—he was dealing with problems of his own at the time. My mom sat with me on the couch. We couldn't take our eyes off each other.

They had my old bedroom ready for me. I had nowhere else to stay, and no money for rent. My parents brushed aside my apologies for being such an inconvenience in their lives. Years later, my brother told me how much he'd resented the attention I got as the prodigal.

They let me sleep a lot and that's what I remember doing. For the first time in twelve years, I had no orders to obey, no policy to apply, no targets to achieve, no products to make, and no statistics to keep. I fell back into the only familiar pattern of life that I knew, and did whatever my father told me to do. I took the Soma tablets he dispensed every two hours—twice the normal dosage of that powerful narcotic. Soma delivers the comforting high of its namesake from Huxley's *Brave New World*. By the second day, I was addicted, and all I had to do to feed my habit was tell my father my neck hurt. Quick as a wish made in *I Dream of Jeannie*, he'd hand me another tablet, as quickly as he'd been handing my mother her cocktails most every night of the forty-plus years they were married.

My father prescribed hot soaks for my neck, and he personally ran the bath water for me—four, maybe six times a day. He told me to take it as hot as I could. He had no idea he was talking to a nascent heavy-duty masochist with drug and alcohol problems. But I didn't know I was a masochist yet, and I didn't believe I had any problems with drugs and alcohol. Scientology had cured me with their Drug Rundown and Purification Program, and I clung to my belief that drugs and alcohol wouldn't hurt me if I took them. What's more, Scientology told me I was free from the *need* to drink or drug, so I felt free to do both for the pleasure of it, not the need. For weeks, four or five times a day, I spent an hour in a steaming hot tub, stoned on narcotics. The drugs made the world look pretty, and that fed my lifelong bone-deep desire to be a pretty girl.

During my first few weeks I had no words to describe my life as ex-cult member and secret girl, so I made art out of it, a series of eight eighteen-by-twenty-four-inch collages. Each one took me two or three days to make. I held off madness by focusing on the precision of extracting images with X-Acto blades, and pasting them just so with rubber cement. Inevitably, I'd look up from my work and catch myself in the mirror, a fat, middle-aged balding man. That's when I'd cut another line into my arm with the same X-Acto blade—my blood went into those collages. The pain of cutting quelled the panic of seeing myself in the mirror. The blood made me smile. Then I'd get back to cut-and-paste. I have one or two collages left. I gave the rest away.

A few months later, the Financial Police were branded a renegade and destructive group within the Church, and they were disbanded. All those big guys were stripped of their rank and assigned to the Rehabilitation Project Force. The Sea Org offered me my job back, and they offered me full amnesty for all my evil deeds. It was my old friend and boss, Dave Renard, who called me on the phone.

"Al, come on back. The Financial Police were assholes. Everything's back to normal. All you have to do is write a confession and sign it. No debt, no RPF."

"I've got no crimes to confess, Dave."

"Al, they're telling me this is your last chance."

"Yeah, they told me that a couple of months ago, too."

Then Dave burst out laughing.

"So, you like to wear women's underwear, huh?"

"G'bye, Dave."

So, why didn't I leap at the chance to return to the arms of the Mother Church? I believed that Scientology worked. I still believe that some Scientology works. But I still wanted to be a girl, and I just figured that meant that Scientology didn't work for me.

——

The Soma took away my appetite. I followed its lead and stopped eating, triggering my mania. As soon as my head could face forward again on its own, I took up jogging. I jogged the length of the boardwalk and back again, four miles a day. I got skinny—again— and for the first time in years, I enjoyed touching myself. I stopped shrinking from the mirror—I stole glances at my reflection whenever I could. Through the lens of my mania, my skin stretched tight across killer cheekbones and collarbones anyone in their right mind would wanna lick. With my flat belly and pouting pelvis I was almost Twiggy. I shaved off my moustache. I took to wearing tight black jeans, a white tank top, and an oversized deconstructed jacket. I wore a wide-brimmed black slouch hat and Holly Golightly sunglasses.

That's how I looked, springtime in New York in 1983. I was a waif leaning against a street lamp—just down the street from the Church of Scientology's new location in Times Square. Six months earlier, I'd loaned my old drinking buddy, Kevin, $750, and now I was close to broke. I was trying to get up my courage to ask him to pay me back, and at the moment I decided to just walk away, Kevin walked out the org's front door. He turned in my direction, spotted me, and grinned. Then he walked over briskly and held out his hand.

"Hello, miss," he said to me.

Oh. My. God. This was not happening. I was Alice through the Looking Glass.

"My name's Kevin. Have you heard about Scientology?"

Inside me, a young girl screamed for joy. I stared at him dumbly. My moustache—he'd never seen me without my moustache. He'd never seen me this skinny or dressed anything like this, ever. Could he be so easily thrown off? Was I starting to look like a girl?

"Would you like to take a free personality test?"

Oh, this was sitcom material, I thought to myself, and I could write about this some day. He took my hand in his and laid his other hand on my forearm.

"C'mon," he said, "it's just a few doors up."

All Scientologists are taught how to control another person's body—it's one of the first things we learn. I allowed him to guide me up the street. I allowed myself to feel like a real girl. I had to put a stop to this. I hadn't lied, not really, not yet. I needed to show him my good intentions. It wasn't my fault he thought I was a girl. The young girl inside me screamed again with joy.

"Kevin. It's me, Al Bornstein."

He froze. Half a dozen emotions flipped across his face like *Wheel of Fortune,* landing on a snarl of rage. I spoke before he could.

"Kevin, I know you're not allowed to talk with me but could you please just pay me back the $750 you owe me?"

"I don't have to give you shit, pervert."

He turned on his heel as if executing an about-face. "Fucking child molester," he said as he walked back into the org.

Child molester. Ah. So that's what they were gonna call me. And of course he didn't have to pay me back—I was Fair Game—but that's one thing they *couldn't* say about me.

After I left the Church of Scientology, I did the best I could to get rid of my funny staring eyes and my compulsive need to acknowledge everything anyone said to me. I didn't talk with many people because I was embarrassed. What would I answer someone who asked me, *So, what do you do?* or *Hey, where have you been for the past twelve years?* I could hide the ex-cult part of me—I could lie, and I did. But I was moving more visibly toward girl every day. Soon I'd reach a tipping point.

I couldn't trust mainstream people with partly girl me. I still didn't have the money to move out, and I didn't have any job skills beyond what I'd learned from L. Ron Hubbard. But one of my dad's patients owned a private middle school in the area, and he got me a job there teaching acting. Soon, I was making an income, and I realized that if I just kept on living with my parents—who seemed genuinely pleased with the arrangement—all the money I was making could go toward exploring the girl in me. I read the *Village Voice* classifieds each week, and I'd circled Ruby's ad. She was a young drag queen in her early twenties who ran a salon in South Jersey for men who wanted to dress like women. And she did house calls. Opportunity knocked soon enough. My father volunteered his services to another medical gig in New Mexico, where he could be Great White Father to the poor savages who lived there.

"Your mother and I are going to be gone for a month. The house is yours, Son. Think you can handle it?"

"I'll be fine, Dad—go save some lives."

As soon as they left, I called to invite Ruby over to the house, and she arrived that evening.

"Oh sweetie," she gushed, "you are going to be so pretty."

I stood in front of her, naked. She eyed me dubiously.

"First, we Nair your chest."

That would be the thick patch of hair that ran from just below my neck to just below my navel. Ruby ran her fingers over my arms, legs, shoulders.

"We're gonna hafta do all these parts of you, baby," she said, "and oh, my honey . . . your back." It took hours. We talked about all the tricks, all the secrets you need to keep, in order to make your boy body look like a girl's. Ruby was tall like me. I was skinny like her. She sidelined in selling women's clothes in larger sizes, and she'd brought an assortment of garments. I bought a bra, foam rubber padding . . . and a gaff—a tight binding spandex g-string for making your outie look like an innie. A gaff is a staple among drag queens. When we'd finally gotten me hairless, Ruby sat me in a chair and did my face. I showed her the short, bobbed brunette wig I'd bought at Lee's.

"Oh, *no* no no," Ruby exclaimed. "We are *not* Miss Mouse."

We tried blonde, platinum blonde, honey blonde, and blonde with black roots. I was too scared. Then we tried the reds. The long, straight hair tickled my shoulders and my forehead as she ran her brush through my . . . my long, beautiful red hair. When she was finished, she spun the chair so I was facing the mirror. I saw pretty girl—the realest girl I'd ever seen me be.

"See? All you needed was help from your drag sister."

We hugged happily. She nuzzled her face into my neck.

"I'm gonna destroy your makeup, lovely."

"Oh! Please do."

She laughed. We kissed. Her skin was impossibly soft. My stubble was already beginning to pop through the makeup on my face.

"Electrolysis," she explained. "When it's your time, I'll show you the best place to go."

My time? Ruby grinned impishly, placed her hands on my shoulders, and pushed me down to my knees in front of her.

"Look," she laughed and turned my head to the mirror on the wall. "We're lesbians!" Yep. That's what we looked like.

Then she turned my face to her cock, and pushed herself forward to my lips. She smelled of roses. I sucked her off greedily. My lipstick left red rings round her cock, and kissy-lips on her balls. We wound up in bed. We fucked for hours, and shared a cigarette after.

"I don't do this with every one of my clients, you know . . . Al?" She sighed, lying in my arms. "I can't call you Al anymore. What's your girl name?"

"Katherine." I liked the name, and it reminded me of a delightful, kind young Sea Org member I'd worked with in New York City.

"Can I call you Miss Kathie for today?"

"You sure can, Miss Ruby."

Ruby squealed happily and rolled herself underneath me.

"Now, fuck me again, Miss Kathie."

I did, and she did me. I saw her again the next week. Then we started dating. She stopped taking money from me, and we spent nights at one or the other of our places. Ruby took me out to a gay bar in South Jersey. The room got quiet as we walked in. The bartender spoke up.

"We don't serve drag queens in here."

"Well that's just fine," chirped Ruby, "because we didn't wanna drink your watered-down booze anyway. And we are *not* drag queens, we are *lezzzz*-bians!" She kissed me. We kissed until they all started clapping for us. Guys bought us drinks all night long. Later that month, my parents returned from their visit to the reservation. Ruby moved to San Francisco, and we never saw each other again.

Becky called me at my parents' home a few days after Mom and Dad returned from the reservation. Becky had left the Sea Org a month after I did—she'd been recovering out on the Philadelphia Main Line with her sister and dad. Could she drive up, she asked, and could we talk about what happens next? Sure, I said. Sure thing.

Three hours later, Becky pulled up the driveway in our red motorcar, freshly washed and waxed. I'd butched up the best I could in a baggy old Brown sweatshirt over some old boy jeans I'd left behind years and years ago. I loped down the steps and across the lawn to greet her. I opened the car door, and she jumped up into my arms for a desperate hug. My parents watched us through the curtains of the living room windows. Becky talked into my shoulder.

"So now that I'm gone too, where are we going to live?" Our heartbeats were beginning to match rhythm—they'd done that for years.

"What did they tell you about me, Becky?"

She pulled herself out of our hug and held me at arm's length. We looked each other up and down. We stroked each other's bones in recognition of our shared hungers. She was still the most beautiful girl I'd known—I was still silly in love with her.

"It's cold out here," she finally said. "Aren't you going to ask me in?"

Her eyes, still so like emeralds.

"No, baby, I'm not asking you in. What did they tell you about me?"

"They said you stole money, and you're a child molester."

"Not true."

"I know that!"

"And what else did they say?"

I knew what else they'd said. Becky looked down at the driveway. I did too. My parents had covered the gravel with more-modern asphalt. I missed the crunch of tires when cars pulled in and out of the drive.

"They said you like to wear women's clothes. That's silly, right?"

Silly hurt my heart, but I hardened my heart.

"No, that part's true."

"I . . . how . . . ? Look at you! You're a man. You've lost too much weight, and I miss your moustache, but it's still you. I love the man you are."

"It's been an act, Becky, I swear! I've always felt I should've been a woman."

She laughed. It helped me harden my heart some more.

"That would explain the makeup you were using on the road."

"Yes it would."

She stopped laughing. I thought I'd been really subtle with that makeup. It was makeup for men, anyway. I used a soft eyeliner and a simple mascara. Becky pressed on.

"But sex," she entreated. "Didn't we have great sex?"

And I thought to myself, *How on earth could an angel like Becky enjoy sex with a freak like me?* She misread the self-directed loathing on my face.

"You didn't like the sex we had?" Her mouth fell open. Tears welled up in the corner of her eyes. And here's where I did that stupid thing people do: we decide to hurt someone for their own good.

"Sex could've been better than it was, right?" Never. It was always amazing.

She told me I must have received some bad auditing. I told her that for twelve years, all my auditing revolved around me wanting to be a girl—even Ron knew about it and *he* couldn't do anything. Oh, was all she said. I asked her did she think she could live with me in skirts. She said no, no she couldn't do that. I shrugged, palms up. Becky shook her head once, and tears flew off her cheeks. She turned and stepped back into the car. I watched as she backed out of the driveway, slowly rolling across the silent asphalt. I watcher her turn and drive down the street and around the corner. There's no such thing as hurting someone for their own good. There's only hurting someone for your own good. That's how I broke it off with Becky, and I am so sorry for doing it that way. I arranged for a legal divorce a few months later.

Nothing was standing between me and the very real possibility of making myself over into a passable girl—but I freaked out at the freak factor that had always overshadowed my dreams of gender change. I didn't think I could live with being a freak. I leapt from my gender quandary like a man jumping from a burning building—I got married again. You know what they say about insanity? That it's doing the same thing over and over again, expecting a different result? Mad, mad me, I gave one last shot at manhood, and got married for a third time—to Janis, a girlfriend of mine from high school. I was up front with her from the start.

"I'm transsexual."

"You're not transsexual," she shot back. "You're a Jewish momma's boy."

I didn't understand her logic but she was Jewish herself, and she said it with such certainty that I allowed for the possibility—and I married her partly because the first night we went to bed, Janis made love to me like I was a woman.

"You've got beautiful breasts, girl."

Janis put a glamour on me. She lay on top of me like she was a guy—stroking and kneading my chest. No one had pinched my nipples before, and I cried out in surprise. Janis traced her hand down my chest to my inner thighs. Taking my cock in her hand, she rubbed her thumb back and forth across its head, calling it my clit. She brought me close to coming, then stopped abruptly—moving her hand down between my legs to rest the length of her middle finger along my scrotum. She knelt down and licked me.

"You taste like roses, girl." I'd just taken a shower—the bath oil had been a g'bye present from Ruby. Before I could tell her that, Janis slowly pushed her middle finger up into the yielding skin of my scrotal sac, which wrapped itself around her finger, resting between my balls. Well, not exactly resting—gently at first, and then more rigorously, she rotated her finger as if she were inside my vagina. Years ago, I'd discovered how to do that for myself, but this was the first time someone was doing it to me. I raised my hips to her.

"Aw, sweet. The little girl wants more."

She gave me more, until I came, all over my belly. It was amazing sex. I'd almost experienced what it might be like to really be a girl. Janis looked as satisfied as I felt. She was smiling, radiantly.

"Well, that proves it," she said, "you're not a transsexual."

"What?"

"You just had great sex, and you were happy with the fantasy. That means you don't need the reality of it."

"What?"

"Jewish boys love their mothers. You love your mother so much, you want to be her. That's all there is to it. It's the same for gay men— they all want to be mommy."

"But that was great sex we just had—amazing great!"

"It was amazing sex for *you*. Which is why we're not going to do it ever again. It only reenforces your momma's boy complex."

Afterward, it was me the guy and Janis the woman sitting across from me in the back garden of the Blue Nile restaurant where Janis was introducing me to Ethiopian food. I was starving myself, but it was delicious enough to eat a few bites. If I closed my eyes and held my breath, I could still feel her finger inside me. Damn. I ordered another beer—was it my fourth or my sixth? Fuck it, I ordered a vodka tonic, a triple.

"And what are you, an alcoholic?"

I scornfully told her I'd completed my Drug Rundown—drugs and alcohol couldn't hurt me anymore.

"Do you know how stupid that sounds?"

———

Janis moved up from Washington, DC, to take a job as an assistant professor at Trenton State College, just across the river from Philadelphia. That's where we'll live, she decided for us. She told me there'd be more of an opportunity for better jobs for me in Philly, and she was right. Some months later, my therapist Greg congratulated me on my ninety days of sobriety. AA had helped. I particularly liked AA's focus on rigorous honesty—and I honestly and rigorously believed myself to be a woman. I never really understood Ron Hubbard's problem with psychiatrists—he kept saying they were all conspiring to take over the world. Greg specialized in helping people return to the real world after a cult experience. We'd spent an entire year on my reintegration, and it all came together in one session.

"We only started calling it PTSD a couple of years ago when we saw that post-traumatic people other than war veterans were experiencing the same symptoms connected with shell shock."

"Post-traumatic. As in after a trauma?"

"Yep."

"Twelve years in Scientology. Could that be seen as a trauma?"

Greg looked at me in disbelief. He took it for granted that my time in the Church was all one big trauma. I hadn't considered that before. Now that I had, I made what to me was the obvious leap.

"Over thirty years of pretending to be a man, making everyone think I really am a man, but I am *not* a man—not ever believing that being a man could ever express the girl I've always known myself to be. Could that be seen as a trauma?"

Greg nodded slowly.

So we dealt with my PTSD, and then we shifted the focus of therapy to my relationship with Janis. She'd been true to her word; she never fucked me like that again, and I'd once again begun to consider girl me. Nevertheless, we'd set a date for the wedding.

"So why are you and Janis getting married?"

"Because I don't want to be a fucking freak. I could never look like a real girl, but I feel like I've got to at least try."

"You still think you're not gay." He'd brought that up one too many times.

"Right. I'm transsexual."

"Convince me."

It didn't occur to me to simply tell Greg that I had no obligation to convince him, and he pressed forward.

"You've had sex with men, right?"

"Yeah, a lot."

"And you enjoyed it, right?"

"Fuck yes, I enjoyed it, Greg. I like sex with guys. I just don't want to live with one." I'd heard a bisexual woman use that line in an AA meeting, and I was proud to be using it myself. But Greg came right back at me.

"I think that makes you homophobic, Al." *Homophobia* was a new word I'd learned at a gay AA meeting, and I was impressed that Greg knew and could use it. "You learned your homophobia from your father and from L. Ron Hubbard, and you internalized it—hook, line, and sinker."

"No, no, no, no, no." I was King Lear again, saying *Never, never, never, never.*

"Al, what's wrong with being gay?"

"What the fuck, Greg? What's wrong with being transsexual?"

We're shouting at each other.

"You really want to be a woman?"

"Goddamnit, Greg, I really *am* a woman!"

Whoa! First time I'd said that. We both let it sink in. I broke the silence.

"My lady sponsor in AA told me she can't sponsor me anymore. She says I've got gender issues and the last thing I needed was a woman as a role model for sobriety."

"So?"

"So, I found myself a not-too-manly-man sponsor."

"And?"

"And he told me to embrace my cross." I shrugged. "He said that's the lesson Jesus taught us all."

Embrace my cross, indeed. My mother believed I had a messiah complex—sort of true. All my life, I've resonated with any expression of the idea that the only way to save the world is to take on its suffering. I made the decision to suffer through one more marriage—just to make sure. It was the wrong cross to embrace. I knew on our wedding day that it wasn't going to work, but I was too afraid to move forward in my transition to girl.

A year after we moved to Philly, I was hired at the start-up office of

Satellite Business Systems, an IBM subsidiary selling long-distance telephone service in the wake of the Ma Bell breakup. About my last twelve years in the Sea Org? I only told a few lies on my resume. The night before my first day at work, I fell asleep wondering how hippie-boy ex-cult closet queen me had ended up at IBM, the bastion of American propriety. At two o'clock that morning, my father woke my mother up with what would be his last words:

"Oh, no! Oh, no! Oh, no!"

Most people when they're hit by a stroke as big as the one that took a day and a night to kill my father, they've got no idea what's happening to them. Like many people, I'd always thought that a stroke was a sort of electrical short in the nervous system, and it fries your brain—stroke, like strike, like lightning strike—but no. While a stroke happens in your brain, it's really a heart-and-blood thing. My father's specialty was cardiothoracic internal medicine. He knew pretty much every way there was to die, and his worst fear was to die of a massive stroke. The technical term is CVA, for cerebral vascular accident. Accident. I guess so. I guess it's an accident that the flow of blood to your brain suddenly cuts off and you feel like you're being slammed in the head with a steel bat.

Oh, no!

I guess it's an accident that immediately after the massive headache, your brain cells start dying and that makes you confused, horribly confused and disoriented: like you don't even know you're lying in the same bed you've been sharing with your wife for the last forty years.

Oh, no!

But as confused as he must have been, a doctor as experienced as my father would have known exactly what was happening to him as it was happening.

Oh, no! Oh, no! Oh, no!

My brother called me with the news. Janis and I jumped in the car and drove the three hours up to the hospital where years earlier my dad had once been chief of staff—the same hospital where my daughter and I were born. My mother and brother were already in the waiting room outside Intensive Care—they were miserable. Janis guided me over to the nurse who'd take me to see my father.

The room was empty except for the bed, my father lying on top of the bed, the heart-monitoring equipment, and the intravenous drip. Everything was white or glass or chrome. My father wore an all-white hospital gown. I don't know where the nursing staff had found that for him—hospital gowns are usually pastel, or flowers. But my father had been chief of staff, and the nurses knew he was not a man to die wearing a pastel gown. The nurse touched a caring hand to my shoulder—she knew me as Doc's son—and left me alone in the room with my dad.

Curled up on top of his hospital bed, my father looked like nothing less than a seventy-five-year-old fetus waiting to be born into death. He was fully cognizant, but he couldn't speak or write a word for the day and a half he lay dying. He couldn't say goodbye. He was angry. He was scared. The few brief moments he lay still, he panted like a dog. Mostly, he thrashed against his restraints. He roared. He sobbed. He gulped for air. I had to tell him something that might comfort him. I took a deep breath . . .

Dad, I'm transsexual. Hush, it'll be fine, I promise. Just listen. Hush. I'm your son, but all along I should have been your daughter. I'm still your child—you're still my father. Listen to me, Daddy—it's not a bad thing. And doesn't it explain everything between us all our lives together?

God, if only I had . . . but no. He was already such a broken thing—I couldn't put him in any more pain. I told him things that mattered to him.

"Dad," not daddy, "I'm still sober. It's been over a year."

It was the truth. He calmed down, he squeezed my hand.

"And it's been six months without a cigarette, Dad."

Also the truth—another squeeze of my hand.

"Today was supposed to be my first day of work at IBM. How about that, Dad? What are you trying to do—kill my shot at making CEO?"

He gurgled. I stroked his hair, like a puppy. Then I lied.

"Janis and I are doing well."

That's how my dad and I had always talked with each other—we told the truth when we could, and we lied when we had to. Over the next twenty-four hours, my mom, Alan, and I took turns sitting with him. It was back to my turn, and there was nothing left for me to say so I sat quietly with him. He cried, but only out of the one eye he could still focus with. I stroked his hair for some minutes. He was lying still, breathing deeply. I did something with my father that I'd never done before—I bent down and kissed his forehead. He made soft little sounds, like a puppy.

"You just rest. No one's going to lose you, Dad."

I put my arms around him, my cheek on his forehead. We were both crying—big wet sloppy tears that real men don't cry. But neither of us were real men, not at that moment—we were lost boys, each in our own way. I held him for a few minutes more.

"I'm right here, Dad. I've got you."

He relaxed back into my arms. It was the kind of sweet moment I'd always wanted with him. And then he was lost.

Oh, no. Oh, no. Oh, no.

CHAPTER 13

Over the Borderline

"So, you never told him how angry you were with him about all his macho demands on you?"

"Nope."

Greg was unsuccessfully prompting me to talk about my father. My heart beat against my ribs.

"The two of you were a time bomb waiting to go off, Al. No wonder you wanted to spit on his grave. That must have been one hell of a funeral."

"Oh, yes. It was."

I didn't cry at the funeral, but now the tears were streaming down my face. I felt shattered—again. It seemed to me like there'd never been a time in my life when I wasn't shattered.

"Al? What?"

"I'm . . . scared. So. Fucking. Scared."

"Of what?"

I didn't have a clue what I was scared of, but I'd learned how to deflect a question like that. I made myself stop crying, and I told Greg he was the only guy in my life that I could talk with about any of my deep truths.

"You know me better than even my AA sponsor."

Greg steepled his fingers in front of his face. I continued.

"You know me better than Janis. You know me better than anyone I know."

He blushed. I'd never heard of transference, and Greg didn't call it to my attention. I was still shaking, and Greg took another tack at cracking my anxiety attack.

"Do you agree with Scientology that you're a suppressive person? A bad person?"

"I'm bad. I do bad things. I hurt people."

"Everyone does."

"I do it a lot. Do you have a disorder for that?"

"Sociopath is as bad as it gets, but Al . . . you're not a bad person. How many times do I have to say that?"

He'd said it a lot, and I never believed him—I figured he had a blind spot, and I knew how to hide in people's blind spots. Greg held up a fat little book and explained to me the importance of the *Diagnostic and Statistical Manual of Mental Disorders III*. I thought to myself, *fuck yes! Finally, a rulebook!*

"People with borderline personality disorder," he said carefully, "are often hostile, uncooperative, manipulative, and impulsive."

Greg looked over his glasses at me and continued.

"People with BPD often turn on the people they're close to."

I sighed audibly with the relief of being named. He explained that this didn't change my diagnosis with PTSD, which was a *mental* disorder. BPD was a *personality* disorder, and a person could have them both at the same time, but not to worry because only 2 percent of all the people in the world are actually diagnosed as borderline.

"Right," I shot back, "and only 2 percent of all the people in the world are declared to be SPs."

Neither of us knew what to say then. I looked away first.

I was working AA as a program of rigorous honesty, and I was honestly a girl. No more trying to be the man that I was not. I needed to move forward in exploring options as a transsexual. Janis said she wasn't a lesbian, and to this day she maintains I'm a momma's boy and not a transsexual. The divorce settlement was easy-peasy-lemon-squeezy. I signed over most everything to Janis: our house, the furniture, and the money in our joint savings account. That seemed fair to both of us. It was my fault, after all—my cross to embrace, not hers.

I moved in to my own place, a first-floor rear studio apartment in a building across the street from Dirty Frank's, Philly's most notorious bar for down-and-out drunks. It was my first home as a girl, and the first thing I did was to shave off the moustache that Janis had insisted I grow back and wear for the length of our marriage. I looked at myself with wonder—my mouth felt naked. A great big part of looking like a man was gone. The apartment didn't get much light, and the walls were a pale mustard brown—layer after layer of nicotine from tenant after tenant. It took the better part of a day to Pine-Sol the smell away and wash the walls, and the better part of a night to paint the place.

One of my first purchases was a full-length mirror. I'd kept on being skinny—Janis was bulimic and I was anorexic, and we didn't talk with each other about our eating disorders. It was easy to tug myself into a pair of black jeans—black girl jeans—*my* black girl jeans. And my simple, black girl tank. And my black Converse girl high-tops. I was going for Nina Hagen, but I couldn't get my eyes quite right. I was chain-smoking like the Old Man—*No!*—I was chain-smoking like Nina Hagen. So I laid one more layer of nicotine onto those walls. I didn't get much sleep the first night. Before dawn, I scrubbed myself clean of any trace of girl, and dressed up like a man to report for my corporate sales job. I was free, alone, and exhilarated. My only direction in life was girl, the freak factor of which still terrified me.

—

Laughing, I touched my upper lip.

"It's a big deal to feel it smooth here, Greg."

"It makes you look pretty."

I blushed. He smiled. I looked up over his shoulder to the window. The snow hadn't yet begun to fall. It was a few days before Christmas and the city was gearing itself up for a blizzard that evening. I was between crises at the moment, so we took the time to reflect on my progress in therapy. I was proud of the degree of self-acceptance and self-confidence I'd achieved. I'd been cross-dressing at home nearly every night—and once a month at a cross-dressers' support group across the river in New Jersey. That meant no time for friends, but

I didn't have any friends anyway—not the kind of friends I could trust with on-my-way-to-being-a-girl me. I'd withdrawn into a world neatly divided into work and girl-practice.

The minute hand of the clock above Greg's head ticked over—it was three minutes before end of session. Greg leaned back in his chair and clasped his hands together behind his head. I knew from a year's experience that this was his body language for *I'm about to drop a big one on you.*

"Merry Christmas, Al."

"Merry Christmas, Greg." I answered more warily than warmly.

Greg got right to the point.

"I wonder how our therapeutic relationship might change, Al . . .," he paused, then continued almost languorously, " . . . if I was to leave my wife and kids . . . and you and I shacked up together."

Outside the snow had just begun to fall. The sky was a dove-grey dotted swiss organza. Greg was talking again. It was difficult to hear him through the roaring in my ears. I'd never before heard anyone use the phrase *shacked up.*

"I'm serious, Al. Think about that—you and me. Have yourself a merry little Christmas, and we'll talk about that next session."

I stood up and held my check out to him across the desk. He reached for my hand . . . not the check, and he pressed my fingers into his own for way too long a time. I turned to leave. He walked me to the door and patted me fondly on my back. Then I was standing outside in a Philadelphia snowstorm.

That night, all my self-harm soothing mechanisms tipped over into the danger zone. I hadn't eaten in a day and a half, and I was super manic—running on empty is what it feels like. I sat on the edge of my bed and alternated between anxiously running my fingers over my bones and lovingly cutting long, deep marks into my arms. I chain-smoked. Janis got the stereo and the TV in the divorce, so I'd bought myself a bedside clock radio at Radio Shack. I found one station that wasn't playing Christmas music, and the radio filled the room with the Go-Go's singing "Can't Stop the World." I finished with five perfectly straight lines across the back of my forearm. They were deeper than I usually cut, but no one would see them under the long-sleeved, button-down shirts I wore to work. I fell asleep around five in the morning, and four hours later I sat hunched over the desk in my sales cubicle. I was on the phone with an AA friend. She was furious.

"It's sexual harassment!"

"OK," I acknowledged—mechanically falling back on Scientology speak.

"You call him right now."

"Yep, I hear ya."

"No, Al, I mean right this minute—and you cancel next week's session. And you cancel every session after that."

"OK, thanks."

"And you never *ever* talk with him again."

It hit me that none of what she was saying ever occurred to me.

"Really?"

"Of course really. Now go, and call me back when you've done that."

I didn't want to speak with Greg, so I called when I knew he'd be in session. I left a message on his answering machine saying I didn't want to speak with him ever again. Two hours later, he called me at my office.

"I am so sorry, Al. That was impossibly wrong of me."

"OK."

"Al, I did a terrible thing. Please, reschedule with me."

My demon walked into the silence. Surprisingly, she was calm and reasonable at first.

"You never believed me when I told you over and over that I'm girl."

"I believe you now, Al."

"Fuck you, Greg. I don't think you do."

"I promise—nothing like that will ever happen again."

"Merry Christmas, Greg. G'bye." I hung up the phone.

My manager Bob was walking by the desk at that moment. He looked at me quizzically.

"Big sale," I told him. "It'll be through by next week." I gave him a big grin and a thumbs-up. He grinned back, gave me his own thumbs-up, and walked on. God, I am such a good liar. I pushed my fingertips hard into my ribs and grinned at the pain of it. *It's Christmas,* I thought to myself, *and bones are the best gift ever.*

It didn't take long to find a new therapist. Mary was a well-known, well-loved, and highly respected butch woman in Philadelphia's sex and gender underworlds. She was close to my age, and more importantly she was known around town for her work with transwomen. In our first session, I ran through the basics: cult member for twelve years, actor, salesman, mariner, married three times. Warily, I showed her my bones and my scars. I spat out the letters PTSD, BPD, and SP. I was careful to display no emotion when I told her about Greg. Mary told me she'd got it, all of it—and by the end of our session, she'd mapped out my journey to genital surgery. It would take a little over a year, she said. I needed to slow down now, she said, and become fully conscious of each step I took toward being girl. Woman. Mary said I should call myself a woman, not a girl.

Under Mary's lesbian-feminist guidance, I learned just how deeply I'd bought into the heterosexist mainstream transsexual narrative of the day: I wanted to look like and take on the woman's role in the misogynist American dream. Mary sent me forth to study feminist theory. I had no idea what that was, beyond the disdain I heard in most men's voices when they spoke the phrase *women's liberation.* I wanted to show my new lesbian therapist that I could make myself a most liberated woman.

"Like Holly Golightly," I announced proudly.

"She's your idea of a liberated woman?"

"Well . . . yeah, for her day. She was."

Mary looked at me doubtfully. Holly was not the best role model for me, not in her eyes, and I needed Mary's approval for my surgery. But she'd only seen the film, and I didn't have the language to describe how Capote crafted thoroughly modern Holly in his novella as a girl who could stand alone on her own two feet, and still be fabulous and delightful. I didn't tell Mary how afraid I was of becoming the other Holly—the wild-thing girl who I'd now figured out was a girl living with BPD. Instead, I kept telling Mary I wanted to be pretty. It made her smile. I was not pretty the day the bandages came off my face.

"It was a terrible accident," I'd told my coworkers at SBS Skyline. "My face went through the windshield." Liar liar me. I'd scheduled plastic surgery to rid myself of the hound-dog bags under my eyes, and to trim my nose down to something that might make my face look more girl.

"I don't want anything turned up or cute," I'd told my surgeon. "Just less . . . wide. If I go ahead with a sex change, I want to be able to look like a woman. If I decide not to at the last minute, I'll wanna look like a man."

"Yep, I can do that," said the surgeon.

"And I don't want a perfect nose—I want a bump, like Charlotte Rampling." I showed my surgeon a photo in a fan magazine.

She grinned and said she could do all of that in her office. She did, and I stayed out of work for nearly a week, healing. My boss and co-workers sent me flowers, like they'd done my first day of work, when my father died. Everyone was sweet and welcoming when I walked back onto the sales floor with my face bandaged up like Claude Rains in *The Invisible Man*.

Two weeks later, when the bandages had all come off, I didn't think my swollen red face looked pretty, but some of my coworkers told me they wished they could be in an accident and come out of it better looking . . . the way I had.

"I was lucky," I lied, "that there was a plastics guy on duty that night."

"You look adorable," gushed one of my gay male coworkers.

"He said I look adorable," I gushed to Mary later that evening.

"Well, you do."

Mary still wanted to yank my attention off adorable and on to the practical reality of living as a woman in a world of misogynists. She sent me across town to Giovanni's Room, Philadelphia's lesbian, gay, and feminist bookstore. Arleen Olshan and Ed Hermance owned and managed the store. They both made me feel comfortable enough to tell them I was on my way to becoming a woman, and that I needed to learn about feminism. Gay Ed looked amused—he turned me over to lesbian Arleen, who looked bemused. Nonetheless, Arleen took me on a shelf-by-shelf book tour of the subject.

In the '80s, feminists were careful to strip themselves of any markers that might lead women back into lockstep with the patriarchy—so there were no books about wanting to be skinny, cute, and sexy. I read book after book about women's rights, and how over history, men had subjugated women into positions of frailty and fealty. A lot of the books I read told me how to escape those traps. Beyond fashion magazines and porn, there weren't any books about the joy of being a sexy woman—so I continued to buy and devour fashion mags and porn.

I had therapy with Mary once, sometimes twice, a week, but I'd cut down on the number of AA meetings I was attending. That left me with four or five nights a week free to do theater at the Wilma Project, a small on-the-edge theater in Philadelphia founded and run by Blanka and Jiri Zizka—a pair of theatrical visionaries from Czechoslovakia. I joined Scientology before I had the opportunity to explore eastern European theater, and in Scientology the only theater was Ron. Jiri had time for lunch with me.

We met at a Center City diner, and sat in a booth across from each other. It was a couple of weeks after I took the bandages off my face. The swelling had gone down, and the redness was gone—so it was androgynous me, chatting with Jiri. Plus, I was acting more and more like a woman. Part of my therapy had been to go out and watch women—not in a creepy way, but simply to observe how women move through the world—posture, gestures, styles of interaction, speech patterns, the expression of different emotions. Jim Barnhill taught me this technique at Brown, to prepare myself for a stage role. I'd take on parts of different people I watched, and part by part I'd become my character. I was good at it—it's part of the mechanics of self-transformation. So, I'd been watching women for months now, and slowly I was becoming one. Sure, I was a man when I was sitting across from Jiri, but more and more of my gestures and mannerisms had already shifted toward girl—I still said girl, not woman, when I thought of myself.

Our conversation got around to his current production, Brecht and Weill's musical *Happy End,* and he asked if I would be interested in auditioning for a role.

"I'm transsexual," I blurted out. "I'm a woman. Well, I will be."

"I can see that," said Jiri without missing a beat. "So, can you sing?"

He explained that he'd written in the character of an emcee who would sometimes be onstage as a man, and sometimes as a woman.

"It might be just the right role for you," he said.

I thought so, too. I auditioned with the song "Pirate Jenny" from *The Threepenny Opera*—and he cast me as the emcee. For the next ten weeks—during rehearsals and performances—I switched dizzily back and forth between being a man and being a woman. I worked as a corporate man by day, and each night, I became not only the bigendered emcee of the show . . . I doubled as the notorious dame known as The Fly, the secret leader of a 1940s gang of cheap, sleazy criminals. I felt like a villainess out of a *Batman* comic. I went through twenty-seven costume changes in each performance. The local Philadelphia papers gave me terrific reviews. The *Philadelphia Gay News* devoted a full page to an interview with me, in which I carefully explained that I wasn't gay. I didn't mention that I was transsexual.

"Sweetie," exclaimed the young gay man who was interviewing me, "you were absolutely adorable in your sequined butterfly outfit. You may not be gay, but you are certainly not straight."

"Adorable," I gushed the next day to Mary. "He called me adorable."

——

"Janis Raymond does not speak for all lesbians," Mary said firmly. "And not all feminists are going to think you're a terrible person."

After I'd exhausted the supply of books about feminism and

women's culture, I asked Arleen if she knew of any books that link transsexuals and feminism. She sighed and told me not to read the slim black paperback she'd pulled from a shelf labeled "Lesbian Separatism"—*The Transsexual Empire: The Making of the She-Male* by radical lesbian feminist Janis Raymond, a learned professor who didn't like transsexual women—nope, not one bit. Her points of view don't bear repeating in this book—beyond saying they were mean enough to make me want to kill myself.

It took me less than a day to come up with a plan: Colorado. I'd take a bus and ask the driver to let me off at the foot of the same mountain I'd fallen off over a decade ago, before I ran into Scientology. This time, I'd be wearing proper hiking boots. I'd bring along a couple of bottles of vodka. I'd climb up as high as I could, find myself a ledge, and drink both bottles. Hypothermia would take me quietly. There'd be no mess for anyone to clean up. And by the time my body thawed out, I'd be a delightful feast for all sorts of God's creatures. Mary was alarmed.

"You're saying you want to kill yourself?"

"No, no," I lied. "I'm saying I wish I was dead. Just because I have a plan doesn't mean I actually want to do it. Geez."

Mary didn't buy it, and I stayed alive for the months of therapy it took to defuse Raymond's transphobic analysis and understand that going through with my gender change didn't mean I was a traitor to feminism. I filed my suicide plan away for future reference.

My final roadblock to accepting my transsexuality was my decades-old quandary: *How could I be a woman if it was women that I loved?* Mary had an answer that worked: the distinction between sexual orientation and gender identity. Sexual orientation, she explained, answers the questions *Who and how do you love?* Gender identity answers the questions *What gender am I and how do I want to express it?* I got the theory of it, but . . .

"So what does that make me? I'm a transsexual. I want to be a woman, and I want to be in love with women."

"Sounds to me like you're a lesbian."

I'd never considered that. On the hierarchy of gender in those days, lesbian was more of a real woman than transsexual—maybe even a higher form of life—just like straight women were more real women than lesbians. I knew all about thetans having no gender, but in real life gender was an immutable caste-like system. And here was Mary, suggesting it was time for me to climb up the gender evolutionary ladder to lesbian. Furthermore, Mary said it was high time I began my real-life test. The RLT was part of the established medical guidelines of the day in which the transsexual must first, prior to any permanent surgery, live a year full-time in their chosen gender. That would mean nonstop girl for a whole year, 24-7. I'd do my best to look like a woman, talk like a woman, act like a woman, and survive like a woman. But before I could start my RLT, there were a few people I had to come out to first.

———

It was a hot August afternoon down the Jersey Shore. My mother and I sat across from each other on the sunporch of her home, the same big house I'd grown up in. We were drinking iced tea. Strong, with extra lemon. No sugar. That's how we both liked our iced tea.

"I have something to tell you, Mom."

"You're gay," she said without missing a beat. It turns out she'd always suspected I was gay, and she thought this moment was a good time to let me know she suspected it.

"Not exactly, Mom," I told her cautiously. "Do you know what a transsexual is?"

A summer breeze whispered through the leaves above the sunporch.

"Transvestite?" she asked. She knew the difference. Of course she knew the difference. Her husband, my father, had been a medical doctor. She knew the difference. It was the truth she didn't want to know, and I pushed forward with the truth.

"Transvestites want to dress up in women's clothes, Mom," I told her. "I'm getting the surgery so I can live as a woman—that makes me a transsexual."

"So, why are you telling me this?" she shot back at me. "Why didn't you just let me go to my grave believing I have two sons?" The fact that my mother had given birth to two sons elevated her status in the conservative Jewish value system she'd grown up with. There I was, threatening to rip that away from her. *Me, me, me. It's all about me.*

I pressed on relentlessly.

"Mom, I'm going to *look* like a woman. I'm going to *talk* like a woman. And if I didn't tell you now, then I'd never be able to talk with you, or see you, again."

My mother stood up slowly and folded her hands across her chest. She spoke evenly and with every ounce of conviction she had.

"You get out of here right now, young man. You just walk out that door. And if you go through with this . . . if you really go through with this . . . don't bother coming back to my house. You won't be welcome here."

I nodded, gulped down the last of my iced tea, and stood up.

"Wait," she said. "What are you going to call yourself?"

"Katherine."

"You were born Albert. It was my father's name."

"OK," I acknowledged.

My mother narrowed her eyes to slits. Everyone in my family knew that look. She called it "making little eyes." It was a tell. She always made little eyes right before she pounced.

"If I have to call you Katherine, then you call me Mrs. Bornstein."

"All right," I acknowledged Scientologically. "I got that."

I made myself leave calmly, with some dignity. She didn't see me crying. I didn't see her crying. Later, my mother told me that she sat there, drinking her iced tea, watching me pull the car out of the driveway into the street, then around the corner and out of sight.

———

"I'm transsexual," I told Bob, the office manager. "And the next step in my therapy is to spend a year living full-time as a woman, and I'd like to continue working here." I used words from the talk I'd rehearsed with Mary.

"And you plan to start this year . . . when?"

"Ah, well, Mr. Dundon . . ."

"Bob."

"Bob. Well, Bob . . . starting like . . . now. I'd like a week off to get all my ducks in a row—mostly a whole new wardrobe—and when I come back, I'm going to be Katherine."

"Katherine."

"Uh-huh."

Bob was taller than I. He had beach boy blond hair and blue eyes—the kind of blue that makes you stop and notice how blue they are.

"Will you still be able to sell?"

"Uh . . . yeah."

"Well, do you think Katherine can sell as much as Al?"

"Uh . . . yeah. Yes!"

"Great. Then take the week off, get yourself ready, buy yourself some smart clothes, and I'll see you next week."

He reached across the desk to shake my hand, thought better about it, and walked out from behind the desk to give me a hug. He was that good of a guy the whole time I knew him. I took a week to run up my charge cards, buying outfits a notch above dress-for-success—and, ta-da!—it was the beginning of me as all girl, all the time.

A week later, I left for work as a woman for the first time. I walked out of my apartment just after sunrise—before rush hour. I didn't want anyone to see me. But as I opened the front door to my apartment building, I found myself face to face with two workmen. They looked at me and grinned. My worst fears had come true, and I was walking through the world like a clown—a man in the dress. But the older guy doffed his cap and spoke cheerfully.

"Good morning, miss. Gosh, I don't know what's more beautiful this morning—the sunrise or you."

He was teasing me. No . . . he wasn't. I'd been reading up on ancient matriarchal cultures, and I silently thanked half a dozen goddesses, who all told me to smile at the guy. I did, and he smiled back. *Yes!*

"Have a lovely day, miss."

The two guys made their way past me and I watched them disappear down the basement stairs. I turned back to the beautiful morning, closed the front door behind me, and walked out into the world as full-time Katherine.

I made even more sales than I'd made as Al. My office mates were all terrific—well, with the exception of our token fundamentalist Christian who seethed when I stepped into his sightline. The women gave me tips on how to sell to guy executives when you're a woman—I learned a whole other set of rules and ploys than I'd ever used. For their part, the guys in the office felt free to tell me I looked good, or even pretty . . . when they thought I did. The days of their silence made me want to crawl under my desk and die.

It was a series of IBM's national vice presidents who gave me a hard time. Three days after I showed up at work as Katherine, a Human Resources veep arrived in Philly on a mission to tell me to man up or I'd be fired. He smugly explained that by wearing women's clothing I was violating IBM's dress code—and they would fire me unless I went back to dressing like the man I legally was. That's when Scientology saved my job. Without missing a beat, I asked to see the dress code in writing. That old Scientology maxim, *If it's not written, it's not true*—it was drilled into us like *Easy does it* is drilled into recovering alcoholics. The vice president smiled confidently and handed me an IBM employee manual, opened to the dress code. I read through a few pages of it.

"Wow, I sure am violating most of this. Too bad I'm not contracted to IBM. I work for SBS Skyline. Bob . . . ?"

"Way ahead of you, Kate." He passed me a copy of the employee manual for SBS Skyline. I flipped through it until I came to the dress code I remembered reading a year earlier. It was simple—one line—and I read it out loud.

"All employees shall wear appropriate business attire."

I smiled and did a pirouette in my fabulous boutique-y business outfit, and that was that. The veep left in a huff, but for the next six weeks our office was visited by some national executive or other who wanted to see the tranny for himself. I got used to it.

The next hurdle at work was the bathroom—building management said a flat no to the ladies room, and I refused to use the men's room. As a solution, they assigned me a private bathroom—six stories up on a floor of the office building where work had been halted months earlier, before construction had been finished. No one worked there anymore and it was creepy to make my way through rubble. There was no door on the bathroom, and I had to bring my own toilet paper. It was humiliating. I stopped drinking coffee and tea at my desk, and I held my pee as long as I could.

My mom and I hadn't spoken with each other for six months—until the night Hurricane Gloria hit the Jersey Shore. I called her from my apartment to see that was she safe. We chatted stiffly, far more polite than we'd ever been with each other.

"How're you doing?" she finally asked me. I was close to tears.

"Not so good, Mom." I told her I was having a hard time at work because I was becoming a woman.

"Oh baby," my mother sighed into the phone. "You think it's rough now—wait till you *are* a woman."

"I *am* a woman, Mom . . . and no one knows it but me." That's when I started to cry.

"Mom, I can't talk anymore." I hung up the phone and cried into my pillow for fifteen, maybe it was twenty, minutes. The phone rang. I knew it was her. I answered on the third ring.

"Hello?"

"Hello . . . Katherine," said my mother for the first time ever.

"Mom . . . I love you so much."

"Stop crying, baby," she said in her most soothing voice. "I love you too. That's why I called. And I called to tell you this . . ." She took a deep breath, then continued.

"No matter how your world falls apart—and honey, that's what happens: we all build ourselves a world, and then it falls apart—but no matter how that happens, you still have the kind heart you've had since you were a child, and that's what really counts. And I will always be here for you, my butzalah. I love you, Katherine."

She assured me she'd easily weather the hurricane. We said our goodbyes and gave each other good wishes and love. After we hung up, I didn't feel like a bad person. I didn't feel empty.

———

SBS Skyline was bought out by MCI, a larger company. I was recruited away to start up an office for a doomed Ford Aerospace bid in the long-distance market. I fled IBM-ish SBS and didn't look back. I now knew enough about Marxist feminism to realize I was sinking deeper and deeper into the misogynist snake pit of capitalism and good old boys that was Corporate America. But there was an alternative—my feminist self-tutoring had led me to read dozens of books and several decks of tarot cards, all chronicling ancient goddess cultures around the world, when matriarchy was the politic of the day. I resolved to find myself work that was steeped in goddess culture. It was easier than I thought. Reading through the *Philadelphia Inquirer* classifieds that night, I came across an ad for adult-phone-line operators. I remembered reading that holy women of the past often served as temple prostitutes. Finally! I'd found a workplace where I could be holy and sexy at the same time!

I knew how to make myself sound like a woman—well, to most people. I could do better on the phone with no man-in-a-dress visual cues. It all turned on pitch—if I could pitch my voice just above the pitch of the person I was talking to, they'd think I was a woman. And I listened to Laurie Anderson albums over and over again until I thought I could speak with just the right mix of playfulness, sing-song snarkiness, and breathy femme nerd girl voice. Nervously, I called the number in the want ad, reminding myself that it was my voice they wanted, not my body. The guy who did the hiring got right to the point.

"All right, lady. Talk dirty to me and make me wanna fuck you."

I was ready for this. I'd rehearsed. I transformed myself into the gum-popping prostitute with a heart of gold, Shirley MacLaine in *Some Came Running*. I lay back on my bed and closed my eyes.

"Tell me, mister. Tell me what it is ya like." I told him I was stroking my pussy, and it made him gasp with pleasure. I was stroking, but it wasn't a pussy yet.

"Tell me," I dared him, " . . . tell me what you want me to be . . . daddy?" I heard him swallow hard—gotcha! "You wanna fuck me, daddy? Is that why you're callin' me?"

"Oh yeah, baby," says the guy. "That's why I'm callin' you."

My hips rose up all by themselves. I was so girl, stretching myself out on top of my bed. I could feel each and every erotic nerve in my cock, my balls, and deep up inside me—it was wonderful, and I sounded that kind of wonderful to this guy.

"Mmmmmm. Want me to suck you and fuck you, daddy?"

"Aw, yeah! That's the stuff—c'mere and suck on daddy's cock."

Half an hour later, he gave me the job. *Et voila!* I am woman, hear me seduce! I worked the graveyard shift, six nights a week. It paid the rent. Some bank had given me my first credit card solely on the basis of my one-year employment history at SBS Skyline. It came with a $25,000 credit line in 1986 dollars. No one ever told me how credit worked, and I never asked. I continued charging up my card and suddenly I'd successfully jumped off the corporate bandwagon into a job as one of the USA's first-ever phone-sex hostesses. Truth.

It wasn't all sex. A lot of it was flirtatious banter—playful, even joyful. Very little of it was mean. I could do a lot of different voices, so I played with the guys. When the line was getting too quiet, I'd speak like three different Munchkins, each saying *follow the yellow brick road.* That led to me being Dorothy and guys spending more money to stay on the line with a real live girl from Kansas. It was my first experience of virtual sex. Using only my voice and my wits as an avatar, I was completely free of my boy-born body. I was a real girl and I was making myself over into one man's sex dream after another. Twice a week, before my phone-sex shifts, I worked another phone line—only it wasn't Oz anymore. It was Kansas.

"I've got a shotgun," came the husky whisper in the receiver I clutched against my ear. "And I'm going to kill myself."

It was my first night on the gay and lesbian hotline at the University of Pennsylvania. A young gay man had received the call from the distraught forty-something transsexual woman, and he passed the call to me, the only tranny on staff. I'd been on the phone with this woman for thirty minutes.

"And if I don't kill myself," she growled, "I'm gonna take aim down at the street and kill people at random. Now, what should I do?"

My supervisor was listening in on the call.

"Keep her on the line," she whispered. "Make her talk about herself . . . or tell her about *yourself*."

"Ummm . . . so, why do you want to be a woman?"

"I *am* a woman, goddamnit!"

Oh Goddess, I thought, *please never let me sound like that.*

"I'm trapped in a man's body," she said, "and I'm sick and tired of people laughing at me when I dress in the clothes I should be wearing."

"I'm a transsexual woman too," I blurted out, "and I hear you. I so hear you."

Long pause.

"No shit?"

"No shit."

Another long pause.

"Have you had your surgery?"

"No, not yet."

"What's stopping you from wanting to kill yourself?"

"Right this minute," I say, "you are. You're keeping me alive by staying alive and talking with me." My supervisor gave me the thumbs-up.

"How can you bear it?" whimpered the tranny on the phone.

"One day at a time," I chirped in my best AA speak.

Silence, then . . .

"I don't really have a gun."

"Ah. Well, I can't tell you how glad I am to hear that." What I couldn't tell her was how ashamed I was that I'd waited thirty min-utes to tell her that I was transsexual too. We wished each other a good evening and hung up. I slammed my fist down on the desk—so hard that the people in the office stopped what they were doing and turned to look at me.

—

It was January 24, 1986, when a judge handed down her approval of my legal name change from Albert Herman Bornstein to Katherine Vandam Bornstein. It was the very same day L. Ron Hubbard died.

The Commodore was seventy-five years old, living alone in a double-wide out on a Church-owned ranch in the desert of Southern California. It was a luxury trailer, but it was a trailer, and it was the best he could do for a hideout. The Old Man had been named as a coconspirator by US government prosecutors, but he hadn't been indicted so he was on the lam. The government had a pretty much iron-clad case against more than twenty Scientologists who'd infiltrated the IRS for years in order, reportedly, to mine personnel files that the Church could leverage into getting itself a nonprofit status. Ron's wife, Mary Sue, had been tried and found guilty, along with ten other Scientologists—they were all serving time in jail. Mary Sue Hubbard adored Ron as deeply as my mom adored my dad. Both women worshipped their men, fought for their men, and placed their men above themselves. Mary Sue and my mother were women of a generation, and I loved them both. Mary Sue Hubbard was behind bars the day the love of her life died alone out in the desert. That's just not right.

Of course he wasn't completely alone. There were a few young Sea Org members assigned to the Commodore's household staff: a cook, a couple of stewards—but it wasn't like the old days when he'd had his pretty young girls in short skirts to light his cigarettes, carry his ashtray, or powder his feet before pulling on his socks. And he had stopped issuing direct orders into any and all Scientology and Sea Org command lines. So he didn't have anyone to order around anymore. David Miscavige was reportedly the only person with whom he'd talk Church business. Well, that's what David Miscavige says.

He died in what had to be a bed that could fold up for storage.

Then again, I could be wrong about any or all of this—I put this story of the Old Man's death together from what I found online. You can google any of this for yourself and see how many sources will confirm what I'm writing about here. L. Ron Hubbard had gone mad. His death certificate shows the presence of prescription drugs in his body—whatever drugs the psychiatrists were giving to mad people back in those days. Go ahead, google it. You can have the PDF of his death certificate on your screen within two minutes. Go ahead, I'll wait.

As the Old Man lay dying, a coup was in progress to determine who was next in command. High-level Church executives were sent to the RPF by the dozen. The player who emerged victorious was David Miscavige, who claims to have been Ron Hubbard's most trusted officer. Maybe that was the case.

———

There's a photo of L. Ron Hubbard taken just before he died. You can find it online easily enough—it's the grainy blotchy one. He's disheveled and unshaven, wearing what looks like a stained nightshirt. His eyes are unfocused and his jaw's gone all slack. It's heartbreaking. Yes, yes, yes, he was a mean old man. But so many of us held him in our hearts like we'd hold daddy. He was a bad daddy to be sure, but he was daddy. No one's come forward online to say they were there when the Old Man was lost, or that they held his hand and cried with him. If I'd been there, I would have.

CHAPTER 14

Stages of Life

When I was first a girl, I was a thirty-eight-year old man and I had to make up for lost time. It wasn't easy. I had to learn girl from the ground up, just like I'd had to learn boy. It wasn't pretty.

When I was first a girl, I'd already perfected my anorexia as a teenaged boy.

When I became a girl, bleeding didn't just happen to me. It took me decades, but I'd learned how to make myself bleed. I used surgical scalpels and razor blades. I used anything sharp.

When I was first a girl, the huge dose of hormones they shot into my hip every week took six months to kick my system over from testosterone to estrogen—and for six months I teetered on the edge of my own private menopause while I watched my penis shrivel.

When I first looked out onto the world from the eyes of a girl, the AIDS epidemic was just starting to peak in the larger cities of the United States. Gay men were dying by the thousands, and it was only the luck of the draw that I wasn't one of them. I was a brand-new lesbian, and AIDS wasn't traveling as swiftly through the sapphic corridors of the sexual underworld.

When I was first a girl, I was ugly beyond any words that could describe my ugliness—compared to the ladies in the magazines. I hadn't yet learned that *Playboy*, *Elle*, and *Vogue* all airbrushed the photos of their models. I thought that sort of beauty was achievable. I was skinny, but the problem with anorexia is that even if you're skinny, you still think you're fat. So when I was first a girl, I looked into mirrors, and all I could see was a fat, middle-aged man in a dress at a crossroads marked *Woman, This Way* and *Theater, That Way.*

I couldn't see any way to live them both, so I danced along the edge of a life not worth living because I couldn't live either. I daydreamed more and more about mountaintops outside Denver, or maybe up in Maine: me, a couple of bottles of vodka, and hypothermia. Perfect way to do it. It was *theater* that saved my life, not *woman*. I was a failure at woman.

I cofounded a lesbian theater company with graphic artist, painter, cartoonist, and comedienne N. Leigh Dunlap. She and I called our company Order Before Midnight because we liked the way it sounded. We produced two shows during which friends both bonded and flew apart from each other . . . and that's show biz.

———

"Are you heading back to Philly?"

"Yes indeedy," I chirped. "I've got time to catch the last train. Give me a ride to the station?"

Cindy had changed herself back into Chuck, and that's what Chuck did for me after our monthly cross-dressers' meetings—he gave me rides to the station. I was in the kitchen helping Sabrina, our hostess, rinse dishes and glasses before loading them into the dishwasher. Sabrina owned a local wig shop, and charged us all a small cover fee for the get-together each month—she made her money on the wigs, clothes, and one-on-one coaching with the ladies. I kept attending those meetings to learn survival tips like just how do you dress a man's body to look like it's a woman's body? How do you make your guy face look like a girl? So I went to learn that sort of thing, but mostly, I kept going to those meetings because I wanted to be sure I wasn't one of those guys myself. I believed I was a real woman, and they were men making believe—that's how I thought.

Month after month, I watched them dress up in frilly clothes, evening gowns, lingerie. But they still acted like guys. They smoked cigars. They punched each other in the arm. They spoke in deep, gravelly voices about their investments, their patios, their barbecue pits, their little women at home. And they took up way too much space . . . and that above everything else is what triggers my anger around guys. So I mostly hung out with Sabrina. We talked about padded shoulders, platforms, and three-color eye-makeup designs.

Chuck was leaning in the kitchen doorway, watching us as we finished. He'd told me months ago that he didn't help out in the kitchen because he was a paying customer. He made a really cute girl, and now he was wearing chinos and a soft, pastel cashmere sweater. He looked like a girl trying to be a boy. He took my breath away. We'd kissed a couple of times. We said goodnight to our hostess and walked down the block to where he'd parked his really cool low-slung muscle car. He held the door open for me.

"It's late," he said. "Stay out at my place tonight. I'll give you a ride to the station early tomorrow morning."

I could sleep in his bed, he said—he'd sleep on the couch. That's not what happened. What happened was that shortly after I fell asleep in his bed, I woke up with pretty girl Cindy on top of me, holding my face between her hands. She . . . he? . . . leaned down and kissed me—brutally—on the mouth. Her stubble would leave a burn mark, I thought. I wasn't kissing her back—she didn't like that, and she told me so. Then he slapped me hard across the face.

"Be good when I tell you to be good," she said and leaned down closer. "And I know you like S and M—I've seen your eyes light up when you've talked about it in meetings." She straddled my chest, positioning her knees on either side of me. He had a good four inches and fifty pounds on me. He grabbed my cock and she leaned down to kiss me again. I groaned into her mouth. He mauled my not yet A-cup-size breasts. I jerked my head away from her mouth.

"Stop! That hurts!"

He slapped me again, and I saw stars. She sat up and edged her hips closer to my face, lifted her peignoir, and pushed his cock up against my lips.

"Suck me off, slut," he growled. "Suck me good." I did, for way too long a time. He went to sleep in his girly-girl bed with the pink satin sheets. I sat up in the kitchen until morning. He drove me to the train station just before dawn. NPR was droning on about Yasser

Arafat. Chuck was chuckling. I wanted to peel the lips off my face. I pressed my cheek hard against the car window. The pain and cold of it felt wonderful.

I lied—Chuck wasn't chuckling, I've just always wanted to write that line.

—

Dr. Stanley Biber enjoyed talking about his days in the Korean War. He'd been a surgeon in MASH 8055, the unit that served as a model for the 4077 of the novel, film, and television series.

"We did meatball surgery," he told me. "We didn't have any of the equipment we needed, so we were always coming up with wacky ideas to get the job done."

I couldn't wait to hear what wacky meatball idea he had in mind for me when we sat down across his desk after my physical exam.

"Your surgery is going to be more complex than usual."

Oh crap.

"Prior to penile inversion—and as part of the procedure—I'm going to have to take two rectangular patches of skin from your butt or your inner thighs, and make them ready to insert."

"Insert where?"

"In your new vagina."

"For why?"

"For depth."

"Huh?"

"Well, your body has been soaking up estrogen for some time now, and as a result, your penis has shrunk considerably."

"And?" It sure sounded like a wacky meatball surgery plan, but he was very patient as he explained it to me.

"Your penis is *short*. It's going to be even shorter in six months when you're back for your surgery—you're not going to have enough depth."

I felt trapped in a vaudeville routine and I didn't know the punch line.

"Depth for *what?!*"

"For penile intercourse! Don't you get it? Your vagina isn't going to be deep enough for the average penis. So I'll use those two patches of your skin to add depth and sensitivity." He sat back, charmingly smug. The tension drained out of my shoulders and I sighed with relief.

"I don't need that kind of depth."

"I beg your pardon?"

"I'm not going to be having any . . . penile intercourse."

"What?"

"I'm a lesbian."

Doc Biber smacked his forehead like he could have had a V-8 and laughed. And we ended our interview like an episode of *M*A*S*H* . . .

"You're a lesbian! Of course! Why didn't you tell me? Nope, we won't need the extra skin. You'll be just fine the way you are."

Loved that guy. We scheduled a surgery date for May 1, 1986. I showed up two days early, because I was as certain as I would ever be. Over the previous two years, I'd made a list of questions, over ninety of them, each challenging my decision to go through with genital-reassignment surgery. It kept coming down to this: life as a man was not a life worth living.

I'd ruled out cross-dressing as an option. The only other options were drag queen, she-male working girl, and real woman—well, as close to that as I could get. I wasn't pretty, graceful, or feminine enough to make it as a drag queen or working girl—and I was too old for any sex work except phone sex, and that market was flooded now anyway. The only road left took me right to the door of the Mount San Rafael Hospital in Trinidad, Colorado, where ol' Doc Biber turned boys into girls and girls into boys with wacky meatball surgery. At the time, the hospital was staffed and run by the Sisters of Charity. The entire week I was there, I resisted the urge to tell them that I'd always wanted to be a bride of Christ so that I could get a divorce like Audrey Hepburn in *The Nun's Story*.

Two days before I checked in to the hospital, I pulled my rented car into the parking lot of the Trail's End Motel on East Main Street.

I couldn't invent a better name for the motel where so many boys like me went to become the girls of their dreams.

Unpacking into the unendingly strange and unpredictable con-figurations of hotel/motel bureau drawers is a requisite skill for trav-elers. Unpacking toiletries into the bathroom, hanging clothes in the closet was easy—I'd done it all hundreds of times during my years as a road warrior registrar for Scientology. But this was my first out-of-state trip since I'd begun living full-time as a woman. Unpacking into the motel room, I was hesitant, awkward. Do you put your bras and panties into the same drawer as your red flannel nightgown? I was figuring all this out for myself when I dropped one of my dain-ties onto the once-bright lemon-lime shag carpet. Bending down, I could see beneath the bureau. The floor was spotless. It touched my heart that someone had taken the time to make everything so clean—knowing it would be a tranny who'd be sleeping in that room. Trinidad's economy depended on trannies, so the townsfolk were for the most part genuinely nice to us.

Then I noticed—all the way in the back, on the floor up against the baseboard—a tube of lipstick and a vial of bright-blue liquid eye-liner. Talismans of trannies past. We left ghosts, all of us trannies. Each of us left behind us the ghost of the man or woman we'd been pretending to be for so long that it hurt enough to make us want to go through with this surgery or kill ourselves. Trail's End was haunted by the ghosts of men who were desperate to become women. Ghosts of women who'd been born with a birth defect, and they were get-ting it fixed so they could be the real women they'd always known themselves to be, right down to the blue eyeliner and the ruby-red lips. I didn't want to touch what some ghost had left behind. Neither did the person who cleaned the floor so spotlessly and left behind the talismans of a Trail's End ghost.

Surgery morning, I lay relaxed on a gurney, high on antihista-mines. Dr. Biber was being affable—I don't remember his chatter, but it was reassuring in a crotchety-old-doctor sort of way. I clutched at the leather bag around my neck that held the powerful rose quartz and Apache tear crystals. Marsha Botzer agreed to carry them into the operating room for me. She was a transwoman, a therapist who counseled other transfolk and escorted many of them from Seattle to Trinidad to get their surgeries. I'd met her the day before. Marsha was my witchy midwife and we are dear friends to this day. I looked up into her smiling face—she knew exactly how excited I was. The nurse started the drip of night-night drugs. Marsha took the bag of crystals from around my neck. The super-duper anesthesia kicked in and it all went dark. When I woke up next I was back in my hospital bed, where I'd lie healing for the next week.

Oh. My. Goddess. It hurt the entire week. That first day all I could do was cry, it hurt so much. My sponsor and friends in Alcoholics Anonymous had warned me not to take painkillers—they could trigger my alcoholism, they'd all said. So I didn't take any post-op painkillers beyond Tylenol. When I became a woman in body, that's when I learned how to deal with searing pain: enjoy it. In my first lucid, tear-free moment, I drew a tarot card at random: the Ace of Cups—Happiness. Now that's what I'm talking about.

A week and a day later, I was back home in Philadelphia. Prior to leaving, I'd been dating Kim, a sweet, gentle butch dyke—she called me her pretty girl. Now that I was back, Kim looked in on me every day. When she determined I was healthy enough, she spent the night. She gave me my first vaginally stimulated full-body orgasm—the kind lesbians write about when they use words like *waves of pleasure*. That's what Kim gave me that night. Waves of pleasure.

Over the next year, I built and tore down bridges in Philadelphia's lesbian community. I was more loudly inquisitive about sadomasochism, and that alone alienated me from a whole lot of lesbians. I cofounded a transsexual-support group and was asked to leave because I was a lesbian and so couldn't be a real transsexual. I served a year on the Philadelphia Mayor's Commission on Sexual Minorities. My brush with theater had caught the attention of my old friend and theater mentor John Emigh, and he invited me to do a presentation at the first-ever Women in Theater (WIT) preconference to the second annual conference of the Association of Theater in Higher Education (ATHE). I never knew there were such organizations.

On the morning of my presentation, all the attendees were listening to the plenary speaker. The audience sat in two sets of bleachers, facing each other. The speaker stood in the middle. Everyone nodded as she wove intricate links between dramaturgy, feminism, and postmodern theory—everyone but me. I had no idea what she was talking about. I didn't even know what the word *plenary* meant. The speaker was saying something about "the male gaze." I heard it as "the male gays." And then, from the bleachers across the room . . .

"I think there's a man here, in drag."

It was supposed to have been a whisper.

"A man? Where? In drag? What?"

"Over there." Two women in the bleachers across from me lifted their heads and gazed at me.

Most people in the room called themselves women. Three of the women were out as lesbians. There was one man—John Emigh. Then there was me, the transsexual.

"Man? There's no man."

Doctor Vicki was one of the conference organizers. She looked at me and judged me woman, then shifted her gaze to the lady next to me, to see if *she* was the man in drag. The other woman's eyes continued to bore into mine. She knew, and she knew that I knew that she knew. (Kindly forgive me—I've always wanted to write a sentence like that.)

"Yes, there is," said the knowing woman. "That's a man right there. In drag." Doctor Sue was another of the conference founders—one of the three out lesbians. Doctor Sue described herself as a working-class, butch, Marxist lesbian theater artist, critic, and theorist. Her blend of identities made me shiver with delight. Most everyone described her as a genius. One or two women quietly described her as prickly.

"Where? I don't see him."

I was wearing a classic audition outfit for my presentation later that afternoon: jeans, black turtleneck, high-tops. I added one bit of girly-girl: a long, flowing, ripped-and-distressed olive-green cotton scarf. It was the morning of my presentation, and Doctor Sue was now saying,

"Him," again in the overloud stage whisper. She pointed at me with an accusing finger. "Look at that. It's a man in drag."

"Don't be silly," giggled Doctor Vicki, "You just don't know what big midwestern girls look like."

I laughed and I cried, all inside myself—anyone watching would have found me particularly attentive to the plenary speaker—whoever she was or whatever she was saying in highly postmodern academese. I was the transsexual in a sea of real women—real *smart* women. What the fuck was I doing here? My fear rose up into my throat, and I mentally checked out, disappearing into myself while the plenary speaker droned on.

"Blah blah hegemony. Blah blah patriarchal blah. Blah blah blah blah fourth wall."

I dove deep inside my mind, to the same place I go when I cut myself—it made me feel tough, like I could take it, whatever they threw at me. Yeah. And I was witchy enough to cast a circle of protection around myself. No one with hurt in their mind could get past my psychic goddess-powered force field. I'd rehearsed my presentation—it was all based on roles I'd already played—so I trusted myself to give 'em a good show no matter how far I checked myself out. I'd done it before—it's never your best performance, it's more like operating a virtual body in a computer game. Yes, I could pull off what I'd rehearsed . . .

First I'd appear as Tolen, the ultra-macho stud guy in Ann Jellicoe's *The Knack . . . and How to Get It*. I was the guy with the knack, and I'd show those women just how to get it. Me, the guy. Then I'd turn my back, breathe, and turn around again as The Fly—gang leader and fabulous drag queen emcee of the Brecht and Weill musical *Happy End*. Drag queen is a gender like no other, and with practice I'd learned to rise to it. Lastly, I'd turn upstage for a second time, breathe, and turn around as Sue, the older lesbian sugar momma of Jane Chambers's *Last Summer at Bluefish Cove*. Then I'd bow, walk offstage, and return after a moment for questions and answers. I was terrified, but I was prepared to act my heart out for 'em.

When John Emigh had first suggested I attend the Women in Theatre pre-conference at ATHE, I'd told him that I wasn't really all that sure I was a woman. He told me that over the past year in academic theater, there had been heated discussions about biology and culture, nature and nurture, in regards to both gender and sexual preference. He admitted to naively—but in the end accurately—thinking it would be great for me to meet this group of people and for them to meet me. John has always been a maker of great mischief.

Here's how that conference went for me: I finished performing my three genders, and I took a bow to total silence. Later some of the women told me that it would have been patriarchal for them to clap at a demonstration. I turned to walk offstage, but Doctor Elin had already begun speaking.

"Your work is dependent on the staged representation of gender, and all you're doing is using actors' tricks to lure us into believing that your enactment was something that was never a construct."

What?

"And what was with the turning around? Were you afraid to face us?"

What?

One woman after another spoke at me, analyzing me with a language I didn't understand. They used the terms *hegemonic* and *the male gaze*. Doctor Sue somehow linked what I did to Marxism—markedly referring to me as a man. I responded as dumbly to their questions as they had responded dumbly to my performance. When every woman in the room had spoken, John Emigh raised his hand to speak. He explained that I'd studied acting with him in college. He said it was one of the most marvelous performances of mine he'd ever seen. He told them that of course it was a staged representation—that's theater, that's acting. Only it was a representation taken from my life, he said. He further told them that of course I was using an actor's bag of tricks—I was an actor, a damned good one. Actors have bags of tricks, he said—that's theater, he reiterated, that's acting. He concluded by telling them that of course I needed to turn around between characters—largely because they were not a welcoming audience. I couldn't speak. John could, and he did—like some wise older doctor in raggedy tweed, with elbow patches. And that's largely the reason I came to dedicate my first book, *Gender Outlaw*, to John Emigh.

As for the eminent Doctor Sue, well, a year later she decided that since she called herself a working-class lesbian, I could call myself a transsexual lesbian—and we have shared a delightful friendship and flirtation to this day.

———

I spent six years in Philadelphia. My compulsive inward focus, along with the obsession with my gender change, took all my conscious energy, and I defaulted to many of the worst traits associated with my identity as a suppressive person living with borderline personality disorder. I'm not being snarky—I really was mean to some people I was close to. In fairness to myself (and being fair to myself is something I'm only now learning to do), I made some lifelong friends in Philly's lesbian communities. It took close to a year to get enough cash together to move. By the time I left, I'd almost completely withdrawn from the worlds of both theater and lesbians. All by myself, I packed my belongings into a dozen cardboard shipping boxes, and sent them off by Greyhound freight.

No one ran me out of town—I slunk away with my tail between my legs. I felt too damned lonely there was no one else like me in the whole fucking city. My ginger cat Gideon and I jumped into the olive-green Volvo wagon I'd picked up from the drive-away company, and I took off for San Francisco, a city that I was sure would be full of freaks like me.

CHAPTER 15

OK, Kid, This Is Where It Gets Complicated

I moved to San Francisco in June 1988, arriving just in time for the Pride Parade. Thousands of lesbians and gay men, and hundreds of drag queens, were either marching or they cheered and waved rainbow flags from both sides of Market Street. There were no transgender contingents. No one used that word yet. There were a few transwomen in the parade, but they were marching as part of something else. There were transsexual men in the parade, but they looked so real they were hard to pick out. Pride Parade, huh? Trannies had nothing to be proud of. Queer historian and academic theorist Susan Stryker said it best. We were onstage at a conference recently when the conversation turned to gay liberation. She leaned over to me and whispered, "Gays and lesbians were liberated. *We* were still an identity disorder." Maybe so, but there I was, in San Francisco.

———

"Kate, come here," Carol exclaimed. "I have the most wonderful thing to tell you!"

It was the second week of my very first job out West, across the bay in Berkeley as an assistant secretary in a small insurance office. Carol was my boss—I typed her letters and made her coffee. She was from Alaska, a big girl and tall like me. She could barely contain her excitement.

"Now, don't you go taking this the wrong way, Miss Kate," she warned me with a grin, "but my brother's in town this week, and he took one look at you and said he wanted you for his wife." She clapped her hands together with joy.

What do you say when a person tells you something like that?

"You gotta forgive him, Kate, he's from a small town in the woods."

"Ah." I nodded my head, pretending to understand.

"But here's the best part: he said that he could tell just by lookin' at you, you'd give him strong sons. He called you good breeding stock." She looked me up and down. "Well, you are."

The following week, I applied for and was hired at the Castro Street offices of *On Our Backs* magazine—a lesbian feminist porn mag with international distribution. Debi Sundahl and Nan Kinney produced *OOB*. Nan did a lot of the photography. Susie Bright (aka Susie Sexpert) was editor in chief. All the content was written by and for lesbians, with photos by and of real lesbians, doing real lesbian sex things with each other. I hadn't been in San Francisco a month and I was spending my workdays talking about porn, in the company of women who knew how to make themselves sexy. At first, I felt intimidated by the women's comfort with their bodies, and the casual ease with which they were simply sexy—all the time. My own style of girl had morphed from androgynous jumpsuits to granny dresses and Doc Martens. Working at *On Our Backs*, I was learning how to show some cleavage. After a few months at *OOB*, I had substantially more cleavage to show. Gluttony replaced starvation and I'd grown positively Rubenesque—and in the company of good women who made porn, I learned how to enjoy my voluptuous tranny body.

I made my way into San Francisco theater via Theatre Rhinoceros, the country's oldest lesbian and gay theater company. I was cast in their 1988 production of Jean Genet's *The Balcony*, directed by Leland Moss, which put me in the dressing room with the city's three leading drag queens: Doris Fish, Miss X, and 'Tippi.' I asked 'Tippi' why there were quote marks around her name. She patiently explained to me that there was only one real Tippi Hedren and she,

'Tippi,' was more of a quotation. Well, I asked her, why didn't she use double quotation marks?

"I'm a simple girl," she told me.

—

"To better embody your character—and Genet's characters are all about their bodies—you first have to disembody your self." Director Leland Moss was addressing the cast at the first rehearsal and read-through of *The Balcony*.

"Some actors wear their roles like clothing," he said. "No matter what part they're playing, you can always easily see who it is beneath the costume."

"It's how drag queens do women, darling," volunteered the elegant Miss X.

Keanu Reeves is that kind of actor, I thought to myself.

"Keanu Reeves is that kind of actor," said Leland. "No matter what part he's playing, you always know it's Keanu Reeves." Leland had several KS lesions on his face and hands. It was hard not to stare.

"The really amazing actors strip themselves down to nothing— they make themselves a blank slate, and you can never guess what they're going to look like or act like in their next film because they completely transform themselves."

"It's how transsexuals do women, darling," opined Doris Fish with an arched eyebrow in my direction.

Gary Oldman, I thought to myself. He'd just played Joe Orton, a year after he played Sid Vicious. The performances are distinct and nuanced.

"Gary Oldman is that kind of actor," pronounced Leland. "You can watch a whole film and not know he was in it until the credits roll."

Doris Fish sat directly across from me. She'd come to rehearsal as a boy—it didn't please her boyfriend to see her as a drag queen. She flashed me a smile—it was impossible to not smile back.

"Lesson one, baby girl," she told me over coffee after our first rehearsal, "drag queens dress up so they can become women, and transsexuals become women so they can dress up."

Doris Fish became my first drag mom. I'd been looking for freaky people who were just like me, and I found them in the queer theater community that gathered itself around Theatre Rhinoceros. Doug Holsclaw, then Rhino's managing director, gave me my first big break—he invited me to write a play for Rhino's next season. I wrote *Hidden: A Gender,* Rhino produced it, and it blew my world wide open.

—

The Loma Prieta earthquake hit the city in October 1989. Two months later, Justin Bond and I were huddled behind the curtain, peering out at audience members who were taking their seats for act II of *Hidden: A Gender.*

"There!" I squealed in a whisper, "audience right, third row, on the aisle. See? She was flirting with me!"

I stepped aside, so Justin could peek through the crack in the curtain.

"Oh hon! She is hot!"

We squealed together. I had a deep crush on Justin from the day I met him—I saw in him the exquisite blend of boy and girl I'd come to believe myself at heart to be. That was the whole point of the play: not man, not woman, but rather both and neither. Beautiful Justin embodied all of that. And the dyke on the aisle who'd been flirting with me? She came backstage to congratulate us after that performance. Her name was Catherine. She and I would become girl-friends for three and a half years, and then she'd become David, my boyfriend. I'm getting way ahead of myself. Neither of us was aware of it at the time but it's his gender change that made us make sense.

Our first date was the afternoon after opening night at a small witchy-Wiccan magic shop, blocks from where Catherine lived in the Lower Haight. We were in the back of the store, standing close to each other, turning dreamcatchers over in our hands. She broke the silence.

"I used to work as a professional dominatrix in a dungeon on upper Market Street."

"Oh yeah?"

We had sex together that night—well, that night and a couple of hours past dawn the next morning. It became clear to both of us that we stood at remarkably similar crossroads of gender identity. We had sex being girls. We had sex being boys. We were boy and girl at random. He had as much fun on top of me as I had fun on top of her. And we both enjoyed being on the bottom. She hurt me in ways that gave me some of the deepest joy I'd ever known—she taught me how to do that for her. We were young and our beauty took each other's breath away. We were driven, both of us, to make art and sex out of our freaky lives because we didn't know any other way to talk about it.

I moved in to her funky one-bedroom apartment in a Victorian house, just off lower Haight Street. Catherine was taking acting lessons in the city. To pay the bills, she'd set up a small bookkeeping business. At night, she worked on her script. We fucked a lot. I did most of the cooking. Catherine made me feel sexy. Looking at my still-voluptuous body through her eyes, I could see pretty girl. That was a first for me—not being skinny, and liking what I saw in the mirror.

I left *On Our Backs* reluctantly. Their schedule didn't allow me time for rehearsals. Instead, I was sitting safely back behind a telephone, selling subscriptions for the San Francisco Symphony. On the side, I wrote for the *Bay Area Reporter,* a weekly gay and lesbian newspaper with a wide readership throughout Northern California. Most of the paper was devoted to AIDS coverage. Hundreds of gay men in the city were dying. It wasn't genocide, but that's sure what it felt like—something was killing off all our sweet sexy boys. Each week, the *BAR* featured ten or more articles on possible cures, government neglect, support groups, and new pockets of the community hit by the epidemic. Way in the back of the paper was me, Little Mary Sunshine. Along with half a dozen arts reporters, I covered theater, film, music, art, books, cultural quirks, and anything for a laugh. Our articles and reviews followed the obituaries, which were often as long as twelve pages a week.

San Francisco was magical for me. I was an out transsexual in the city. I was writing articles from a tranny point of view. People recognized me in the street as a transsexual. It had been such a relief for me when I could stop pretending to be a man. Well, it was a similar relief not to have to pretend I was a woman.

———

December 1992, I toured with the company of *Hidden: A Gender* to off-off Broadway at Performance Space 122 in New York City. A month later, we returned to the Bay Area for an encore production on Theatre Rhino's main stage. At the same time, Catherine had written and performed her first play, *Permission,* based on her experience as a professional dominatrix. Late nights, after some heavy don't-we-just-rock-the-world-with-our-art sex, we lay in bed, face to face.

"So, what's really up," I asked her, "with the female-to-male trans character in your show?"

When you write a play, you're casting a spell. You imagine your characters, you write them down, then you watch them come to life. And there's a bit of you in every single character you write. The trans character in the play had to be Catherine. But . . .

"Well, you know, I've always wanted to be a Beatle, Katie. But I'm not going to transition."

"Oh yes you will."

David was splitting off from me, I could feel it. It wasn't all that many years ago I'd spun myself into a cocoon. I knew what it looked like. And I was splitting off from David. Just as he was exploring his gender more deeply, I was exploring sex—well, more accurately, it was sadomasochism I'd been exploring.

The Second Annual Gay and Lesbian Writers Conference hit the city, and I was asked to speak on a playwrights' panel. I scribbled out a piece, published later by Amy Scholder as "Transsexual Lesbian Playwright Tells All," in her anthology *High Risk,* coedited with Ira Silverberg.

After the panel, I was approached by a lean, sharp-eyed butch dyke with ginger hair and a disarming grin that filled her wide, Irish American face. She was maybe ten years younger than I. She wore jeans, boots that were well worn and well looked after, a plaid shirt, and a well-loved leather jacket. I wore a white tank top and my old jeans jacket from the '70s, the one with the American flag sewed onto the back and sleeves. I was wearing bright red cowboy boots into which I'd tucked my favorite pair of tight faded and torn jeans. Peeking out from her back left pocket, I could see the tip of a black handkerchief. It matched the black hankie I wore in my back *right* pocket. She was signaling that she was a heavy-duty sadist and I was flagging myself as a heavy-duty masochist.

"I'm Caitlin, Caitlin Sullivan. Your talk was fucking amazing. I never heard a transsexual talk so candidly about being transsexual before."

"Life's better without secrets."

"I saw you walking around earlier, and I just thought you were this amazing tall redhead babe hippie-chick dyke, and then . . ."

"And then you got a closer look."

"Yeah. Love the jacket. Did you get that in the '70s? I had one back then. My parents were hippies. Well, sort of—they were college professors. What have you written? What are you working on?"

She guided me over to a corner table, where we talked about theater as revolution. Caitlin was in town with three friends of hers, Sailor and Lula and their slave girl, Gabriella. Catherine was in rehearsal for another show, so she didn't join us for dinner that night. The four Seattleites wanted genuine Mission District burritos, so I took them to El Toro, around the corner from the city's finest Latina drag bar. At El Toro, $4.50 bought you a huge burrito and unlimited free refills for sides of chips and salsa. The people who ate and worked at El Toro were used to all sorts of people in that part of town, but I don't think they'd ever seen anything like Sailor, Lula, and Gabriella. I sure hadn't seen anything like them.

Growing up, it never occurred to me that there were people who wanted to belong to other people who in turn wanted to own them. I was a Jew—we are a race of slaves and every day we're ready to fight for our freedom because you never know when some anti-Semitic jerk is going to cross your path with a chip on his shoulder. It never occurred to me I could want to be a slave—not until my first year in college, when I read *The Story of O*, the 1954 SM classic, written by Anne Desclos under the pen name Pauline Réage. Olympia Press published the first English edition in 1965, and I snagged a copy in 1966. The book is written in the first person by a woman who becomes a willing sex slave—twenty-four hours a day, seven days a week.

Sailor, Lula, Caitlin, and I sat down at a table against the back wall of the taqueria.

"Dinner's on us, gorgeous," purred Lula, the femme of the pair. "Tell the girl what you want, and she'll get it for you." *Gorgeous.* She called me gorgeous. Lula handed some cash over to Gabriella, aka *the girl.* There's no table service at El Toro as there is in more traditional taquerias. You wait in line and, step by step, you instruct the person behind the counter just how to build the burrito of your dreams. A little bit of this, just so much of that, peppers—yes—but only so many. It's a dance, ordering a burrito, and it's hard to order a burrito for someone you don't know well. *The girl* stood next to me, her hands folded behind her back. I told her what I wanted. She listened and repeated my burrito preferences back to me. Without another word, *the girl* took her place in line to order and pay for the burritos for all of us.

"I don't know anything about a world like yours," I said. "But I'd like to."

Lula laughed delightedly. Sailor, the butch, told me she'd e mail me a reading list. Caitlin just grinned and watched us flirt. *The girl* returned to our table with our burritos, and dropped to her knees on the floor between Sailor and Lula. Everyone got quiet and began to enjoy their meal. My burrito was made exactly the way I liked it. Lula hand-fed *the girl* pieces of her own burrito. *The girl* was careful to lick Lula's fingers clean.

———

My father and L. Ron Hubbard both taught me that the key to making life worth living is to be of service—that's all, just make yourself useful. All my life, I had the fantasy of being useful sexually, and now I saw it was possible—but I didn't think it would be possible with Catherine. I suspected Catherine was transsexual—she'd given me enough hints. But I didn't get the message loud and clear until the moment she announced it on national television. We were guests on *The Phil Donahue Show,* in the days when Phil was still bigger than Oprah. The segment was called "Transsexual Lesbians and Their Partners." At the very end of the show, Phil asked Catherine how she managed to be so sympathetic to and understanding of my experience as a transsexual. Catherine looked right at the camera and said, "Well, actually, Phil, I have a few gender issues myself, and right now I'm coming out as a transsexual man." The camera panned to me, slack-jawed in disbelief. Cut to commercial and end of show.

A few weeks later, I was standing in Modern Times Bookstore listening to Marjorie Garber talk about her new book, *Vested Interests.* I'd reviewed it favorably for the *BAR,* highlighting her theory that the presence of just one person with a gender other than man or woman reveals gender to be a *space,* one that includes many more than two genders. Pleased with my write-up, Routledge Press editor Bill Germano asked me to introduce Professor Garber at the bookstore that evening. Later that night, he asked me if I'd ever thought about writing a book about my own take on gender. I answered him truthfully that I'd never considered it. I wouldn't know where to begin and I wasn't all that sure of where it might end if I started to write it.

Bill asked me to send him any and all pieces I'd written about gender. I sent him all my articles for the *BAR,* a copy of the play *Hidden: A Gender,* and the script for a new solo performance piece I'd begun touring with, called *The Opposite Sex Is Neither.* It made for a hefty pile of paper. The Internet was a baby in those days, so I sent Bill a large box filled with finished pieces and rambling notes I'd accumulated over the previous four years. He read it all and proclaimed that there was a book in there someplace. Two and a half years later, it would be published as *Gender Outlaw: On Men, Women, and the Rest of Us.* I stole the "and the rest of us" part of the subtitle from an Apple ad campaign. *Ms.* magazine would declare *Gender Outlaw* "an ode to paradox." But that would come two and a half years later, and I had a whole lot of paradox to explore before I could finish the book.

Paradox was roaring back into my life with a vengeance. I'd only tiptoed into paradox by saying I'm not a man and not a woman. There was the old unresolved paradox of "I'm a thetan with no gender," along with how Scientologists laughed at me because I wanted to be a girl. Plus, I was juggling a couple of body-level paradoxes: I was a forty-year-old-man with a surgically constructed vagina, walking through the world calling myself girl. Paradoxically, I was asking women to somehow include me in their number. Paradox? I laugh at paradox. *Ha!* From the moment I learned the word *fuck* when I was ten years old, I've lived my life with *What the fuck am I? Where the fuck do I belong? Who's ever gonna call me family, knowing who and what I really am?* Paradox? Bring it on.

The first paradox up for examination was Catherine deciding for sure that she was going to become David. Two days after his decision, he was diagnosed with breast cancer. He fought her cancer like the trooper she'd always been—he even parlayed a mastectomy into a partial chest reconstruction by a hotshot plastic surgeon. And that opened the door to my next paradox: I was now a lesbian with a boyfriend, but I *wasn't* a real lesbian and he *wasn't* a real boy—so did that make us a heterosexual couple the other way round? Don't talk to me about paradox.

But the paradox that raised the most hackles was my political stand on women-only spaces that forbade admission to transwomen: I thought every private space has the right to admit whomever they want—I told them I thought it was their responsibility to define the word *woman*. And I told the transwomen to stop acting like men with a sense of entitlement. So everyone was pissed off at me. I wrote a Thanksgiving piece about the war between lesbian separatists and trans activists. I called it "A Plague on Both Your Houses." And that's what led Leslie Feinberg, quintessential transgender warrior, to draw her sword in defense of me, quintessential transgender fool.

Leslie would be coming to town to talk at the San Francisco Women's Center—a bastion of womanhood, nearly a women-only space. Transwomen were tolerated but not encouraged to attend. The women at SFWC were willing to dialogue with the intent to resolve the conflict. So they'd asked Leslie to speak on the subject of how the struggle for women's rights and the struggle for trans rights were essentially one and the same. Trans activists at the time applauded the center's step in the right direction.

Leslie Feinberg more than anyone else managed to unite the trans community around a struggle for freedom. As a socialist leader fighting for queer rights within socialism, and trans rights in the lesbian and gay community, Leslie took the word *warrior* seriously— anything short of violence. In the spirit of inclusivity, Leslie asked me to accompany her onstage so we could be one sort of boy and one sort of girl. Leslie wrote a call to arms. I wrote a fun piece called "My Girlfriend Is Becoming the Man of My Dreams"—less of a struggle, more of a giggle.

A week before my engagement with Leslie Feinberg, I played Portland, Oregon, for a pre-Christmas 1992 weekend run of my solo show, *The Opposite Sex Is Neither,* produced and promoted by a guy who called himself Howie Baggadonutz. None of us on the queer performance circuit ever knew him by any other name. It was a fun two-night gig for me. My stand on "women-only" spaces and my re-fusal to claim a male or female gender got me picketed by Portland transwomen holding up signs: "Kate Bornstein Is Transphobic" and "Kate Bornstein Is Not Transexual" and "Bornstein Doesn't Speak for Me." That was the first time I saw the word *transphobic*.

It was scary making my way into the theater both nights through the phalanx of a dozen or so tall, angry women holding those signs and shaking their fists at me. But I was learning to embrace my cross and love the notoriety. It was an adventure, and I wanted to make it a delightful adventure—so I made it a point to thank and agree with all the trannies who insisted "Bornstein Doesn't Speak for Me."

"Of course I don't speak for you," I told each of them, "and I promise that I'll never say that I do."

Inside, the Portland audiences were warm and appreciative. They laughed in all the right places, and the Kleenex came out just when

I hoped it would. That was my first visit to Portland and I still think about moving there. I returned home on an early afternoon flight, a week before winter solstice. It was the night I was supposed to speak at the Women's Center with Leslie Feinberg (whose pronouns of choice at the time were "she" and "her.") David was mostly recovered from surgery and chemo, and the holiday magic was holding at bay the tension of our awkward attempts at becoming boyfriend and girlfriend. David was being gallant, which made it my part of our dance to be gracious. It's how we could love each other. I took a cab in from the airport, we hugged for a long time, I took off my San Francisco four-season leather jacket, and sat myself down next to my answering machine with a pen and a pad of paper. I'd been gone five or six days, and the answering machine was blinking furiously. Most of the messages were booking inquiries and deadline reminders. Then I played the message from Sailor.

"You've got email, girl. Answer it."

I shivered—maybe I whimpered out loud. David rolled his eyes— he was accustomed to me jumping up to obey random orders from Sailor and her partner Lula. I walked quickly over to my computer, turned it on, and read my email. Then I did what they'd instructed— it didn't take a long time. After I finished, I washed up and wrote them a passionate response. Life was good. Then I played the next message on my answering machine.

"Hey, Kate. It's Susan Stryker. This isn't going to be easy to say. Look, I admire your work, and I think you've got the right to speak your opinions. But I don't think you know what effect those opinions are having on other people. I'm calling to tell you that Transgender Nation is going to protest your talk tonight. When you get up to speak, they're going to stand up and turn their backs on you."

I've long since begged for and received Susan's forgiveness for calling her back and flipping out on her with what I learned in several rounds of therapy to be L. Ron Hubbard's hair-trigger temper and my father's bottomless rage in response to challenge. David spoke up after I slammed down the receiver.

"Call Leslie Feinberg right now," he ordered gently. "Tell her what they're planning to do. Tell her I'm asking her to draw her sword on my behalf. I'd do it myself, you know I would, but no one in the Women's Center is going to listen to me with all my male privilege. Leslie can help you. Call her."

Leslie was horrified to hear the plan. I was scheduled to open the evening for her. Before I was introduced, Leslie took the stage and asked the women of Transgender Nation to let me speak. She told them she trusted me to be well intentioned.

"It's not good politics," she said from the podium, "to turn on our own. Family is family, and there are far too few of us."

Everyone clapped, including many of the transwomen. I walked out on the stage and faced the audience of attentive women. I spoke, and no one turned their backs on me. There were young women and crones—lesbians and straight women—women of color and white women—and there were around two dozen transwomen scattered all about the audience. Fool that I was, I made them laugh . . . a lot. They were laughing when they gave me a standing ovation after my talk. Leslie gave me a good daddy hug and launched into her call for arms. Warrior that she was, Leslie brought the audience to their feet half a dozen times—they cheered, whistled, and stomped their feet.

David and I were the first to leave. It was a twenty-minute walk home through the cold and foggy December night.

"I'm not an activist, David."

"Of course not, missy. You never were."

"I go for the cheap laugh—what does that make me?"

"You're a mad, mad artist, my dear, and you are awfully cute."

"And you're my knight in shining armor."

"I'll always draw my sword for you, Katie Bornstein. Or I'll find someone who can."

He's been true to his word to this day.

———

I spent the next two years bouncing in and out of San Francisco for weeks at a time, alternately selling symphony subscriptions and touring with one or another of my shows. Every free moment I had, I wrote pieces of *Gender Outlaw,* even out on the road. There were no laptops in the early '90s. I carried my Mac Classic, which weighed in at twelve pounds. Add two more pounds for the heavily padded canvas backpack. Then add a keyboard, mouse, power cord, a speedy 600-baud Hayes modem, and four or five reference books, and I was touring the country with a good twenty-five to thirty pounds of livelihood strapped to my back. Walking through airports and train stations was a cardiovascular workout. And every free moment I had out on the road—bit by bit—I'd write more of the book.

I'd assumed that my readers would be lesbians and gays, bisexuals, and transgender folks. Bill Germano added college students to the list, because Routledge was an academic press. Given my experience at the academic Women in Theater conference, I wasn't sure I'd know how to speak academese, but Bill convinced me to trust that my own voice would get my points across—which happily turned out to be exactly what happened.

I'd been fat and voluptuous since I'd moved to San Francisco. The stress level of writing a book helped me not eat. When I met Bill, I weighed just over 200 pounds. Two years later, when the book came out, I was down to 155. Yes, yes, I was back to anorexia again, but there was a difference: this was the first time I was starving myself *as a girl.* I could wear skinny girl clothes, like in the magazines. It was intoxicating.

Gender Outlaw was published in May of 1994. It was a big hit—before me, no one had spoken quite so accessibly about the notion of not being a man *or* a woman—and my life became more public than it ever had been before. I wanted to hide away home, but it didn't feel like home with David anymore. He'd been on testosterone long enough to give him facial hair and a baritone speaking voice. I taught him how to shave. I wanted less to do with him as a man, and he wanted less to do with me as a sadomasochist.

David wrote a new solo show for himself, *FTM: A Transsexual Journey from Female to Male,* which he was busy touring to fringe festivals in cities around North America. I'd written a second solo show,

Virtually Yours, as part of my agreement with Routledge to write a new show so they could piggyback a *Gender Outlaw* book tour on the performance schedule. I'd played San Francisco, and the show was booked to open at PS 122 in New York City in June 1994, followed by a three-week run in Santa Monica. People would come in droves to all the performances, and one for one they would leave in tears. Big mistake in that show: not nearly enough laugh lines.

—

Months before we ever did anything physical with each other, Sailor had come right out and asked me on the phone . . .

"How do you know you really want that kind of pain?"

"How do you know I don't?"

Sailor and Lula and I had been speculating what the three of us might look like—me belonging to the two of them. How would that work? I was still David's girlfriend. But Sailor and Lula told me over and over how much they wanted to give me "some good pain." I didn't know what that meant, but I wanted with all my heart to prove to them I could take it. The cruel geography of our lives frustrated any real physical contact. But those ladies were smart, and that's part of why I'd been falling in love with them. They wanted to hurt me, and I wanted to take it, and so Sailor and Lula worked out a plan to test my desire that Sailor later bragged about as having been both sly and literally theatrical.

"When are you next going onstage?"

I told her I had a performance coming up on the weekend, three days away. Sailor laughed.

"OK, here's what you're going to do. Sometime Friday night, while you're onstage, you're going to dig your fingernail into your own hand until you draw blood. Call us as soon as you get home from the theater that night."

I wore my nails long and red back then, so it was easy. The end of the show is a blackout. Then the lights come up, and I take my bows and say my thank-yous. That's when I did it. Slowly, I drove a long red fingernail into the flesh of my right palm. Audience members were cheering. They were watching what they thought were tears of joy—they were righter than they thought.

Sailor and Lula were thrilled when I told them. Sailor says she remembers that being able to cause me pain over that much of a distance was the beginning of the ownership.

———

David and I weren't having sex with each other anymore. My long-distance slave sessions with Sailor and Lula had grown increasingly inventive. They kept me spellbound with the very real joy I felt in obedience, service, and the mind-boggling paradox of pleasurable consensual slavery. I made the decision to leave San Francisco when I realized there was no place for me in that town any more than there'd been a place for me in Philadelphia.

The mainstream lesbian community didn't want anything to do with me because (a) I was transsexual, (b) I had a boyfriend, and (c) I was a sadomasochist. Even the sadomasochist dykes in the city steered clear of me because I played with pointy things and I wanted them to draw my blood. Sailor and Lula were deep into blood sports, along with a fairly large number of Seattle SM dykes. Seattle might could be a home, I reckoned, and I made up my mind to call Sailor and Lula to ask if they would consider owning me in real life. After six years in San Francisco, I'd move up to Seattle. The three of us were thrilled. Lula drove down to San Francisco to help me move, about two weeks before I was supposed to start rehearsals in New York.

———

The morning I moved to Seattle, David was out on the sidewalk in front of our apartment, selling all his girl stuff to young lesbians with baby carriages. Lula and I walked carefully through his sidewalk display on our way to the car with the last remaining boxes of my own belongings—the stuff I didn't trust to Greyhound.

David and I had come shooting at each other like two comets through space, both of us coming from a point light years away from each other. When we finally met, we were caught up in each other's gravity and there we spun around each other for almost five years: a binary star system, each of us trying to burn as brightly in the world as we possibly could. We saw that in each other—the drive to become a star. Art, politics, desire, and identity all whirled into a perfect cosmic storm. Ultimately, our sex-and-gender polarities shifted and we repelled each other, shooting off light years away from each other in opposite directions.

CHAPTER 16

Girl

I scrubbed the oak plank floors in their living room with as much love and care as I'd cared for the teakwood decks on the Flagship *Apollo*. I used Murphy's oil soap, as Lula had instructed me, and I rinsed with fresh water.

"Murphy's is the only way to get blood out of sheets and towels, girl," Lula had said. "Keep that in mind, it'll come in handy real soon." Then she left.

I was mopping when she returned a few hours later.

"Girl, is that hot water in that bucket?"

"No, ma'am."

Most people who enter into a master/slave agreement take the time to iron out in great detail the duties and expectations of their period of service. There are plenty of well-written books with hard-won advice, all intended to make your master/slave relationship safe and the most fun possible.

"You go back there right now and you refill that bucket with hot water."

I ran off to do as I was told. I could hear her laughter through the kitchen door. At least I'd made her laugh. That counted for something. There are all sorts of slaves and masters, and countless ways to live out a loving master/slave relationship. Pick an adjective, any adjective. Now, stick that in front of the word *sadomasochist*. That's how many kinds of SM folks there are in the world. If you were giving yourself heart, mind, soul, and body to a pair of sadists, you'd want to know what sort of sadist you'd be owned by. Kind? Mean? Comical? Deep into the dark arts?

If you were going to say *Yes, I'll be your slave* to someone, you'd want to know up front what you're getting into, before anyone put a collar on you—because that's what they do, they put a collar on you to mark you as property. For example, you'd want to know something about the future of your own sex life, right? Like whether or not you'd have one. Was there going to be any sex with your owners, or would most of your service involve cleaning their house and baking their bread? If June Cleaver in chains was your future persona, you'd want to know if you were going to get an erotic kick out of it, right? Before the first single tail whip kissed your shoulder and made you scream, you'd have agreed upon a definition of words like *fun, pleasurable, maybe,* and *no.* You'd have worked out just who had the latitude to do what, with what, and to whom.

Well, Sailor and Lula and I didn't know any of that about each other. We just jumped right into it, like a puppy pile, each of us taking a leap of faith. It was plain dumb luck that it worked out as wonderfully well as it did. That we blew apart so fiercely doesn't change how filled with wonder that year was for all of us, beginning with the thirteen-hour drive up the Pacific Northwest coast from San Francisco to Seattle. It was midafternoon when Lula and I crossed the Golden Gate Bridge. Babylon by the Bay looks her sweetest when the midday sun is burning off the fog. We pulled into the Emerald City at sunrise. Well, rain-rise. The sun rarely rises visibly in Oz.

Lula drove first shift. I was under strict orders to watch how she drove, and when it came my turn, it had better feel to her as though she herself was at the wheel. I knew how to do that. In the Sea Org, the Commodore taught all his drivers that the perfect ride on land or sea has got to be smooth for the passenger—never a sudden movement or stop. So I watched Lula drive between seven and twelve miles per hour above the speed limit. We stopped every two hours for oil. We stopped before the engine began to smoke. When I took the wheel, Lula watched me with an unwavering gaze. For the next two hours I drove like she did. Oh, so easy. It's what I'd trained to do as an actor—act like someone else. Finally I pulled over to pour a quart of oil into the not-yet-smoking engine.

"Good girl."

"This girl is pleased she has pleased you, ma'am." Lula had told me she was always to be addressed as ma'am, or Miss Lula. Sailor was always to be called ma'am. Slaves never talk about themselves in the first person, and most aren't called by their birth or taken names. Your owners get to call you whatever they like—they get to name you. Sailor and Lula called me *girl*. While I was in service, I called myself *this one*, or *this girl*.

"Girl, wake up! I'm dozing off and I need to talk."

"Yes, ma'am."

"Quick! How would you pronounce the name of that town?" The exit sign read "Puyallup." I struggled with the word, and with every wrong answer she pinched my thigh. Hard. Ten minutes later or so, she took mercy and told me, Pyoo-AH-lup. Who the fuck would have guessed that?

"How's that thigh of yours?"

"It's burning, ma'am."

"Change the burning feeling into love, honey. Then bring that hot love up into your heart."

If I'd wanted a big, bad, mean sadist, it wasn't Lula who would be that for me. That would be Sailor's job. We had maybe another half hour more to go when for one moment, the sun broke brilliantly through the clouds and I got my first look at Mount Rainier, the largest mountain on Seattle's horizon.

"Aw, she came out for you. That's a good sign, my girl."

We parked in front of their apartment. Lula took my chin in her hand and turned my face toward me.

"Is this the right way to hold your neck still with your what's-it-called?"

I was still calling the condition *spasmodic torticollis*, and I told her yes.

"Am I holding your neck so you can look me in the eyes comfortably?"

"Yes ma'am, thank you, ma'am."

She told me that every time she held me like that in the future, it would be an order for me to tell the truth, completely, no matter the consequences.

"So, are you bulimic?" she asked, looking into my eyes. "I am. Sometimes."

"This one is anorexic, ma'am. Sometimes, not always."

"Are you starving yourself now?"

"No, ma'am. But this girl feels fat, ma'am."

"You're not fat. And you be sure to tell me when you feel like you wanna starve yourself. I don't want any skin-and-bones slave in my house."

"Yes, ma'am, thank you, ma'am."

I'd never talked so casually about my eating disorder and body image.

"One thing I should warn you about me, girl."

"Ma'am?"

"I fart—a lot—and they are stinky farts."

"Really, ma'am? And all this time I thought we were driving by rose gardens."

Still smiling, still holding my chin so still I couldn't move it, Lula slapped me across the cheek. Hard. She did everything hard. Then we kissed. Yes, hard.

—

It's come to the point in this story that I need to write a great deal more graphically about sadomasochism. I know and respect that it's not going to be easy for everyone to read this. Permit me please, this close to the end of the book, to say that I know that my grandchildren may be reading these words. You, dear reader, could be my daughter. That's been on my mind since I first sat down to write this book six years ago. The sex stuff was hard enough to write about, and I've been trying to keep it all playfully hot . . . but how do I talk SM to my daughter? I think I've figured out how to do it. Nonetheless, I'm going to give any reader an opportunity to skip over the hard parts. So, everyone can keep on reading for now. I promise I'll give you plenty of warning.

My first exposure to sadomasochism was porn. Most porn makes SM look violent—all that black leather, all those whips, all that pushing people around and forcing them to do stuff beyond the daydreams of an average sexual imagination. But that's *porn* violence—it's *fiction* violence. Some aspects of real SM absolutely look like violence—to me, that's hot—but it's not violence, because it's been agreed upon by two or more rational consenting adults. It may not appeal to everyone, but it is not violence.

Look, even the *language* of sadomasochism is a giggle. When sadomasochists do sadomasochism, we call it *playing*. Isn't that marvelous? And our instruments of pain? Those whips you hear about, the chains, the rope, the rack, and so forth? Toys. They're all called *toys*. Including the slaves—we're toys, as well. Using words like *play* and *toy* reminds sadomasochists why we go through all that pain, why we cherish the welts and bruises and scars—because we are playing, for the fun and for the sheer ecstatic joy of it.

My publicist and dear friend Gail Leondar-Wright grows queasy at my more graphic descriptions of sadomasochism. So for Gail and for you, dear reader, I'm saying *that* section is coming up real soon. It will suffice if you know that the first night we played, it lasted nearly ten nonstop hours. There was no fucking, not in the usual hetero or homo sense of the word. Sailor and Lula used lots and lots of toys on me. We were a trio of happy kids, adults, and every age in between. I delighted them with just how much I could take, and they left wonderful marks on me that I wore like they were the crown jewels of England. Then they put a collar on me. That collar said without words to other sadomasochists: *Hands off. This person is owned property.* We stopped just before dawn—they took me to an all-night place to eat. I had a bacon, lettuce, and tomato sandwich on lightly toasted rye—to this day, my post-play comfort food of choice. That night, I slept on a pallet at the foot of their bed. Pretty picture, happy ending. If that delights you, if that's all you want to know, then please skip to the middle of page 218 and start with the sentence "The WildRose Cafe was a lesbian coffeehouse, restaurant, bar and pool hall, and performance space all in one." Otherwise, you're welcome to read on and look at the three of us in a lot more detail.

———

Still here? Thank you for your trust.

Here's what I remember about the first night the three of us played together, the day after I arrived in Seattle. First off, they played as a team. It was the two of them topping the one of me. I was their bottom, and they hurt me a whole lot. They cut me open and watched me bleed. They scarred me for life and I loved every minute of it. All of us did.

Most sadists develop preferences for the toys they use. Lula was happy just to hurt me any way she could. She liked it when I screamed, and screaming comes easy when someone's hurting you really really really a whole lot. Lots of screaming was a big part of our play date. It delighted Lula to use kitchen utensils in wacky, inventive ways—it also appealed to her sense of thrift, because professionally made toys can cost a lot of money. Lula spent all her toy money on canes. They made her squeal in pleasure as loud as I screamed in pain. Sailor laughed and laughed. Canes hurt you twice: first, as they strike your skin, they bruise you deeply. Then your skin wraps itself around the cane at the place of impact. Because canes are so flexible, they rebound away from your body before your skin can unwrap itself, and that's the second hurt: the cane rips your skin open after it hits you. I hate canes. Lula, bless her heart, loved them. What was a girl to do?

Sailor was a cutter, like me. She used an antique straight razor. Later, I learned that she sharpened it daily on a leather strop that hung by her sink. She could have ordered me to care for her razor. I would have kept it sharp, clean, and at the ready. But it was protocol in our world to ask before you touch anyone's toys—including us slaves. The straight razor was Sailor's talisman, something that gave Sailor power and made her vulnerable at the same time.

That first night, Sailor used her razor to carve two long deep lines down the length of my back from my shoulders to just above my butt. The next day, I'd look in the mirror and see the cello pattern. Sailor finished the second score at the base of my spine, and just as she lifted her blade, I began a long, deeply satisfying laugh. When I could catch my breath, I got a single word out.

"Wings."

"What's that, girl?"

"Wings. My wings are breaking their way out of me. Watch out for the blood and feathers." We all laughed, but damn me to hell if I couldn't feel them. Lula was whispering into my ear.

"This is going to help you remember those brand-new wings of yours, girl." She rubbed two fists full of coarse sea salt into the long bloody scores on my back, and I screamed.

"Oh shush, you big baby," Lula laughed, "the salt's good for you."

I can feel my wings to this day—long, strong, beautiful wings. Sailor had cut them free for me that night, and Lula made me remember them. Angel wings in bottom space. Oh yes. It was a feeling of strength and freedom and *yes* that I can call up to this day.

I know we played for hours and hours more. I remember that they laid me across a table—on my back. My bloody wings screamed in protest—no, it was me screaming. Still. An hour before dawn—the hour of the wolf, she called it—Sailor cut a wolf's skull into my chest. Wolves were her animal spirit guide. Sailor and Lula had freed my wings, they told me, so I could fly as high as I dared. Wolf, they said, would be there to protect me. I'd never felt so safe, so secure, or so well cared for.

The sun had been up for a few hours. Sailor was standing over me; the sun shone through the window. Her face, inches from my own, eclipsed the light. Sailor spoke softly from the shadow within a halo of sunlight.

"What would you do for me, girl?"

"Anything, ma'am. Anything for you."

OK—never, never, *never* tell a sadist you'll do anything they want. Seriously. Especially not after they've been building up their bloodlust for the past ten hours. Sailor carefully put her hands around my throat. Lula stood off to one side, watching us quietly—she knew what was coming. Sailor tightened her grip on my throat, just enough so I'd notice.

"Oh, this is what I really want to do, girl."

"Do," was all I could say. "Please, ma'am. Do."

She slowly tightened her fingers until I wasn't breathing—couldn't breathe. Blood red clouds gathered at the edges of my vision. I could see Sailor's eyes fill with wonder. The world around me and inside me seemed to stop, and all I could think was . . . *at last*. At long, long last.

It was Lula who stopped us. She gently loosened Sailor's fingers from around my throat. I looked up at Sailor, questioningly. She nodded. Only then did I take a long, slow, deep breath of air. Flashbulbs and fireworks—red, yellow, and white—were going off at the edges of my lines of sight. Sailor sat back, grinning.

When she saw that I was breathing again, Lula took my chin in her hand and slapped me hard across my face with her open palm.

"You are my toy, girl, and I don't want you broken yet."

Lula kissed me full and gently on the mouth.

Yet?

Sailor fastened a simple leather collar around my neck—loose but tight enough that I'd know all the time I was wearing their collar.

"You belong to us now, girl."

———

The WildRose Cafe was a lesbian coffeehouse, restaurant, bar and pool hall, and performance space all in one. Bryher, the owner and manager, had designed it that way. She was an easygoing old-school butch. She'd once been a good and fair county judge, but the level of crime she had to deal with on a daily basis got to be too much for her, so she quit being a judge to open the WildRose as a haven and hangout for Seattle's fledgling lesbian community. She told us it was her life's work to take care of all her girls. She made it her business to know our lives, and she knew all about my life within the first week. Everyone had a crush on Bryher—and I do believe Bryher had a crush on every one of us.

It was early morning, a couple of days after I'd arrived in town. I was sitting—very gingerly—at a booth, writing notes for a book idea that Caitlin Sullivan and I had been tossing back and forth. We'd been having fun playing around online with virtual identities and cybersex. We joked that we were doing research for a book. Sailor and Lula ordered me to write it with her. I was lost in my notes when I heard . . .

"Hi. My name is PJ. Mind if I sit down?"

I looked up from my notebook to see that PJ was a butch dyke, maybe ten years younger than I, dressed casually in black. She wasn't goth—her blacks weren't so much a fashion statement as they were the promise of dangerous games in the dark. I shuddered involuntarily with delight. PJ later told me she thought I was afraid of her.

"Just for a minute, really."

"Oh sure, sure. Please, have a seat. My name is Kate."

PJ slid into the seat across from me. In contrast to her understated sexy blacks, I was positively Pippi Longstocking, minus the pigtails. I was a strawberry blonde, with a shoulder-length pageboy. I wore an olive-green A-line dress over a cream-colored blouse. Brown knee-high boots completed my ensemble. My eyes were perfectly done. My hetero relationship with David had altered my fashion statement toward elegantly acceptable. My mother had been thrilled.

"Kate," PJ was saying, "do you know what sort of bar this is?"

"Beg pardon?"

Bryher had sauntered over to our table and was standing off to one side, out of PJ's line of sight—our eyes met. PJ lowered her voice and confided in me.

"This is a lesbian bar."

Aw, man. I braced for the onslaught of political correctness. *You aren't a real woman,* she'd say. *You aren't a lesbian. You're a man,* she'd say, *and this is a women's bar.* I'd heard that line for so many years now. How would I respond to it here? Me, the new tranny on the block. PJ pressed on. Her tone of voice was kinder than I'd feared.

"We don't get too many straight women here, and well . . ." PJ blushed handsomely. "Kate, you're a lovely lady, and I just want you to know that some other lady in here might try to hit on you."

"PJ! That's so sweet of you! But I *am* a lesbian, really."

Relief flooded PJ's body. She slouched comfortably in the booth across from me. She told me she made a living making leather clothing and toys for the SM dyke community. Then she apologized for using the word *dyke,* and asked me if I knew what sadomasochism was.

"Oh PJ, yes I do—thank you for asking. I'm a bottom, PJ, and you should know that I'm also a transsexual."

Slow takes are some of the best moments in comedy.

"And Kate's a writer, PJ." Bryher joined us, sliding into the booth next to PJ. "With a book out. How about that? I told her the WildRose was a good place to chill and write, so that's what she's doing."

Bryher's endorsement shifted the look on PJ's face from confusion to wonder, like the sun coming out from behind a cloud . . . and then slowly back to confusion.

"I guess it's my fashion statement . . . huh, Bryher?"

"You do look like a straight girl, Kate."

"I've had a boyfriend for so long, Bryher," I whined, "and since I hit town, I haven't had a minute to do any shopping!"

"Sailor and Lula working you pretty hard, are they?"

PJ had to stop us there. "Sailor and Lula and . . . you?"

My owners were highly respected ladies among the Seattle SM dykes. They had a reputation, I discovered, and now I was becoming part of it. I looked down at the tabletop, slowly opened the top of my blouse two buttons lower than necessary, and ran a finger along my black leather collar.

Bryher grinned. "All three of you are lucky gals."

"All three of us are more than lucky," announced Sailor, who'd appeared out of nowhere—like a supernatural being, "we are jumpin' for joy. Aren't we, Sugarpop?" Lula sauntered over to Sailor's side, kissed her full on the mouth, then leaned herself in and under Sailor's arm like she was born to be there. Everyone who knew them was floored by the grand romance that was Sailor and Lula.

"No more writing today," Lula drawled. "We're here to take our girl shopping. *Up!*" She snapped her fingers and I got to my feet as quickly as I could. Bryher and PJ rose together in a gentlemanly gesture. I blew them a kiss and scampered to Lula's side—the three of us fairly pranced out of the WildRose. For the year we were together, Lula always walked between me and Sailor.

"You need a pair of black boots and a black leather jacket. Brown won't cut it."

"Aw, my very own SM fashion consultant."

Lula punched me not-so-lightly on the arm.

"Ow!"

"Oooooh, she said ouch, Sailor. Do I get to hit her again?"

"Yes you do, Sugarpop."

Lula laughed and hit me again, harder—driving her knuckles into my upper arm. I was skinny, and her knuckles met bone. I gasped—then quickly remembered to mentally direct the pain into my heart. The small bolt of knuckles-on-bone pain struck my soul. I shivered and slithered gratefully into a mind/spirit place of joy that I was learning to call *bottom space*.

"Thank you, ma'am."

"That's my girl."

"Your girl, ma'am." My eyes were lowered.

Slaves don't look anyone in the eye unless we're invited to or ordered to. On one hand, this was easy for me, given my beta wolf childhood. But for twelve years, I'd obeyed Scientology canon that insisted on maintaining unflinching eye contact whenever you talked with someone. Looking away all the time, even down at the floor, was a relief—and it made the moments of looking someone in the eye more meaningful. All sorts of emotions from adoration to loathing can pass between two people who are looking into each other's eyes. SM players looking into each other's eyes are opening their souls. It's rarely an act of aggression. Eye gazing is almost always an act of trust. As a slave girl, I was not permitted that intimacy without permission. So, with my eyes cast down and Lula in the middle, the three of us left to get me all dressed up like a proper Seattle dyke slave girl.

—

Later that night Gabriella was hosting the annual SM dyke summer picnic in her backyard. I'd arranged to meet up with Sailor and Lula at the barbecue. Now I was home trying on each piece and accessory of my new dykewear. Gideon watched my every move from the windowsill. He was my big boy ginger cat who'd traveled with me from Philadelphia to San Francisco. Now he was my Seattle boy—oh, how I loved that cat. The story of our twelve years and twenty-two homes together is for another book. We shared a sweet little two-bedroom, two-story townhouse on Capitol Hill, with an unfinished basement and a dweeby little redwood deck—well, it was more of a boardwalk laid down just above the weeds out back. I lived just across the street and down the alley from Sailor and Lula's back door. From a deep sleep, I could be dressed and at their place—to fulfill any wish of theirs, diabolical, delicious, or mundane—in under five minutes. They always timed me. That little townhouse in Capitol Hill was a wonderful place to call home.

I had wheels. A friend had driven my Toyota station wagon up to Seattle, loaded with the very last of my stuff. It was about twenty minutes to the barbecue at Gabriella's house. I arrived earlier than I was ordered to be there, so I waited two minutes out on the front porch to be right on time. Gabriella told me not to bother ringing the bell, just walk in and come out back. No one in the SM dyke community locked their doors, unless they were going out to work or for a long round of errands. As a member of the community, you just walked into someone's house and announced yourself. *Welcome* was the default voice of our households. Still, I was the new kid in town, a flamboyantly out transsexual to boot, and I was meeting for the first time the women who would become my community.

I stood on Gabriella's front porch, properly clad in my new blacks—skinny black jeans and a low-cut black tank that showed off both my collar and my cleavage. I patted my right back pocket to make sure the black bandana was peeking out just enough to be seen. I'd clipped my few keys to a belt loop—also on the right, the side for bottoms. I was the new bottom, and I wanted to get it right. Taking a deep breath, I walked into the house and out into the backyard. I stepped out into the bright sunlight. Everyone in the yard stopped talking and looked at me with varying degrees of amusement and astonishment.

They were all wearing laid-back summer wear in all sorts of fun bright colors that screamed *Party Time!* There were butches in Bermuda shorts and Hawaiian shirts. There were femmes in brightly colored sundresses. And there was me, the tranny new girl, in my understated perfectly rumpled blacks. Lula walked up to me and slapped me across the face.

"Silly rabbit! This is a summer barbecue." She turned to the smiling but still silent yard. "Everyone, this is Kate. She's my and Sailor's new girl and I apologize for her dreadful fashion sense."

Femmes tittered. Butches guffawed. I reddened.

"We'll help you teach her," shouted one woman.

"Yeah, send her my way for a night or a weekend," shouted another.

I grinned stupidly until Lula pulled my face down to hers, kissed me, then broke away to face the ladies and gents.

"And yes, she's transsexual. We think it's weird too, but isn't she cute?"

A moment of silence, and then . . .

"I still say send her my way!"

Applause. Laughter. A couple of wolf whistles. Lula smacked me on my bottom—hard, with a paddle. I gasped. Sailor took the paddle from Lula. I turned the other cheek, and Sailor whacked me even harder.

"Now get out of here, girl. Go home, get fun, and come right back."

Then I was standing back out on the front stoop. My butt was still stinging from the paddle. I took a deep breath, bringing the pain up into my heart as love. That's all it took to get me into bottom space, lots of love.

———

Two weeks later, I opened *Virtually Yours* in New York City. My mother was in the audience. I had to warn her about the clothespin scene in which I take on the character of a young dyke who tells the audience that she has no name. Her name was taken away from her the day she agreed to belong to her lover. She was just called *girl.*

Prescient me, I wrote that bit before I left David. As the young dyke bottom tells the audience the story of their romance, she attaches clothespins across her arms and chest. She explains that they don't hurt going on—they only hurt when you take 'em off, ten or fifteen minutes later. *It's the absence that hurts,* she says. Then I'd ask audience members to please please take the clothespins off me. I'm grateful to the gallant young Ben Brantley of the *New York Times,* who spoke so elegantly of the moment: "Ms. Bornstein scores a sly, unsettling coup de theatre playing an eager masochist who draws unwitting audience members into the role of sadist."

Before the show started, I told my mom that I was using fake clothespins—I'd had them specially made, I told her, and it didn't really hurt. She looked at me skeptically, but she accepted my lie as truth. I'd got her a seat in the front row, and at the moment I began to attach the clothespins to my body, she turned around to the rest of the audience and in a loud whisper said,

"They're *fake* clothespins! He's not really hurting himself."

It was clear to audience members that night that the new thin bright-red wet scars on my chest formed the shape of a wolf's head. I'd tried covering them up with body makeup, but the stage lighting in the small theater was intensely hot, and the makeup washed away in my perspiration. It looked like they were still bleeding, the marks Sailor and Lula had cut into me only a week earlier.

———

May 9 is a major Scientology holiday, the anniversary of the 1950 publication of *Dianetics: The Modern Science of Mental Health* by L. Ron Hubbard. Scientologists call it Book One, or DMSMH. It was the book that led to it all: auditing, the Sea Org, management by statistics, e-meters, ethics conditions. It wasn't lost on me that the 1994 publication date of *Gender Outlaw* was only three days later, on May 12.

My book had been on the shelves for a few months. A whole lot of people were liking it. I hadn't expected such a whoopee response. I thought it would be a fun book for the couple of transsexuals and students who might agree with some of what I had to say. I thought some students who knew a thing or two about postmodern theory might be able to use what I wrote to come up with some really clever idea. I thought a couple of lesbians and gay men would be amused.

I even wrote my email address in the book because email was still new, and I figured the only people reading the book would most likely be friendly nerds . . . which in fact they've turned out to be. Very friendly. But it was thousands, not dozens, who were buying and reading the hardback—so many, in fact, that the book went into a paperback release a year later and hasn't gone out of print since. The first six months of the first hardback edition, I received twelve marriage proposals, and so many invitations to festivals, conferences, and play parties in cities around the world that I couldn't say yes to all the invites. I'd lived a traveling life as a slave in the Sea Org, but I'd never traveled then the way I traveled when I was a slave to a pair of SM dykes.

———

Midsummer Day, Vienna, 1994. I was attending the city's first-ever Transgender Film Festival. I was a guest of honor at a luncheon panel. Think academic dinner theater. The woman seated next to me looked like a French runway model, which in fact she turned out to be. She had two fingers up inside me. I toyed with my strudel for a while. Then she said . . .

"Get up. We're going outside."

I don't know if any of the people passing by the end of the alley turned their heads to see her slam me up against the brick wall and fuck me so goddamn good that we spent the night together and did it again the next morning, behind the last row of the next festival screening. Her name was Petra. That's when I learned to respect and adore public sex. Oh! I was learning so much stuff!

———

My joy that so many people were embracing *Gender Outlaw* was two-fold: I wasn't hiding anymore, and I was finding common ground with a whole lot of people. From all around the world, women—not all of them transwomen—were emailing me with thanks for articulating the nature of their own gender traps. And guys—heterosexual men—emailed to thank me for a theory they could use to justify the dawn of their effete metrosexuality. A few transsexuals wrote and cursed me out. Their chief complaint was that my retelling of *thetans have no gender* invalidated their own gender journeys to becoming real women. Even more transwomen and transmen wrote to tell me that before reading *Gender Outlaw,* they'd always felt alone in the understanding of themselves as not-quite-woman and not-very-much-man. Every week, people emailed me describing themselves in shades and combinations of gender I'd never imagined. At first, I answered every email I received, but the volume and intimacy of so many letters led me to shutting down the email account I'd named in the book. A few years later, a very nice woman took my AOL email handle. She has that address to this day and she tells me she still gets email from readers to me. She forwards some on to me every now and then.

I was doing a lot of radio—dozens of morning shock-jock shows, and a couple of local NPR talk shows. Plus, I was regularly showing up as a television guest on *Good Morning, This City, That City,* or *Another City.* Those gigs didn't pay, but I totally enjoyed doing them, and they made my publishers ecstatic. I was still a slave girl, but I wasn't out about that yet.

"No, you can't wear your collar on national television."

"Please? I wore it to Europe."

"And you had an affair with a floozy. Girl, you are a famous author now. You are not going to wear your collar on television."

"She's not a floozy. She's smart. She's an activist."

"You're not wearing your collar on television. What would people think?"

"They'll think it's very Madonna. Please, ma'am?"

I rarely bucked Lula's will. She knelt down next to me and turned my eyes to hers.

"What's the truth of it, girl? Tell."

I told her I was too scared to take it off. I told her I didn't know who I'd be if I didn't belong to her. She nuzzled my ear with her lips.

"OK, you goofy little thing," she whispered, "you can wear it." And before I could say *thank you, ma'am,* she bit my ear.

"Ow!"

"And don't say ouch!" She bit me again, even harder.

I squealed, and we both burst out laughing.

———

I was still touring theaters and colleges with both *Op Sex* and *Virtually Yours,* making enough money to pay the bills. When I wasn't on tour, I was a full-time household slave. We only played together a couple of times a month. Sailor and Lula had their own lives that didn't include me. Most of my time at home in Seattle was spent learning how to cook exquisitely, clean meticulously, and run errands without having to be asked.

I was still exploring gender. Lula became my femme role model, while Sailor coaxed out the boy in me. *Boy,* not *man*—these are two different genders. Sailor and I shaved together. I never could afford to finish my facial electrolysis, and Sailor's chin sprouted hairs she liked to shave every now and then. So it was the two of us in the mirror, our faces lathered—the butch dyke and her tranny slave girl. Sailor used the same straight razor she'd used to cut free my wings. I used a disposable Gillette. Shaving was a buddy thing. Sailor and I got to be boys together. Boys, not men. I was beginning to see more and more details and permutations in the matrix of sex and gender. I was beginning to feel comfortable and less ashamed of being a girl who's partly a boy.

At the same time, Caitlin and I were trying to nail down what happens to a person when both their identity and their desire are fluid, not fixed, expressions of life—what happens to two people like that in relationship with each other? Caitlin and I had spent over a year online, exploring our identities through other people's eyes using text-based cybersex in online chat rooms. I never played myself. I was variously a skateboard dude, a lesbian *Star Trek* officer, or food for some vampire. I also showed up regularly in an online jazz bar as the dame in a tight red dress. Wherever I went, whatever I became, there was *someone* who wanted to have cybersex with me. Caitlin had experienced the same thing whenever she surfed online avatars. We were much closer to writing our book about all this. She got all excited when she talked about it.

"It's all about traction! We change who we are, sure, but we're always changing into someone who's recognizable. There's always some sort of recognizable identity that gives us traction with someone else."

"Right! Without an identity, desire is all slippery-slidery—like ice. What we're doing online proves that identity is the traction that makes desire possible."

"Right, *and* I think the stuff you're doing with gender, Kate, is part of a missing key to identity, but . . . slippery-slidery? That can never go in a book."

"Right, Caitlin. Slippery-slidery never goes in a book."

———

Paperback sales of *Gender Outlaw* continued to grow, and Bill Germano at Routledge asked me to do a follow-up book. I told him no thanks, that I'd written everything I knew about gender and all I had left was questions.

"Then figure out how to write a book that asks your questions," he suggested, "and don't you dare try to write *The Zen of Gender*, or *The Tao According to Kate*." Rats. That's really what I'd wanted to do— spooky how he knew that.

I told all this to Malaga Baldi, my new literary agent. Doesn't she have the best name ever? After a few weeks of bouncing ideas back and forth with her, I came up with a compromise that worked: a primary-school workbook format. All the pieces fell into place, and soon I had a contract and a fair advance for *My Gender Workbook*. What a wonderful life I was living! And then—like a sickening twist in a David Lynch film—it all went bad. No, it all went really really bad.

Writing this part of the story, I called Sailor and Lula to ask for dates, and the order in which all of it unfolded. None of us could remember it all, but we all agree it was a terrible time for all three of us, and that our breakup and what followed was a time completely worthy of the last hour of any Tarantino serial-killer romance film.

First, Sailor fell in love with Martha. You don't need to know who Martha is, or why they fell in love. Sailor told Lula, and Lula told me that Sailor had been seeing Martha secretly for over six weeks.

Oh no.

Then, I confessed that I'd fallen in love with Sailor. I'd seen it coming for half a year, and I was quiet for all that time. In my dreams, Sailor was daddy, and all that *daddy* had ever meant to me from all the way back to *Father Knows Best* and *Leave It To Beaver*. She didn't love me back, not that way. But Lula had trusted me to play with the two of them and not cross that particular emotional line—*she* was daddy's girl, and she'd trusted me to keep my relationship with Sailor on the level of slave and bottom. I'd gone too far.

Lula lost it, badly. She checked herself into a psych ward, where she was quickly diagnosed with bipolar disorder. Lula remained on the ward for a couple of weeks, refusing to speak with me or Sailor.

Oh no.

Then my mom died.

Oh fucking no.

———

December 10, 1994. Alan was living with my mom on the Jersey Shore. She was on heavy-duty painkillers. He hadn't recovered from his second divorce. The two of them rambled around the big old house like ghosts, looking after each other's needs.

I was visiting because three days earlier, the doctors had told my mom that she was definitely dying, and it was time for her to go into hospice care. I didn't know what that meant, and I was too embarrassed to ask. I'd flown in from Seattle to Newark, New Jersey. From there, it was a bus ride to the train station, and an hour's ride down to Asbury Park. My brother picked me up in his white Jeep Wrangler. We drove back to their house in silence.

I kissed my mom hello, and dropped my bags upstairs in my old bedroom. I was unpacking when she called up to me.

"Albert, come downstairs. I want to talk with you and your brother."

She was on a heavy dose of morphine, and she knew who I was. We'd grown close enough that names and pronouns didn't matter. Alan and I sat across from her.

"I want you two to know my last wish."

"Mom, don't talk like that."

"Alan, let her talk the way she wants to talk."

"Fuck you, Albert. You're never here, what do you know?"

"*Kate!* It's Kate! *God,* you can be *such* a dick." He wasn't on morphine. There was no excuse for him fucking with my name.

"Boys—children! Stop it! Listen to me. The doctors say I've got another year left. I don't want to spend it watching the two of you at each other's throats. You've been fighting for seven years now, and that's quite enough. I want you to promise me that after I'm gone, you'll look after each other the same as I would look after both of you."

Our mom had never given up on either of us. She'd always defended us both, fiercely.

"Now, promise me that."

We promised. I hugged my brother for the first time in over five years—he hugged back. It was our first brother/sister hug, and we didn't know where to put our bodies, but at least we tried. A few hours later, Alan left with a small overnight bag to spend the night with his girlfriend, Deb. This would be the first night in weeks that they'd have a night alone with each other, out of my mom's house.

"You've got Deb's number. Call me if you need anything."

"We'll be just fine," my mother and I chorused cheerily.

At the time, Caitlin and I were into serial-killer films: Quentin Tarantino, David Lynch, Oliver Stone. She'd recommended I watch *Kalifornia,* a film starring Scientologist Juliette Lewis. I don't know what possessed me to rent the ultraviolent film and watch it that night with my dying mother who was high out of her mind on morphine and white wine. I watched her lit cigarette fall from her mouth into her lap three times in less than half an hour. Each time, I jumped up and grabbed the burning cigarette off her lap. Each time, I scared her badly. Neither of us ended up seeing much of the film. We watched each other. I told her I loved her. She smiled. I turned off the film before the end. We watched the news and the weather, then I walked her up to her bedroom. I helped her undress, wash, and get into bed. I stayed up a few more hours, watching bad television, then I went to sleep in my bedroom, down the hall from my parents' bedroom. It had been their bedroom all my life.

I woke up late the next morning, maybe ten o'clock. Mom wasn't up yet. I was glad she was getting some extra rest. I made myself breakfast. Eleven o'clock, and she still wasn't up. I walked upstairs, knocked on her door. No answer. I pushed the door open, and looked in. She was lying on her back, her mouth was open wide. Her eyes were closed.

"Mom?"

I walked to her side and bent down to kiss her. She was cool to the touch. Something like a mirror shattered inside me. I fell to my knees beside the bed and sobbed into her chest. *I'm sorry*, I said over and over. *I love you, I love you, I love you. I'm so sorry. Mommy.* I'd never called her Mommy before that moment, but when I talk to her now I do.

Months earlier, I was paying her a birthday visit in September. She was driving me back to the train station, and she asked me about the scars she'd seen on my chest a few months earlier—the ones that looked like a wolf's head.

"Those girls you're with now," she said evenly, her eyes on the road. "They did that to you?"

"You really want to know the answer to that?" We drove in silence for a while and she said yes, yes she did—so I told her yes, Mom. Those girls had done that to me.

"Did it make you feel happy, them doing . . . that?"

I told her yes, yes it had. We drove five more minutes in silence until we reached the train station.

"Your father and I, we liked our sex rough."

Then it was three months later, and there I was kneeling by the bed where she and my dad had done their rough sex. I picked up the phone on her bedside table and called my brother at Deb's house.

"Alan, she's gone. Mom's gone."

"What do you mean, she's gone? What? Where'd she go?"

"Alan, Mom's gone. I'm in her bedroom now. She's gone."

He never forgave himself for not being there the night she died. I've never forgiven myself for making her watch *Kalifornia* the night before she passed on. Whatever was I thinking? The night my mom died, my friend and mentor Holly Hughes took the train down from New York City to sit with me in the living room of my mother's house, the house I'd grown up in on the Jersey Shore. It was me, Holly, and my brother—who was only slightly more sociable than Boo Radley at the time. Holly held my hand as we sat on the couch. The next night, Lula called me from Seattle. We hadn't spoken for weeks, not since the day I told her I'd fallen so head over heels in love with Sailor.

"So, I heard your mom died."

"Yes, ma'am. Last night, in her sleep."

"She was blessed. And Katie, it's not ma'am anymore."

"Yeah? Well, it's not Mom anymore either."

"Yuk yuk, always the joker. How you holding up?"

"You really wanna talk with me, after what I did to you?"

"Love trumps rage, baby girl. You lost your mom. That's the sort of thing that brings families back together again. I love you, you know that."

"Oh god, I love you too."

"Oh, you love everyone."

I heard her drop coins into the phone.

"Hey, where are you?"

"On the ward, on one of the pay phones in the hall."

"You OK?"

"Oh, Katie! It is *so Girl, Interrupted* in here." It was one of our favorite books—we often read it out loud to each other.

"Are you OK?"

"Yeah, I am. The meds they've got me on are actually keeping my poor little brain balanced."

"Glad to hear it. I sure as fuck want my own little brain balanced. How's your heart, Miss Lula?"

"Broken to pieces, Miss Katie."

We both sighed.

"I'm so glad you called, ma' . . . Lula."

She laughed. "You're always going to be my good girl, Katie. That's part of who we are and who we're always going to be to each other. But now it's time to find out the rest of who we are. That oughta be a kick."

"Love you, Miss Lula."

"Love you back, Katie. Hang in there. Your mom loved you for lots of good reasons."

—

My mom left Alan and me a hefty chunk of money to split. I'd never had a lump sum of money before. I felt I didn't deserve it, or that I was less deserving of that kind of money than others. The only thing that gave me any pleasure with that inheritance was to give most of it away. Giving presents was a family tradition, and I went on a spending spree buying things for people. I always told them it was a gift from my mom. I got to pass on money from my mom to David, to finish his masculinizing chest surgery. He'd given me my first computer. We'd spent years as the lover of each other's dreams. How do you ever repay a guy for that?

I bought new computers for young queer writers. I bought fabulous shoes for a lot of my friends.

Mom paid for Caitlin to take a month's writing retreat in her beloved Santa Barbara. We had a contract for our book idea, and we were writing excitedly. Amy Scholder had asked to see what we had. She was publishing her own line of books under the High Risk imprint. We pitched our idea for a romance/action/mystery/cybersex/adventure novel, and she said yes right away. So, Caitlin could write for a solid month. I was home, writing both *My Gender Workbook* and the book with Caitlin, *Nearly Roadkill*—which kept my mind off the big breakup, and it kept me away from shopping for a while.

Then I got the phone call from transgender activist and author Riki Wilchins.

"Kate, we need you to come to Falls City, Nebraska, for a protest and a vigil."

"A what? Where?"

"Brandon Teena's murderer is going on trial. There's going to be TV coverage, and a documentary film crew. We want to show a unified presence of transgender people."

"What are you talking about?"

"Are you OK, Kate? Look, you've got experience with being on television. You know how to talk to the camera and handle interviewers. Can you do it?"

"Who's Brandon Teena?"

"What?"

"Brandon Teena? Murder trial? Who is he?"

"Kate, where have you been for the past two years?"

"Oh, Riki, that's exactly what I'm trying to figure out myself."

"Can you be there?"

"Yeah, sure."

—

Cars and trucks circled the block. Young men yelled out their windows.

"You fucking transsexuals, get out of here!"

You're probably familiar with the film *Boys Don't Cry*. Hilary Swank took home the Oscar for best actress. Chloë Sevigny was nominated for best supporting actress. The film is based on the real-life story of Brandon Teena. Swank plays Brandon, a hot young female-to-male transboy who tomcatted his way through the girlfriends of some badass guys in the heartland of America. They raped him and they killed him. I've never seen the film. I hear it's amazing, but it's hard to even talk about without weeping.

Kimberly Peirce wrote and directed the film. She and I met up at the trial in Falls City. At the time, she was an earnest young butch dyke who went by the name of Kim. She wore New York City blacks, which are a bit classier than Seattle blacks. My own fashion statement was caught in mourning, somewhere between Seattle slave-girl grunge and old-school high-femme goth. Neither of us fit right in, there in Falls City, Nebraska. We wandered around together in the small park that surrounded the courthouse, telling each other stories. Suddenly, Riki was in my face, cameraman in tow.

"This is Kate Bornstein," Riki was explaining. "Kate is a prominent writer and activist on behalf of transgender rights."

I was? The guys in the cars kept on shouting.

"Take one step out here, morphodites! We're gonna kill you."

"Kate, come here."

Riki directed the cameraman to a grassy bit of knoll, aimed him at me, and ran off in search of the news anchor. I asked the cameraman about the kids screaming from the cars.

"Go home to San Francisco, you ass-fuckers!"

The cameraman missed my point completely, and dove into a technical monologue about directional microphones, assuring me that wouldn't be a problem for the interview.

"Die, you faggots!"

Riki returned arm in arm with the handsome-ish news anchor for Falls City TV. He was crisp and clean in his two-piece suit and say-nothing tie. His sweaty neck only rolled over his collar just a teensy bit. He was as startled to see me as I was dismayed to see him. It was a terrible interview. The news anchor thought I was a complete freak. I thought he was creepy. The guys in the street kept hollering.

"Gonna cut your balls off, when I catch you!"

I thought of my mom, who couldn't comfort me through this one.

"Got a broomstick here for up your ass, you faggots."

I reached up to my throat, where I wore no collar, and I broke into tears.

Riki salvaged the interview, but she's never again asked me to be a spokesperson. She was furious. I tried to explain I didn't know a thing about transgender rights. I tried to explain I was never very good at sound-bite summations.

"Oh, Kate, please. What about the Geraldo show when you said, 'The plumbing works, and so does the electricity'?"

I returned her fury. "That was about *sex*! I give great sound bites when it's about sex, but I always fuck up politics. I'm sorry, OK? Count me here as a body, Riki. I'll hold up a sign. But I can't talk about this trial or this . . ." My voice trailed off to nothing, all by itself. I waved a hand, turned my back, and walked over to where Kim had been watching the shouting match. She and I joined arms and walked off together along the pathways through the courthouse lawn.

"Die, you fucking faggots, die!"

Kim was pleased to be seen as a faggot, and waved cheerily back at the guys in the cars. That's when they started throwing beer cans at us. Only then did the police clear them off the streets. With the way more or less safe, Kim and I walked the few blocks back to the hotel together, and sketched out our plan to go visit the murder scene the next day. Well, it was Kim's plan, not mine. She'd been following the story for years. It was all culminating in her script. She wanted to see for herself the cottage out in the woods where the murders had taken place. Murders, plural. The good old guys also killed a guy who happened to be visiting Brandon's place when they came to kill him. Kim wanted to get a good feel for the place. She'd planned on going alone. I wheedled my way into coming along. Not that I wanted to go, I just didn't want her to go alone. I reminded Kim there's safety in numbers, and she agreed.

Before we could go, we had to find a way to blend in better with the crowd. I borrowed a khaki skirt and cream sweater from one of the other transwomen. I bought a matching pair of sensible flats at Payless Shoes down the block, across the street from the Woolworth's department store where we bought Kim a pair of jeans and checkered shirt in the boys' department.

It was midafternoon when we rented ourselves a car as mother and son, and that's how we drove to Humboldt, Nebraska. It's a small town of maybe three hundred to five hundred people. We parked in the town square and walked into the only restaurant. The place was also the only bar. It was dinnertime, after-work time, time-for-a-beer time. Drunk, angry guys argued at the bar. A couple of them looked at me, leering at my cleavage. I buried myself in the menu. Kim and I both settled on the meatloaf. The guys at the bar were talking loudly.

"Goddamn transmaphrodites. If I ever see one of 'em, I'm gonna do it the favor of shooting off its cock."

"You seen 'em, parading around the courthouse like that?"

"Hell yes. Bunch of freaks."

"You wanna kill 'em clean, like they did to that he-she, Tina."

Mother and son finished their dinner, paid the nice waitress, and discreetly left the restaurant where the guys were still coming up with plan after plan to mutilate the morphodites who had descended on Falls City.

It was a twenty-minute drive from the Humboldt town square to the small shack in the woods. Years earlier the place had been surrounded by yellow police tape, but someone had torn it down. Tape still hung from the trees like Spanish moss. No one was patrolling the area. We soon stood at the front door. It was unlocked—Kim pushed the door open, and we looked in. Brandon's murderers hadn't killed him clean—not him or his houseguest.

A blood stain the size of a child's inflatable pool covered the floor of the front room. We stepped around it to look into the bedroom. Dark splatter stains on the floor and walls. Another stain, deep into the mattress on the floor. It was a dirt-cheap rental shack out in the woods. Who would bother to clean it up?

Later that night, mother and son shared a room in a motel outside of Humboldt. Kim wrote furiously. On television, thirty or forty transsexuals continued their vigil at the courthouse in Falls City. The next day, a documentary film crew asked me for an interview. I was dressed in my raggedy mix of Seattle black. Kimberly had stayed in the hotel room that day, writing. The camera rolled, I heard the word *Action!* The nice lady making the documentary film was as gentle as she could be when she asked me about the trial. I didn't know about the trial. I told her about the crime scene. I managed to get some words out this time before I broke into tears.

Over the next couple of years, Kim checked in with me every now and then to see if I wanted to read her script before it went into production. I told her how sorry I was that I couldn't do that. Since then, I've apologized to Kimberly for that—and for not seeing her film. Kimberly told me she understands. I flew back from Nebraska just in time to help Lula check out of the psych ward and move into her apartment.

—

After five years of true wild-at-heart romance with Sailor, Lula was moving into a place of her own. Together, we packed up Lula's stuff at the old apartment. Sailor had already moved out her own stuff, so half the closets were empty, and most of the bookshelves were bare. All three of our hearts were broken. The two of them weren't talking with each other, but we all agreed that each of them could stay friends with and talk to me. At the bottom was the understanding that it gave me great pleasure to simply please them. We agreed to not talk bad about the others. This arrangement worked out well for everyone: Lula and I shared our mania, Sailor and I shared our depression. We stayed alive.

For the second time in my life, no one owned me. No parents, no teachers, no L. Ron Hubbard, no bosses, no wives or Sea Org officers. I wasn't a slave to anyone. I had a community. No, I had several communities. There were the Seattle SM dykes, my writing and theater collaborators, and a small clutch of high femmes. David and I had successfully transformed our relationship as lovers into a relationship as mates, so we visited each other every couple of months. A lot of people were ready and willing to help me heal, but I couldn't find any happiness inside myself, so I retreated into a familiar daily pattern of writing and service.

Mornings, I wrote *Nearly Roadkill* with Caitlin. Well, she wrote in Santa Barbara, and later in her place a few blocks away from me. We wrote online and by exchanging drafts back and forth—each of us had our reasons for being a hermit. We wrote a funny book, though—full of smart gender theory and an eerily prescient view of the Internet under the thumb of government and corporate America.

Afternoons were for Lula. Online, we'd discovered Linda Hamilton's workout program for her role as Sarah Connor in *Terminator 2*. I bought us a small home gym and fed us a diet of tofu hot dogs and diet soda. We worked out for two hours in the morning and another two hours in the late afternoon. We looked great, and as part of our conjoined mania, Lula and I went overboard shopping. From beyond the grave, my mother bought us designer dresses, one-of-a-kind shoes, and only the very finest piercing jewelry in town. Looking great is enough to keep you alive, when nothing else is doing the trick. Lula and I kept each other alive and looking great.

In the evenings, after Lula left, Sailor came over to my house. I was able to channel my crush on her into a more grounded and realistic caring for her. She was gaunt and anguished. I fed her. For a year, I'd learned what she liked and what she didn't like. She mostly liked to talk, so most nights we sat naked across from each other in a hot tub on my dweeby little back porch, under the always cloudy Seattle skies.

Around one in the morning, Sailor would amble off home. That was my time to sit down to write quizzes, puzzles, games, and guidelines for the gender workbook. I wrote listening to the soundtrack from that favorite childhood television show of mine, *The Little Rascals*. It made me feel like a kid, so I could be playful with the writing.

I was smoking two or more packs of cigarettes a day. I stayed off alcohol, but I'd started smoking marijuana again. I grew more and more withdrawn, living only to be of service to Sailor and Lula and—through my writing—to anyone who might want to read my books after I was dead, which one afternoon suddenly looked a lot closer to me than it ever had before. I was sitting in front of my doctor at the free queer clinic. She was telling me that they'd confirmed my diagnosis of chronic lymphocytic leukemia.

That afternoon, I talked Big Gay Mark into giving me the ankh tat on the back of my left hand. In Neil Gaiman's graphic novel world of *The Sandman,* the ankh is the sigil of Death Herself. I wanted to mark the place where She kissed me on the hand. I chose my left hand for the kiss, because in SM wearing anything on the left marks a person as a top. I wasn't ready to bottom to Lady Death just yet. I had a few things to do, and then I'd bow to my inevitable liaison with Her Ladyship.

That's the day I called my ex-wife, Molly—Jessica's mom, who hung up on me as soon as I spoke my name. It was the same day I'd walked up the stairs to the bathroom in my little townhouse and carved a valentine heart into my chest. Later, as the endorphins from my cutting wore off, I dusted off the suicide plans I'd made for myself in Philadelphia—the mountain, the vodka, the hypothermia still looked good to me. On his recent visits, David and I had scoped out some good trails up Mount Rainier. I knew what trail to take that would get me the farthest away from—and out of sight of—other hikers. I'd take a box of sourdough pretzels and a couple of bottles of vodka and greet Lady Death through the comfy veil of my chilling body. Critters would pick my bones clean. No muss, no fuss. I decided to wait until both books were finished—that was only fair. It was femmes who saved my life—femmes and the film *Romy and Michele's High School Reunion.*

I was hanging out with a small clique of smart ladies who did cute just right and dared people to call them dumb. They were good-hearted ladies who did sexy to a sizzling tee and dared the larger culture around them to call them evil. I considered myself their mascot, a femme in training. All of us dressed the best we could, putting our wardrobes together from sales, thrift shops, or our own sewing machines. I didn't know how to sew, and anyway—no matter what I bought—I'd look in the mirror and see myself as a man in a dress. Sure, I knew I wasn't a man. But I also knew I wasn't a woman. Neither meant a goddamn thing to me anymore. I'd fallen back on my primal need to be cute and sexy, but I looked like an old man. It had been ten years since my genital surgery. I'd tried my best, and I gave up trying.

Nearly Roadkill was finally finished and published. It took a while to come up with a good, short first draft of *My Gender Workbook*. The day I sent that file off to Bill Germano and UPS'd him the hard copy, I went out and bought myself the two quarts of vodka. I packed them into my backpack, along with a box of pretzels and a comfy blanket. I saw no need for lying down on bare rocks. I owned a pair of good hiking shoes that David had helped me pick out on his last visit to Seattle. I was all set to go . . . but it was raining. I know, duh, Seattle. But still . . . I didn't want to die in the rain, and the weather report predicted clear skies before midnight. So I took myself and my suicide-kit-in-a-backpack to the movies.

It was the Seattle premiere of *Romy and Michele's High School Reunion*, promoted as a girly-girl buddy film. I could really use a girly-girl buddy. The last bus out to Mount Rainier left half an hour after the movie would get out. If I missed it, I could just walk home, get in my car, and drive to the fucking mountain. The theater went dark—twenty mind-numbing minutes later, the feature began.

Mira Sorvino plays Romy White, ten years out of high school. She works as a receptionist in a car dealership. She hangs out all the time—really, all the time—with Michele Weinberger, played by Lisa Kudrow. Michele makes designer clothes for the two of them, in which they both look head-turningly stunning. The subtitle of the film is *The Blonde Leading the Blonde*. Sure, the film rags on blondes—but blondes I know who've seen that film know that the heart of the film is how deeply the two friends love each other. I'd learned that misogyny plays out as *cute is dumb* and *sexy is evil*—but that didn't seem to apply to either of the girls in the film. And cute sexy women aren't supposed to be best friends—they're supposed to be clawing each other's eyes out.

I left the theater wishing I had a friend like Romy or Michele— and that made me smile, because Lula and I had our times like that. Could two cute, sexy women really have such a deep friendship? Outside the theater, I looked up into the sky and let the big, fat drops of rain fall onto my face. It was too damned uncomfortable a night to die. On the walk home, my new hiking shoes kept my feet warm and dry—good choice of shoes.

I woke up the next morning wanting to be Lisa Kudrow—or maybe I wanted to be her character, Michele—it wasn't clear. But somewhere in the night—maybe in the dreams I don't remember having—I'd discovered a big piece to the puzzle, a punch line hidden away in blonde jokes where blonde is cute and cute is dumb: cute blondes, I realized, don't have to be smart in order to get a man to take care of them—guys will do anything for a cute blonde. But that realization didn't work for me because (a) I was a redhead, (b) I was smart, and (c) I didn't want a man to take care of me. God, I was even too fucked up to be a blonde in a blonde joke. I hadn't tasted vodka in twelve years, but I could taste it now—it sent an almost sexual shiver through my body.

It was raining, but nowhere near as hard as the night before— it wasn't even umbrella rain, but still . . . fuck. I hoisted the suicide backpack over my shoulder and walked the six or seven blocks to catch the matinee. Walking through the rain was fine, it's what Seattleites do. The idea of dying in the rain creeped me out—I'd spent too long a time living on a ship, when rain meant danger, and I didn't want to die feeling scared. The ticket-taker guy raised an eyebrow at the clinking from my backpack.

"No drinks allowed in the theater, ma'am."

"Oh. What? These? No, they're for . . . later. I can leave 'em with you if you want? Or I could show them to you on the way out, how's that?"

The guy shrugged and waved me on in. I sat in the same seat as the night before. There were maybe a dozen other people in the theater. I was impatient to see the film.

Romy and Michele are sexy ladies, but not even a Bible-thumping fundamentalist would consider them evil. Why? I watched the film, throwing myself into Lisa Kudrow's character. By the end of the film, I'd figured it out: the girls are sexy, but only for each other. Scene after scene, they fend off guys' advances. Yes, Romy had a crush on a high school football star—he turned out to be a complete jerk. And the class nerd had a crush on Michele—the two of them get together only when Michele insists that Romy be part of their relationship.

The ladies have only got eyes for each other because they are so gosh-darned sexy cute. They're delightful. They were everything I wanted to be—but it was a fairy tale, right? It was fiction—but, I reasoned with myself, isn't all mythology fiction? Over the next three days, I watched that movie five more times. I stopped bringing my suicide backpack with me.

It's clear by the end of the film that on top of being cute and sexy, the two women are smart and talented. Despite that cultural impossibility, they find a great way to live well with each other, presumably into their old age. My life's journey was all coming together now, like the final scene in an Agatha Christie mystery. Back when I began to focus on my journey as a transsexual, my first *aha* moment was the realization that I'd bought into a cultural mandate that real women only love men. I broke that rule and I went through with my gender change to became a femme lesbian . . . and by golly, I'd immediately fallen into a similar trap: I believed and blindly obeyed the subcultural mandate that real femmes only love butches!

"I fell for Sailor because she was butch, Lula."

"Kate," Lula admonished, "you loved a whole lot more about Sailor than that."

"Yeah, well, there was the fact that she's just like my dad, right down to his bullheadedness."

"The girl can be stubborn."

"Yeah, just like me. And the last thing I need in my life is someone who's beating up on me all the time. I do enough of that to myself."

"Katie, that all sounds good, but you adore Sailor. I've watched your face."

"I adore her, Lula, yes—but I wasn't in love with her. I loved playing with her."

"Girl, you did a lot more than play with Sailor. You flirted your ass off with her. You flirt your ass off with anything that's butch!"

"Well, sure. But that's playing, too."

"You play with a lot of butches that way, sweetie, and they think you're leading them on."

"No, I'm dancing with them. It's fun to flirt with daddy, you know that. It's not my fault if they expect more than that."

Then the great big words fell out of my mouth. "It wasn't Sailor I fell in love with, Lula, it was you. You're my best friend."

No, Lula didn't fall into my arms and confess her love for me. She loved butches. But I'd figured out cute, and I'd figured out sexy. Most importantly, I'd discovered the nature of my desire: *I wanted to be the kind of girl I was attracted to.* The answer was clear: stay alive and go blonde. Not like Romy or Michele—I couldn't pull off that much girly. I went blonde like Geena Davis in *The Long Kiss Goodnight.* I could do that kind of kick-ass cute and sexy. I was still buff from my workouts with Lula, and when I looked in the mirror, I saw a boy looking hot in girl clothes. Boy, not man—two different genders.

———

"I've even figured out the whole daddy thing!"

"Oh yeah?" Lula reached out and lightly touched the scar of the heart on my chest. "What about you being Jessica's daddy?"

I took a deep breath, then told her I'd figured out that one too.

"What? You're gonna go find her and get her out of that fucking cult?"

"No. I could probably find her if I looked hard enough. But if I showed up on her doorstep, all I'd do would be to get her in big trouble with the only people in the world she thinks are good. No . . . I'm gonna do what Romy and Michele would do."

"And that would be?"

"I'm gonna move to New York, and I'm gonna be a star."

"Oh, Katie—not really."

"Lula, I'm gonna be a *tranny* star! It can't be that hard, cuz there's not all that much competition. And when I'm a star, that's gonna make it easy for Jessica to find me—if ever she wants to."

Lula threw her arms around my shoulders. I lifted her in a loving hug.

"You'd make a good daddy, Katie, even if you are a pretty girl. I hope Jessica finds that out one day."

"Yeah, well I hope so, too."

Stardom. I was sure I could do it. The new understanding of my desires, on top of the new awareness of my mortality, made me confident enough to believe I could do it. There wasn't much of Mom's money left, so I sold my car for the money to make the move to New York, where I wouldn't need a car anyway. I rented a big old U-Haul.

All my dyke friends came by to help me pack the truck, and to wish me well on my journey to stardom. We laughed and danced and sang songs in the courtyard of my townhouse row—we were a Bollywood grand finale of booty-shaking SM dykes. It was after ten at night before everyone left. I headed out first thing in the morning—me, my ginger cat Gideon, and Robin, a butch dyke who looked just like a young Christopher Walken.

Mount Rainier shed her clouds to wish us a safe journey. We drove for hours into the rosy golden arms of the rising sun. Life was worth living, oh yes, and I had a song in my heart.

EPILOGUE
Hello, Sweetie

Two weeks after we left Seattle, Robin dropped me off in New York City. I did not become a star, and as of this writing, that's still the case. Gideon and I settled down together in yet another home—a midtown studio apartment that I sublet from Barbara Carrellas, the woman who became the Romy to my Michelle. Barbara and I have been girly-girl pals, writers, performers, theater people, dog people, cat people, co-creators, and life partners for fourteen years now. I started working on *A Queer and Pleasant Danger* six years ago—it was a solo performance piece before it was a book. It's pleasing to look back at my life and realize that nearly all of my written work has had its roots in theater.

My slow dance with suicide back in Seattle was the last time I've seriously considered killing myself. Oh, I've still got what my therapist calls passive suicidal ideation—days in my life when I wonder, *Won't it all be over soon—please?* But for all my leanings toward self-destruction, the fact remains that for over sixty-three years, I have found a reason to go on living every day of my life.

My chronic lymphocytic leukemia was diagnosed fourteen years ago at stage zero out of four, and it was only a couple of years ago that it kicked up a notch to stage one. The CLL slows me down a bit, but it's certainly not going to kill me. Over the past six or seven years, I've had three close calls with Death, and I'm still here. I keep finding more and more to enjoy out of life—more and more to laugh about, so I don't mind if Her Ladyship takes her time coming for me. That's a first for me—not craving Death's company—and that says to me I'm liking more and more the person I'm still becoming.

The day I left the Church of Scientology, I became the lowest of their low—a danger to everyone everywhere. With a lot of help from my friends, I've recently begun to believe I may not be such an evil fuck after all. Now I'm trying to reconcile what *several* religions and subcultures believe to be my evil nature with my heart's desire to be a source of compassion and delight as I walk through the world. I may have found a way along a Buddhist life path called *bodhisattva*.

A couple of years ago, I attended a three-day teaching with His Holiness, the Dalai Lama. Me, my partner Barbara, and about seven hundred other people at the Beacon Theatre in New York City. I swore an oath that day. The Dalai Lama asked all of us who wanted to pursue the path of bodhisattva to take this pledge:

> As long as space remains,
> As long as sentient beings remain,
> Until then, may I too remain,
> And dispel the miseries of the world.

Heck, I spent all that time in the Sea Org living with the notion that *we come back,* and that was only for a billion years. So—no stepping off the great wheel of life and death for me, not until *everyone* does. It's so Jonathan Livingston Seagull. There's even a version of bodhisattva that appeals to masochists: with each reincarnation, you become a lower-level being than your last lifetime—until you get to the bottom of the heap. Why would you do that? Because your subsequent and inevitable enlightenment will be so big, so bright, and so intense, that all sentient beings everywhere will benefit from its radiance. This makes a great deal of sense to me. I've been doing a lot of that in just this one lifetime. At most crossroads of my life, I've opted for the path more outlawed, less culturally approved. I sure hope those Buddhists are right about my subsequent and inevitable enlightenment. But even if they're not, it's been a way fun journey on the way down.

A few years ago, and quite by accident, I learned that I'm a grandparent. Imagine that. I've a pair of teenage grandchildren, Christopher and his sister—I believe her name is Celaina. I'm not sure how old they are, but I hear that they're both old enough to have signed their billion-year contracts with the Sea Org. Around the same time, I also discovered that Jessica is holding down a high-level job in the Sea Org. Not everyone gets as far up in the organization as she has— it's hard to believe, but I realize I'm proud of her. I've known all along she's a powerful thetan.

I'm reasonably sure I know where Jessica lives these days. So how come I'm sitting at this computer and not knocking on her door right this minute? Well, in her world, that would be a kiss of death. Jessica has spent her entire life in Scientology—it's all she knows. I can't just march in and fuck that up. No. But I did write this book on the outside chance that you, dear reader, are Jessica, so . . .

Hello, Sweetie.

I'm pretty sure the last time we spent any length of time together was the drive home from school the day you asked me about God. You were eight, maybe nine.

Thank you for reading my words. I know it couldn't have been easy. As for the truth of it—well, parts of it—you can ask your mom. I doubt she's going to want to read this, but give her my love anyway, will you? We loved each other, your mom and I. We were best mates for years and in love with each other for such a brief time. We had stars in our eyes, the planet was ours, and we wanted to share it with you. You were born into a whole lot of love.

Jessica for beauty and *Leah* for strength—it was the most magical name your mom and I could think of for you—I hope both names have served you well. I know you changed your last name to your stepfather's last name shortly after I left. I want you to know there's no hard feelings.

I have fifteen photographs of you, including those you sent to my mom. She kept them in a drawer by her bedside, and I found them there after she died. That means that your grandma loved you a whole lot, to keep you by her bedside like that—and so did your grandpa. You melted his heart every time you'd come toddling around the corner. I've never seen him as mellow and sweet—you brought out the best in him. He never got it, why you didn't ever come visit them, neither did my mom. No guilt—I did the same damn thing to them when I was in the Sea Org. I understand why you didn't visit them—they were both in touch with me, and that made them potential sources of trouble for both you and the Church. Besides, it's hard to talk with wogs about anything other than getting them onto Ron's Bridge to Total Freedom. And oh honey—the way they talk out here would drive you crazy! No one acknowledges anything, *and* they interrupt all the time. People communicate with each other a whole lot better where you are than we do out here.

I wonder, do you ever think of leaving? I'd be a bad SP if I didn't at least ask. I want you to know that if you ever do choose to leave, I'd take you in or find you a place with some good friends who could help get you a place of your own. Now wouldn't *that* throw a monkey wrench into the lives of just about everyone you and I both know and love? Yikes! Mind you, I'm not asking you to leave or even get back in touch with me. I *am* letting you know that it's an option, and that you'd be welcome.

You look like me, did you know that? And I look like my father. He was a good-looking guy, and I'm guessing you're a beautiful woman. There's a *lot* of photos of me on the Internet—match them up with photos of yourself. You and I have my father's eyes. It's eerie. Are you allowed to look at my blog? Or does the filter the Church makes you put on your computer keep you away from my website? I've done my best to make myself easy to find for a long time now, on the chance you ever choose to look for me. Oh God, I'm so hungry to know more about you. I search for you on the Internet a couple of times a month to see if there's any news of your whereabouts, your doings—nothing so far. I'll keep looking.

I wonder—do you believe that Scientology is a religion? I am *not* being snarky, flippant, or disrespectful. The reason I'm asking is that in the old days, we all knew Scientology *wasn't* a religion. When we first met, your mom and I understood that Scientology was an applied religious philosophy—one that we *chose* to subscribe to. Sweetie, do you feel free to choose your own beliefs over those of L. Ron Hubbard? Do you know that you have a basic human right to seek and find your own beliefs without fear of punishment or retribution? There are a great many compassionate, mindful people in the world, and they got that way without Scientology. All I'm saying is that you have options and you have the right to choose from them.

It's breathtaking *fun*, setting your own course in life. Sweetie, there are whole worlds to explore where people would welcome you *and* your questions *and* your ideas— worlds where people would respect your desires. There so many ways to see and understand. . . well . . . God.

When you were little, you asked me *what's God, Daddy?* Scientology teaches that's for everyone to find out for themselves. So, Jessica, please let me turn the question back to you: what's God? You're nearly forty now, how much time have you devoted to discovering the face and glory and peace and comfort and strength and love of God for yourself? I'm not talking about OT abilities or even freedom—I'm talking about what Ron calls the common urge of humanity to survive as part of something that's bigger than all of life, spirit, and the physical universe. Out here in the wog world, I've discovered that every time you find something that makes your life more worth living, that's another clue to solving the mystery that some people call God—I call it *The Great Big Good.* So . . . have you found that for yourself? Oh honey, I could show you some real fun places to look!

Jessica, I'm sorry for any suffering I caused you, and for the mistakes and decisions I made that caused you pain. I am truly sorry. I know that Scientology is supposed to erase all the pain and suffering you've ever felt in this and every other lifetime. Nonetheless, I am sorry that I've been an agent of pain and suffering in your life the way my father was an agent of pain and suffering in my life. I'm sorry for all the years I wasn't there for you. As hard as I tried not to be him, I was more distant with you than my own father was with me.

An ex-Sea Org member recently told me you're worried that someone did incorrect spiritual counseling on me, and that's why I'm so weird and fucked up. Please, don't worry. I'm doing OK out here in the world. I'm grateful for the life I've had, the opportunities I've been given to learn some of the harder lessons of compassion and forgiveness.

Yep, I've learned me some lessons, I've got me some street smarts—from some mighty strange streets—and I'd like to pass them on to you. Because that's what parents do. We're supposed to pass stuff on to our children—what we know, what we've learned, our wishes for you, and our blessings before we die.

Here we go.

One: Cute is a valid way to express yourself, just like any other way you want to express the kind of man or woman or boy or girl or whatever it is you feel like being. Remember, *thetans have no gender*, and anyway, you don't need a gender to do cute. And what's more, it's precisely because thetans have no gender that you get to fall in love with any thetan or thetans, no matter the gender of their body.

Two: Never fuck anyone you wouldn't wanna be.

Three: Watch and read a lot of science fiction and fantasy—the good stuff. People like to rag on L. Ron Hubbard because he was a science fiction writer. That was never his problem. His problem was that he was a *mediocre* science fiction writer. If you like the Old Man's stuff, there's some amazing good SciFi and fantasy writers out here who could open your eyes in wonder with spiritual yum. They didn't have to make a religion out of their work, they're simply good guides.

Four: For all the traveling I've done, I found that all roads in life lead nowhere. So you might as well choose the road that has the most heart, and is the most fun. And if we both do that, then who knows? Maybe our roads will cross again some day, some lifetime.

Five: If nothing else I've said makes sense or rings true, please do this one thing—for no one else but yourself: *Do whatever it takes to make your life more worth living.* Anything, and I do mean *anything*—even if it goes against L. Ron Hubbard's teaching. There's only one rule that matters, sweetie: *Don't be mean.* This is the kind of rule that lets everyone, even people like me, do some good in the world.

OK, gotta wrap up now. Sixty-three years, and I still hate goodbyes more than anything else.

Christopher, Celaina—everything I've offered your mom, I'm offering to you. It's easy to get in touch with me on the interwebs.

Jessica Leah, my girl. I love you. Whatever path you choose, I wish you all the comfort and peace and strength you need to keep on going. I'm so glad to have had this opportunity to talk to you.

Love and Respect Always,

Me

Some Notes on My Scientology Sources

I'm in awe of the ex-Scientologists and Sea Org members who first wrote about the One Whose Name Shall Not Be Spoken—they paved my way in putting words to the unspeakable trauma that was life in the Church and Sea Org:

Ali's Smile / Naked Scientology, by William S. Burroughs (1978)

Bare-Faced Messiah: The True Story of L. Ron Hubbard, by Russell Miller (1987)

L. Ron Hubbard: Messiah or Madman? by Bent Corydon and L. Ron Hubbard Jr. (1987)

A Piece of Blue Sky: Scientology, Dianetics, and L. Ron Hubbard Exposed, by Jon Atack (1990)

My Billion Year Contract: Memoir of a Former Scientologist, by Nancy Many (2009)—Nancy and I served together in the Sea Org.

Blown for Good: Behind the Iron Curtain of Scientology, by Marc Morgan Headley (2009)

Counterfeit Dreams: One Man's Journey into and out of the World of Scientology, by Jefferson Hawkins (2010)

The Symphony of Leif, by Paul Y. Csige (2010)

The Road to Xenu: Life inside Scientology, by Margery Wakefield (2010)

Understanding Scientology: The Demon Cult, by Margery Wakefield (2010)

Scientology—Abuse at the Top, by Amy Scobee (2010)

I've also drawn material from the original versions of books by L. Ron Hubbard (before they were edited by David Miscavige): *Introduction to Scientology Ethics*; *The History of Man*; *Scientology 0–8: The Book of Basics*; and *Dianetics: The Modern Science of Mental Health*. I'm also a graduate of the Organizational Executive Course and the Flag Executive Briefing Course where—despite my completion certificates having been canceled because I'm such a rabid SP—I learned a great deal of L. Ron Hubbard's philosophy of management.

For much of what I've written here about the Church, its leader David Miscavige, and founder L. Ron Hubbard, I'm indebted to Janet Reitman for her book *Inside Scientology: The Story of America's Most Secretive Religion* (2011). More thanks are due to journalist Lawrence Wright for his meticulously fact-checked *New Yorker* article, "The Apostate: Paul Haggis vs. the Church of Scientology" (February 14, 2011).

Paulette Cooper wrote the first tell-all book about Scientology, *The Scandal of Scientology*. I'm in awe of her courage. For years following the 1971 publication, she was the target of what the Church called Operation PC Freakout.

Special thanks to Mark Bunker for his comprehensive website *Xenu TV*, filled with links to documents, books, and sworn testimonies. Thanks also to Tony Ortega, editor in chief of the *Village Voice*, for his one-man journalistic mission to uncover and bring to light so many lies told by the Church of Scientology at the *Village Voice* blog *Runnin' Scared*. Thanks also to Mark "Marty" Rathbun for his blog *Moving On Up a Little Higher,* which daily chronicles Church misdeeds. I check these blogs several times a day. There are also links to court documents, sworn depositions, and video testimony by current and ex-Scientologists on a website called, arcanely enough, Operation Clambake (www.xenu.net). There's one more website that fascinates me, *Ex-Scientology Kids*, where I one day hope to find word of my daughter and her children.

Acknowledgments

In 1998 I wrote an essay for Jessica called "Message in a Bottle." An upmarket news and entertainment website bought the story. This was back when no one was publishing pieces about Scientology because everyone was so afraid of retribution. A week before posting it online, the website editors let me know their lawyers didn't want to run the piece—they sent me a kill fee. Years later, that essay morphed into a solo performance piece called *Kate Bornstein Is a Queer and Pleasant Danger,* which I performed at the eleventh annual Performance Studies International at Brown University. John Emigh, perpetual Trickster in my life, talked me into writing and performing that show. Adam Immerwahr designed the lighting. My BFF Kaylynn Raschke was both my eloquent dramaturge and elegant production designer.

My literary agent, Malaga Baldi, suggested I expand the solo show into memoir. For the last six years, she has cheered me on and held my hand through the times I thought I couldn't write any more. Thank you, Miss Malaga.

Early on, it was Mary Dorman and Amy Scholder who helped me push through my well-founded fear of possible retribution from the Church of Scientology. Crystal Yakacki and Dan Simon at Seven Stories Press first picked up the book, and several years later graciously turned the project over to Beacon Press.

For the next two years, this book came of age under the kind, nononsense, and patient guidance of my editor, Gayatri Patnaik, and editorial assistant Rachael Marks. I appreciate all the encouragement from other Beacon Press folks: Helene Atwan, Tom Hallock, Pamela MacColl, Reshma Melwani, Susan Lumenello, Bob Kosturko, and P J Tierney. Thanks also to Alan J. Kaufman for legally vetting the book.

And big hugs and kisses to the ever so lovely Lane Jantzen and the distribution staff at Random House.

I've gone through several medical emergencies while writing this book. Thank-yous go to Drs. Michael Blechman, Joseph Martz, Myron Schwartz, Paula Rackoff, Donald Kastenbaum, Ariel Ostad, Adam Geyer, Bruce Culliney, "Broadway Benny" Sheinkin, and Rachel Saunders-Pullman. Dr. Rona Vail at Callen-Lorde Clinic in New York City has been my primary care physician—I am secretly crushed out on her.

My spirit needed careful tending-to these past six years. Thanks to Julia Ritchie, my life coach and therapist, for keeping me conscious enough to write *Hello, Cruel World* and most of this book. And thanks to all the several therapists who are now guiding me through Dialectic Behavioral Therapy.

I wrote this book on a series of three Apple MacBook Pros. I wrote and kept an outline and timeline in OmniOutliner Pro. From the outline, I imported notes into Scrivener, where I wrote a chapter at a time, which I'd then export and polish in Pages.

Thanks to my booking agents who kept me on the road: Jean Caiani at SpeakOut Now; Ellie Deegan at The Lecture Bureau; and Seraphin Hedges and Lisa Tusay at PhinLi Bookings.

I've gotten a slew of tattoos over the course of writing this book—all of them were lovingly inked onto me by Pat Sinatra of Pat's Tats in Kingston, New York.

Thank you to my dear shipmates Holly Carlson, Carl Carlson, Sandy Holeman, Rabbi Ira, Captain Bob, and Papa Neil. And—happy ending—I've been in touch with Marion, the lady I left when Molly asked me to marry her. Marion and I had dinner together not all that long ago, when a speaking tour landed me in her city. She graciously forgave me for being such a rat.

A special shout-out to Rheva Acevedo. She and I were shipmates throughout our years in the Sea Org, so we've known each other for over forty years. Now I'm her friend, the perverted socialist; and she's my friend, the Tea Party maven. Together, Rheva and I prove that love transcends politics.

I owe so much to my Seattle pals. I miss them—they kept me honest while I lived there, and ever since then. Thanks to my shape-shifting mentor, dear Jack O'Rion Dragon Excalibur Barker. Thanks to Caitlin Sullivan and Ann Pancake for shelter in so many storms. Ava Apple and Kristen Knapick continue to teach me how to be a girl and a lady. Lainy Beitler and Julia Kaplan are the hostesses with the mostest. Thanks to Sailor for my scars. Thanks and love to Lula for everything, especially the stuff I couldn't write about.

Thanks to close friends and early readers who were there for me by Skype, text, email, and phone. I have a story to write about each of these folks—some of those stories didn't make it into the book, but they've all made it into my heart: David Harrison, Holly Hughes, Mx. Justin V Bond, Sandy Stone, Marsha Botzer, Diane DiMassa, S. Bear Bergman, T Cooper, Erin Markey, Ullie Emigh, Eric Emigh, Lori E. Seid, Scott Turner Schofield, Felicia Luna Lemus, Tony Lioce (and all of his amazing family), Tony Phillips, Abe Rybeck, Sam Feder, Roz Kaveney, Virginia Mollenkott, Judy Reilly, Lana Kane, Kar Winslow, Lynn Birks, Judith Witt, Gwen Smith, M. Gail Harris, Jon Charnas, Serge Nicholson, Gayle Landers, Susan Stryker, Cayenne Woods, Christine Smith, Marilyn S. Miller, Andy Schwartz, Alexis Van Hurkman, and Elsa Sjunnisen.

I'm indebted to students, faculty, and staff of the dozens of colleges, universities, high schools, and youth groups who listened to me read early drafts of this work over the years. Thanks also to my Twitter twibe, now numbering close to ten thousand—you kept me alive in the hardest of times while I was writing this, and I'm grateful. I'm part of a Battlestar Galactica board game group. We all met on Twitter, and we've played half a dozen times over the last couple of years—so, thank you, @Lauravogel, @mxroo, @eyeandy, @catalystparadox, @penguinsquid, @siniful, and @saravibes for the fun and camaraderie, and for letting me play Caprica Six so many times. Thanks also to all the people on Twitter who've posted to #stayalive. It worked. I did, and so did most all of them.

If you enjoyed reading this book, you owe thanks to Barbara Car-rellas, who put up with the six years of madness it took for me to write it. Barbara read every page of this book before it went to my editor, and the words on the cutting room floor are going to be a lot of fun to read after I'm dead and gone. For the past fourteen years, Barbara has been my sister traveler in life. We've kept each other going. We call each other Imzadi—it's an old *Star Trek* term, totally worth a google.